Teaching for Comprehension in Reading

Grades K–2

by **GAY SU PINNELL & PATRICIA L. SCHARER**

with

Diane E. DeFord • Irene C. Fountas • Mary Fried

Justina Henry • Carol A. Lyons • Andrea McCarrier

Lynda Hamilton Mudre • Barbara Joan Wiley

NEW YORK • TORONTO • LONDON • AUCKLAND • SYDNEY

MEXICO CITY • NEW DELHI • HONG KONG • BUENOS AIRES

Excerpt on page 90 from *Owl Moon* by Jane Yolen. Copyright © 1987 by Jane Yolen, text.
Used by permission of Philomel Books, a division of Penguin Young Readers Group,
a Member of Penguin Group (USA) Inc., 345 Hudson St., New York, NY 10014. All rights reserved.

Figures on pages 18, 218, and 219 are from *Guiding Readers and Writers, Grades 3–6: Teaching Comprehension, Genre, and Content Literacy* by Irene Fountas and Gay Su Pinnell.
Copyright © 2001 by Irene Fountas and Gay Su Pinnell. Published by Heinemann, a division of
Reed Elsevier, Inc., Portsmouth, NH. Used by permission of the authors and publisher.

Cover and interior design by Maria Lilja
Cover photo © by David Pollack/CORBIS
Copyedited by Kay Mallett and AnJanette Brush

ISBN: 0-439-54258-8

Printed in the U.S.A.

1 2 3 4 5 6 7 8 9 10   23   09 08 07 06 05 04 03

We dedicate this book to
the children and teachers who
have taught us so much.

We send special thanks to
all of the teachers and children
who have contributed so much
to the chapters in this book.

Contents

Introduction

This book has emerged from our work with teachers and children in an instructional context called *guided reading*. In 1996, Fountas and Pinnell described guided reading as an instructional context in which a teacher helps readers extend the range and effectiveness of the strategies that make up a reading process. (See *Guided Reading: Good First Teaching for All Students.*) As teachers in guided reading, we work with a small group of students who are alike in their reading behaviors and the level of text that they can process with ease and understanding. Through selecting and introducing appropriate texts, supporting students as they read, and revisiting the texts to discuss the meaning and teach for processing strategies, we provide a strong instructional frame that enables readers to take on texts that offer challenges and opportunities to learn.

Over the years, we have found that guided reading "ups the ante" for individual readers. What they learn in guided reading they apply in their independent reading; ultimately, they develop systems of strategies that allow them to expand their abilities by reading increasingly challenging and varied texts. That is, readers learn to read better simply by reading. Guided reading supports the process.

This book examines central questions that we have discussed with teachers over the years as they learned to use guided reading and worked to deepen their understanding of it—questions that range from the complex process of comprehension to the equally complex topic of classroom management. Our central focus is

comprehension, which is the goal of all reading. Our teaching in guided reading is directed toward helping children to understand the texts that they read. In exploring this topic, however, we realize that teaching for comprehension is not the sole purview of guided reading. Children learn to understand texts in just about every context in which they encounter them—hearing them read aloud, reading them as independent work, exploring them at productive work centers, discussing them as literature, and reading together in small groups. All of these contexts are significant in the process. As teachers, we always have in mind the interrelated systems of strategies that work together to help individuals read with understanding.

We are constantly learning from our own teaching and that of others. In this book we share our latest thinking about teaching for comprehension in grades kindergarten through two. The first part, "Expanding Our Understanding: The Foundation for Successful Teaching," presents four chapters that examine comprehension from different perspectives. The first chapter, "What Does It Mean to Comprehend a Text?" focuses on the comprehending process. Pinnell describes the integrated systems of strategies that allow readers to sustain processing, solve words, monitor their reading, gather information, make predictions, maintain fluency, and adjust their reading for different texts and purposes. She also describes strategies that allow readers to go beyond the literal meaning of the text to make inferences and connections, summarize and synthesize information, and engage in analysis and criticism. In Chapter 2, "Teaching for Comprehension Across the Language and Literacy Framework," Pinnell and Fountas discuss the role of a broad language and literacy framework in supporting readers' growth in comprehension. Chapter 3, by Lyons, "The Role of Emotion in Memory and Comprehension," presents emotion as a critical factor in comprehension because it is directly related to the meaning-making process. Lyons offers important new information on the structure of the brain and argues that success and feelings of accomplishment are important factors as young children build a reading process. In the final chapter in this section, "From Primary to Intermediate Grades: How Do Children Change as Readers?" Pinnell and Fountas describe the important changes in behavior that we see in our students between the end of first grade and the beginning of third grade. Changes in learners imply the need for changes in our teaching.

The seven chapters in Part II focus on teaching, with emphasis on guided reading. These chapters underscore the idea that comprehension is not something that happens *after* reading. Readers begin to comprehend from the moment they think about reading a text (building expectations and making those first connections) to long after reading it (talking about it with others, using the information, or connecting to subsequent texts). This part of the book explores text selection and introduction, teacher-student interactions, teaching for fluency, and a variety of ways to support readers' comprehension both in guided reading and other contexts.

Chapter 5, "The Literary Path to Comprehension: Writer's Craft and Guided Reading," by Scharer, introduces the section. She explores the literary path to comprehension and argues that the literary quality of texts is a valid consideration in selecting books for introduction in guided reading. Reading and learning about literary texts can have a big payoff, both for students' expansion of reading strategies and for their enjoyment and awareness of literary aspects of texts. In Chapter 6, "Scaffolding the First Reading of a Book for Children Who Are Learning to Read," Fried focuses on a critical component of guided reading lessons: the support that teachers give students as they engage with a novel text.

In a discussion of "Teaching Versus Prompting: Supporting Comprehension in Guided Reading" in Chapter 7, Mudre helps us reflect on the powerful teaching interactions that support students' reading of texts during guided reading. Her focus is on prompting and encouraging readers to think while reading, thus deepening their understanding of texts. McCarrier, in Chapter 8, "Teaching for Phrasing and Fluency: Connections to Comprehension," explores the deep connections between fluency and comprehension and provides some specific examples of how teachers can help young children develop phrased, fluent reading. In Chapter 9, "Teaching for Comprehension in Guided and Independent Reading," Henry discusses the connections between guided and independent reading and suggests ways to support comprehension across those settings.

Extending the meaning of texts through writing or drawing is another way to support comprehension and is the focus of Chapter 10, "Extending the Meaning of Texts: Beyond the Book in Guided Reading." In it, Pinnell discusses systematic ways to help children reflect on their reading to extend comprehension. In Part II's final chapter, "Interactive Read-Aloud: Supporting and Expanding Strategies for Comprehension," DeFord explores interactive read-aloud as a vital context for supporting young readers' growth in comprehending strategies. She emphasizes how teachers can make effective use of interactive read-aloud to help children extend their comprehending strategies. Reading aloud is described as a powerful and necessary way to demonstrate the importance of books (and taking meaning from texts) every single day in the classroom.

The three chapters in Part III focus on the organizational support systems that are essential for good teaching and effective learning to take place. Good management, organization, and planning must receive careful and detailed attention

to achieve two goals: (1) children engage in productive, independent reading and writing while the teacher is working with small groups in guided reading; and (2) children gradually increase their ability to sustain themselves in sole activities as readers and writers. Both of these factors, when present, contribute to the children's wealth of experience in reading as well as to understanding.

Chapter 12, by Wiley and Henry, features managed independent learning as ongoing problem-solving. The term managed independent learning implies juxtaposing seemingly different concepts: clear directions and independence, or structure and choice. The authors address the important question: What makes managed independent learning work? In Chapter 13, "Shifting Teaching and Management to Meet Learners' Changing Needs: Transitions from Primary to Intermediate," Pinnell and Fountas take a look at how decisions about teaching and classroom management shift as children become more sophisticated as readers and writers. They examine teaching and organization in grade two, a transition time between primary and intermediate grades. The final chapter, Chapter 14, presents a collection of frequently-posed questions and answers about classroom management.

It is our hope that the chapters in this book will initiate important conversations among educators about effective ways to support students as they not only learn to read, but begin to love reading.

G. S. Pinnell

P. L. Scharer

Part I

Expanding Our Understanding: The Foundation for Successful Teaching

The chapters in Part I provide insights into the systems of strategies readers use to process continuous text. First, we explore what it means to comprehend, followed by a discussion of how comprehension is developed in multifaceted ways across the teaching in the language and literacy framework. Chapter 3 focuses on intriguing information about how the brain works and provides insights into the connections between emotion and cognition. Chapter 4 focuses specifically on the important shifts in processing and behavior that take place over the primary years.

—— CHAPTER 1 ——

What Does It Mean to Comprehend a Text?

Gay Su Pinnell

People often speak of *reading* and *comprehending* as two different (although connected) processes. We hear statements such as this: "Well, he can read it, but he doesn't understand it." In this chapter, I take the position that reading *is* comprehending; without understanding, a person may be noticing and responding to graphic symbols but not processing them in the meaningful way that is required of readers.

You can usually tell when there is at least a gap in comprehension while listening to someone read aloud. How does it sound when this gap occurs? The phrasing is off; the reading may sound staccato or wooden; many words will be mispronounced; there may even be stumbling and long pauses. That's not the way good reading sounds.

When we hear someone read aloud with ease and fluency, that person is actually communicating the meaning of the text by accessing the syntax that the writer intended. We even praise performers who give us wonderful interpretations of texts by infusing them with emotion and drama, although drama is not necessary for ordinary oral reading.

For good readers, silent reading is also characterized by ease and fluency. Their eyes move over the page while the meaning echoes in their minds. It is very hard for us to know exactly what is happening here, but we know that silent reading is more rapid than oral reading, possibly because less attention must be given to precise word pronunciation or expression. It may also be that comprehension is deeper because more attention is freed for thinking while reading—that is, if the text is right for the reader. We cannot see comprehension, but we can tell much about it by observing readers as they talk or write about what they have read.

Reflecting on Our Own Reading

To reflect on the idea of comprehension, think about some texts you have read recently. It could be any kind of text—mystery, biography, a news journal, or historical fiction. Chances are, your reading was slightly different with each of these texts. Last year, I read *The Poisonwood Bible* by Barbara Kingsolver (1998). This wonderful novel is the story of a family with four daughters who go as missionaries to what was then the Congo. As I began the book, I had some expectations. I have traveled in Africa, although in another part. I knew missionaries had hard lives, frequently encountering illness, poverty, and the distrust (often deserved) of native peoples that they came to convert. I remembered missionaries who spoke in my small-town church, seeking donations for their work. From an adult

standpoint, I knew that missionary zeal sometimes violated local customs and sought to destroy indigenous culture. But I also knew that the missionaries who succeeded were those who placed more importance on helping people than on converting them. I also had vague memories of the Congo and the struggles there in the 1960s. Overall, the knowledge I brought to this book was scant and fragmented, but as I opened the book, whatever I knew was brought to bear.

At first I found this book quite challenging. The story is told in the voices of five female characters—a mother and four sisters. The narrative spans 30 years, from 1960 to 1990, during which the family encounters physical hardship and problems caused by their own ignorance. As I read, I found myself recalling the 1960s and the 1970s. I remembered the events that influenced my own life, such as the Civil Rights Movement and the Vietnam War. As a socially aware person, I was surprised that such a chaotic history had taken place in the Congo without my close attention. I remember Patrice Lumumba, Congo's first Prime Minister, being discussed on the news, and I remember my parents talking about him; I did not remember that he was murdered.

The Poisonwood Bible is a story of commitment, love, and tragedy. I am still comprehending it as I discuss it with friends (and I try to get them to read it when I can). It is the kind of story that you remember and want to talk about. For the rest of my life, I will be just a little bit more alert to information about the Congo, and probably will remain curious about its history. At the same time, I learned more about the relationships between women in a family—how people differ and how they deal with the challenges created by those differences. This story has everything to do with relationships among people of different races, and it presents every permutation of those relationships. While reading this book, it would be unusual for readers not to examine their own biases, the old mental tapes that influence our connections across racial barriers; certainly that happened to me.

My description of my comprehension of *The Poisonwood Bible* may seem far too detailed, but, in fact, it represents only a fragment of my thinking about this book. There may be other texts that would not require so much description; but all of them require more thinking than can be described in words. When we comprehend, we use imagination, imagery, memory, reflection, and connection. Our minds focus on the concepts and ideas we are reading but, with lightning swiftness, branch out to our own memories, to other texts we have read (or seen on the movie, TV, or video screen), and to what we have previously learned about the world. I could describe my reading as systems of cognitive strategies. Of course, hundreds of connections and actions are taking place in my brain while I read and as I think about my reading afterwards; we can only hypothesize about what is happening in the mind when we read.

Systems of Strategies for Comprehending Texts

STRATEGY:	DEFINITION:
Strategies for Sustaining Reading	**Systems of strategies sustain a reader's processing of a text and allow for the use of various sources of information, including meaning, language knowledge, and the visual information in print.**
1. Solving Words	During the reading of continuous text, readers employ a range of strategies to figure out words while maintaining a sense of meaning.
2. Monitoring and Correcting	Readers constantly check on themselves as to whether reading makes sense, sounds right, and matches the visual information in print, and they self-correct when necessary for meaning and accuracy.
3. Gathering	Readers search for and pick up essential information from the text so that they can fit it into their general interpretation.
4. Predicting	Readers anticipate the meaning and language of a text in a way that makes their processing more efficient.
5. Maintaining Fluency	Readers process the print at a good rate, pausing appropriately, dividing the text into phrase units, and stressing words as prompted by meaning; in silent and oral reading, strategies work together to sustain rate and fluency.
6. Adjusting	Readers vary their rate and style of reading according to purpose and the type of text they are processing.
Strategies for Expanding Meaning	**Systems of strategies provide for the reader to go beyond the literal text and construct unique interpretations.**
7. Connecting	Before, during, and after they process a text, readers make connections to what they already know; they connect to their personal experiences, their knowledge of the world, and the other texts they have read or experienced.
8. Inferring	Readers go beyond the words of a given text to make judgments about what is implied but not stated.
9. Summarizing	As they process a text, readers accumulate information in summary form so that they can remember it in their ongoing interpretations.
10. Synthesizing	Readers reconfigure information, integrating it with their own prior knowledge, drawn from personal, world, and text experiences; readers may think differently after reading a text.
11. Analyzing	Readers examine the elements of a text closely to look at the writer's craft and understand the features (language, organization, etc.) that make a text work.
12. Critiquing	Before, during, and after reading a text, readers make judgments about it.

From Fountas, I.C., & Pinnell, G.S. 2001. *Guiding Readers and Writers, Grades 3–6: Teaching Comprehension, Genre, and Content Literacy.* Portsmouth, NH: Heinemann.

FIGURE 1-1

As teachers of reading, we think constantly about the reading process and what is going on in the minds of our students. If we can develop a way of thinking and talking about comprehension, it will inform our teaching and the way we support students. We can categorize the kinds of strategies that are going on in the head while reading. Thinking about these strategies will help support the kind of deep comprehension that we want our students to experience.

Strategies for Comprehending Texts

Strategies are "in-the-head" operations that we cannot see, but we know they are there because students give us evidence of them through their behavior while reading and after they read. I will describe 12 strategies. We must be cautious when labeling strategies, because there are an uncounted number of them taking place in the human brain. The 12 I examine, however, deal directly with the demands that texts make on readers. In other words, we will be talking about what it takes to read and understand a written text. The first six strategies are called *sustaining strategies* because they have to do with the basic processing of a text with understanding. The second six are called *expanding strategies* because they involve going beyond the text to construct meaning in the mind. (See Fountas & Pinnell 2001.) These strategies are shown in Figure 1-1.

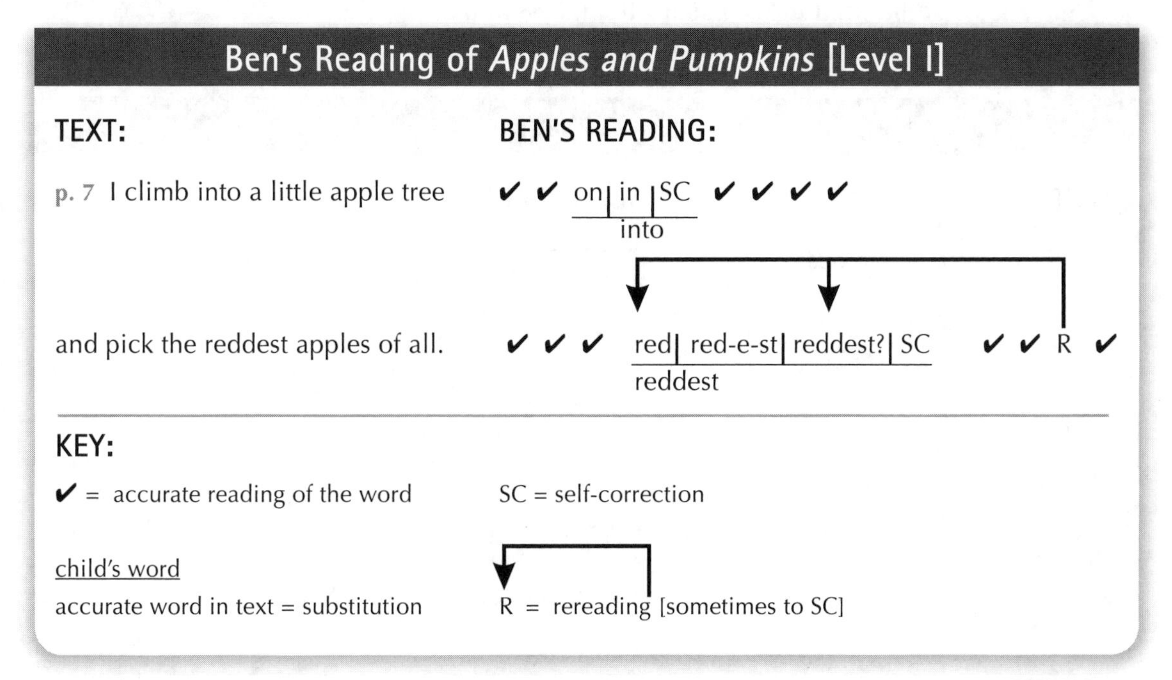

FIGURE 1-2

Strategies for Sustaining Reading

Sustaining strategies are what readers do to process a text. Processing a text means orchestrating several different kinds of information while eyes move across print. It involves keeping a focus on meaning—that is, understanding a text while at the same time recognizing and decoding words. The following six categories describe the processing of text.

SOLVING WORDS

Readers use a range of strategies to take words apart and understand word meanings while reading continuous text. For example, as shown in Figure 1-2, Ben was reading *Apples and Pumpkins* (Rockwell 1989) [Level I]. He substituted "on" for "into," but quickly changed his substitution to "in" and then to the accurate word. Ben probably was predicting from his knowledge of language when he said "on," but he noticed a known word, "in," and then picked up more visual information. Ben was solving words, but also making them fit with visual information as well as with meaning and language structure. Later in the same sentence, he did more complex word-solving. He substituted "red" for "reddest," an unknown word, hesitating briefly as if noticing that "red" was not quite right, yet he kept going to the word "of." Then, he stopped and returned to the word "reddest," this time analyzing the word left to right to decode the ending "-est." His rising tone after the self-correction may have indicated that the word still sounded a bit strange to him.

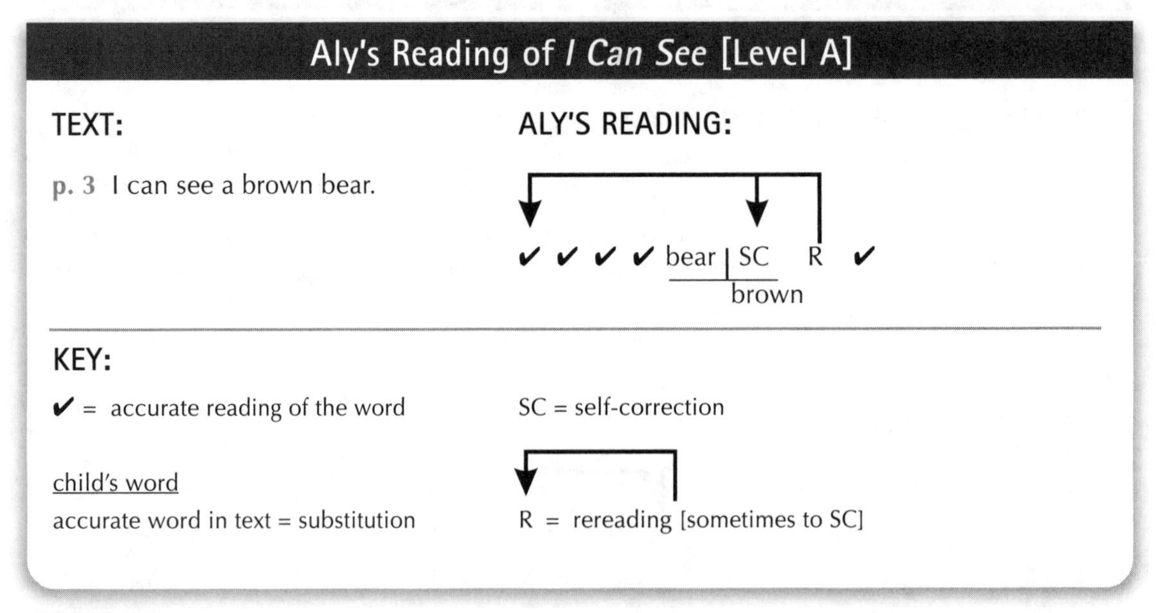

FIGURE 1-3

Good readers rapidly recognize known words and use letters, letter clusters, and syllables to break up unfamiliar words for analysis. While they are capable of analyzing words left to right, they tend to efficiently use everything they know, including word parts and base words, to solve unfamiliar words. Good readers combine word-solving in flexible ways and use language and text meaning to construct individual word meaning. Efficient word-solvers devote maximum attention to understanding a text.

MONITORING AND CORRECTING

Good readers constantly check on themselves to regulate performance. This process is largely unconscious in mature readers, but overt in beginning readers. You can tell they are checking themselves by observing their behavior. An early example of monitoring is shown in Figure 1-3.

Aly, an emergent reader, was carefully pointing to each word as she read this easy text, *I Can See* (Klein 2000) [Level A]. She had just developed the concept that one spoken word was matched with a word on the page (as defined by white space). When she substituted "bear" for "brown" (relying on a predictable language pattern that made sense), she simply ran out of words, so to speak. Another attempt to read the line led to self-correction. The important thing is that, even though her understanding was at a beginning level, Aly was using what she knew to check on herself as a reader and, finally, to self-correct.

The beginning of monitoring emerges as young readers notice the mismatch between their responses and the print. For a text reading "will see," for example, a reader may say "see," but stop, knowing that "see" does not start like "will." Monitoring and correcting refer not only to accurate reading of print but to comprehension. Good readers notice when they do not understand and they search for more information. Ben's oral reading, shown in Figure 1-2, indicates that he was closely monitoring his reading at the sentence level. In fact, the final repetition of the line indicates his confirmation in making all sources fit together.

More sophisticated readers constantly check on their understanding of a text. If it does not make sense, or if they have lost the thread of a story, good readers will scan back in the text looking for information they may have missed. They will even reread from the point of confusion.

GATHERING

Readers continuously pick up information from the print and put it together. As they process a text, they locate and use the important ideas, and they grasp the literal meaning because they have read and understood the words. They also use the information provided by print features such as punctuation, font changes, and headings, and graphic features like diagrams or maps. Gathering refers to a reader grasping the basic information provided by the text—which may be quite a complicated process, given the different sources of information available to readers of sophisticated texts.

To understand *Three Days on a River in a Red Canoe* (Williams 1981), for example, readers would need from the beginning to build an idea of a journey that has a great deal of meaning for the narrator. The illustrations show a hand-drawn map of the river and travelers' provisions and equipment. Readers would also notice that the people in the story were not wealthy; they put their money together to buy a used canoe and had to be budget-conscious in purchasing equipment and supplies.

The details in this story bring to life the adventure of traveling for three days by canoe. The story also includes informational material, such as illustrated directions for setting up a tent, tying knots, making a small cooking fire, and cooking dumplings and a stew from dried fruit, which is conveyed through a character's journal. When the story ends with this sentence, "It seems I can still hear the sound of the river running over the rocks," a good

Sarah's Reading of *Apples and Pumpkins* [Level I]

TEXT:	SARAH'S READING:
p. 18 On Halloween night	p. 18 On Halloween night [pause]
we put our pumpkin on the doorstep.	we put our pumpkin on the doorstep. [pause]
My mother gives away lots of	My mother gives away lots [pause] of
our red and shiny apples.	our red and shiny apples
for trick or treat,	for trick or treat, [brief pause, turning page quickly]
p. 19 while I go trick-or-treating	p. 19 while I go trick-or-treating [pause]
up and down our street.	up and down our street.

FIGURE 1-4

reader will understand why the little girl has that special feeling because the basic information has been gathered and comprehended.

PREDICTING

As they read, readers continually anticipate what will follow. Prediction may take place at the sentence, paragraph, or larger text level. Readers use their knowledge of language, for example, to keep moving forward, and they use language redundancy to their advantage. Consider this sentence: "The seven sisters guarded the tomb of their mother until the trumpets signaled the soldiers' retreat." The "s" in "sisters" and the plural possessive "their" are signaled by the word "seven." The predictive value of this redundancy means that the word-solving, as well as checking and confirming accuracy, are more efficient; they take less attention, leaving more attention for interpretation and meaning-making.

Readers also predict at the text level, thinking forward to what might happen. In *Three Days on a River in a Red Canoe*, for example, the reader might wonder on page three how the extra paddle, the 20 feet of rope, and the packages of freeze-dried chicken and dried apricots would be used. The details foreshadow potential adventures.

MAINTAINING FLUENCY

When good readers process a text orally they reproduce the author's intended syntax (grammatical structure), which is signaled by punctuation and sentence structure, in order to read in phrases and at a good rate. According to Fountas and Pinnell (2001), a good oral/silent reading rate for levels H–M is 75–100 words per minute (WPM). For levels L–P, a good oral rate is 100–124 WPM, and a good silent reading rate is 115–140 WPM. Fluency is not simply *fast* reading. You may have students who read robotically but fast, running right over the punctuation and displaying no awareness of phrasing. In fact, fluency is deeply related to comprehension, as indicated by a study of fourth-graders' oral reading behavior (Pinnell, Pikulski, Wixson, Campbell, Gough, & Beatty 1995). When asked to read orally an easy text (for the third time), students who scored higher on the reading comprehension test of the National Assessment of Educational Progress also read with far greater fluency than lower-scoring students.

The rate of reading is related to:

- the reader's anticipation of meaning.
- the ability to quickly recognize and solve words.
- the ability to recognize and use punctuation.
- the reader's knowledge and ability to use syntactic patterns (language structure).

As Sarah read the last part of *Apples and Pumpkins*, she paused to indicate her interpretation of the meaning of the story, as shown in Figure 1-4. Sarah was processing this Level I text with ease. She made brief pauses where she sensed a phrase unit. These phrase units were not always signaled by commas or periods, but were sometimes left to the reader's interpretation. After the word "treat," which is set off by a comma, the sentence continues on the next page—sometimes a difficult layout for a transitional reader like Sarah. Recognizing that the sentence continued on, she paused briefly and turned the page quickly, letting her voice pattern indicate that the sentence was ongoing. Her pause after "trick-or-treating" emphasized the conclusion of the story.

Once word-by-word matching is established and the finger is used only occasionally to mark the reader's place, fluency with phrasing is an important goal. Kit provided evidence that she thinks phrasing is important, as shown in Figure 1-5. While reading *How Have I Grown?* (Reid 1993) [Level H], she paused dramatically after the word "my," which is set off by a comma, and she ended this last sentence of the book by strongly stressing the last word. She was reading a text that was well within her control and constructing meaning throughout the process.

ADJUSTING

Good readers approach different reading tasks in different ways, making adjustments as they go. Narrative texts, for example, are meant to be read from beginning to end as the story unfolds. As pointed out earlier, readers may slow down to problem-solve or scan back in the text to pick up information. Informational texts may sometimes be read in any order; readers may scan the table of contents or index for the information they want and go to a specific page or section. They may skim the text to search for information, then focus in to read something intently. Some parts of the text may be skipped. When readers are trying to learn something new or remember information from a text, they may reread several times. All of these ways of reading are useful, and good readers know when and how to apply them.

Kit's Reading of *How Have I Grown?* [Level H]

TEXT:	KIT'S READING:
p. 32 My, how I've grown!	p. 32 My [pause], how I've grown! [stress on last word]

FIGURE 1-5

How Have I Grown? is a long text for an early reader—32 pages. The layout, closely tied to illustrations, is unpredictable because the print is clustered next to illustrations in several different places on the page. It appears at the left, top, bottom, or to the left and right of smaller pictures. The sentence structure is equally unpredictable. As she read this book, Kit found some of the words (e.g., "measure" and "compare") challenging, but most of the text was within her control. Each time she turned the page, though, she carefully searched for the print and paused to give close attention to the pictures as she constructed meaning. She adjusted the way she read to deal with the tricky parts of the text.

In reading *Three Days on a River in a Red Canoe*, a reader could skip the insets that provide instructions in specific areas; in fact, that adjustment might be quite productive, allowing readers to follow a general account of the journey without interruption. They might return to the story—and this wonderful book certainly warrants careful study and rereading—and at that time enjoy the instructional pages.

Strategies for Expanding Meaning

Strategies for expanding meaning allow readers to go beyond the specific text that is being processed. To an extent, an individual's experience with a text is different from every other person's reading of it, because he or she brings a unique set of experiences and background to the reading. Understanding is expanded when readers make connections, infer, summarize, synthesize, analyze, and critique a text. While these expanding strategies become quite sophisticated in advanced readers, their roots are in the earliest experiences of learning to read.

MAKING CONNECTIONS

Before, during, and after they process a text, readers make connections to what they already know. All of us have funds of knowledge built through our experiences with the world, including the following:

- **Personal experiences.** Throughout life, we learn about human problems, relationships, circumstances, and places. These experiences help us predict what is likely to happen or judge whether characters or their problems are realistic.
- **World knowledge.** Through content area study and other learning experiences, we build knowledge of the world and its phenomena. This knowledge helps us understand concepts in the texts we read and to judge their accuracy.
- **Text knowledge.** Everything we read builds knowledge of texts. While reading one text, we often make connections to another we have read or experienced. In reading *The Poisonwood Bible*, described earlier in this chapter, I made connections to two other

texts I had read: *The Flame Trees of Thika: Memories of an African Childhood* (Huxley 1981) and *Out of Africa* (Dineson 1992). These two texts, both nonfiction and focusing on wealthy Caucasian colonists, told quite a different story from *The Poisonwood Bible.*

From their earliest experiences, children make connections while reading. Figure 1-6 describes comments made by children during the teacher's introduction of *My Cat Muffin* (Gardner 1996) [Level B]. For a level B book, this text has somewhat challenging concepts (e.g., *kind, smart, brave*) that require connections and interpretation. The children in this group spontaneously made connections between their personal experiences and what they knew about cats. The teacher used some of the language of the story but invited children to comment. She went on to explore other concepts, not only as shown in the illustrations, but in connection to what children knew about ideas such as *kind* and *brave.*

Introduction and Comments—*My Cat Muffin* [Level B]

TEACHER:	TEXT:	CHILDREN'S RESPONSES:
This story is about a cat called Muffin. The title is "My Cat Muffin."	"My Cat Muffin"	**John:** I've got a cat. **Twyla:** (repeat) My Cat Muffin. The cat's name is Muffin.
Look at page 1. There's Muffin.	"My cat Muffin is funny."	**Twyla:** She's got on shoes. **Andy:** ...and glasses. **John:** (laughs)
Do you think Muffin is funny, Sammy?		**Sammy:** A cat doesn't wear clothes and glasses.
On the next page Muffin is chasing a butterfly. Look at those little marks by her feet. The illustrator wants to show that Muffin is moving very fast.	"My cat Muffin is fast."	**Twyla:** She's jumping up. **Sammy:** But she's running too.
So your cat is fast just like Muffin, John.		**John:** My cat can really run fast.

FIGURE 1-6

INFERRING

Good readers go beyond the literal meaning of a text. They wonder *why* and think about *what if.* They think about what is implied in the writer's message, not what is precisely stated. Once when I was reading *The Trek* (Jonas 1985) to a group of first graders, I realized that some of them did not understand that the little girl who tells the story is using her imagination. In this story, a little girl begins by saying, "My mother doesn't walk me to school anymore" (p. 1). She goes on to say, "But she doesn't know we live on the edge of a jungle" (p. 4). The text is straightforward. The little girl talks about seeing animals everywhere she goes—at the waterhole and while walking through the desert, swimming the river, and going through the jungle. She and her friend use their skills to hide from the animals and finally make it to school. The illustrations by Donald Cruz, however, reveal that the animals are only in the girls' imaginations. You have to look closely to see a hippo in the pile of watermelons at the market, a swan in a pile of newspapers, and lizards in vines climbing a brick wall. This text can be visited again and again, once the concept is understood. A discussion with the children helped them to think about their own imaginary play, in which they almost see people, animals, and objects. They began to understand that the

Discussion of *Henry and Mudge Get the Cold Shivers* [Level J]

TEACHER:	CHILDREN'S RESPONSES:
That was a really good ending to that story, wasn't it?	**Nadia:** Henry was really glad Mudge wasn't sick anymore. Because when Henry was sick he liked it, but he didn't like it when Mudge was sick.
How do you think Henry felt when Mudge was sick?	**Desiree:** He was scared because Mudge hadn't ever been sick and he didn't think dogs could be sick. Mudge was just lying there and acting funny.
	Nadia: He wouldn't eat. You go to a vet when your dog is sick and he gets a shot. I bet the doctor gave him a shot when she told Henry to go out of the room. But he didn't want to go because he thought she would hurt Mudge.

FIGURE 1-7

illustrator was showing readers what the little girl imagined, and they even went on to make comments such as these:

"It's more fun for her to walk to school if she imagines animals there."

"She likes to do it with her friend—like playing instead of walking."

"She used to be scared but now she just thinks the animals are fun."

Reading aloud to children is a great way to help them begin to think beyond a text. You can encourage readers to go beyond the text in guided and independent reading as well.

As shown in Figure 1-7, during a discussion of *Henry and Mudge Get the Cold Shivers* (Rylant 1989) [Level J] the children were able to talk about what Henry feels as a character, something that was not elaborated in the text.

SUMMARIZING

Readers put together information as they process a text. Summarizing does not refer simply to a concise statement of the important events or facts after reading a text; readers summarize as they go to help them remember important information. In reading *Henry and Mudge Get the Cold Shivers*, for example, readers' implicit summary statements of what happened when Henry got sick helped them comprehend and appreciate the situation when Mudge got sick. Henry's sick days involved getting Popsicles, comic books, and crackers from his parents (and Mudge always got the crackers). Mudge's doctor said that he had a cold and joked that the dog was asking for comic books. So Mudge's illness parallels Henry's, except that Mudge got ice cubes, rubber toys, and crackers (which Henry ate). The reader's awareness of this parallel structure is made possible because of ongoing summarizing of information during the reading. Of course, readers also summarize information after reading, remembering the gist of a longer story so that the information can be accessed for different purposes.

SYNTHESIZING

After reading a text, you may realize that your own view of the world has changed slightly. This happens when you integrate new information with your existing knowledge to expand or adjust your concepts. It may also happen when you encounter human problems in a story and, after reading, believe you understand a situation or person better. After reading the tale of the city mouse and the country mouse in *City Mouse-Country Mouse and Two More Mouse Tales from Aesop* (Wallner 1970) [Level J], for example, children might have a better understanding of why the country mouse did not like the city in spite of the wonderful food and grand surroundings. After reading *Three Days on a River in a Red Canoe*, readers might have a better sense of the hardship and adventure involved in taking a

camping trip down a river. They might also build an underlying sense of the environment, including an appreciation for clean water and animals, as well as a sense of how to behave in a canoe to avoid danger.

ANALYZING

As they grow in sophistication, readers begin to examine the elements of a text more closely. Appreciating the writing of a text is part of comprehension; it also contributes to the young writer's sense of how to put words and phrases together to create quality writing. You would not involve primary children in formal analysis of the texts they read, but it is important for them to experience high-quality texts and notice the writing. While reading *Three Days on a River in a Red Canoe*, for example, readers could notice how the drawings add to the quality of the journal; they could also notice how the writer switches from telling the story to providing directions. It would not be necessary for them to identify the genre, but noticing aspects of the writer's craft sets the scene for later knowledge of text structure.

A group of second graders was reading *Martin and the Tooth Fairy* (Chardiet 1990) [Level K]. One reader noticed: "They really sound like kids talking. And it's good that the author gives all these step-by-step details because you can really see how Martin gets in trouble a little bit at a time."

These students were skeptical about the tooth fairy giving money for other people's teeth in the first place, so they hypothesized that Martin was not going to make money on the teeth he bought from his friends. All along, they were wondering how he would get out of the mess he had gotten himself into. Noticing how texts are put together enhances readers' overall understanding of the text.

A second-grade reader noticed that Frog and Toad have particular ways of talking that made them seem funny. The whimsical language of *Frog and Toad Are Friends* (Lobel 1970) [Level K] adds to the warmth and personality of the characters. For example:

> Oh, drat, said Toad.
> Not only do my feet hurt,
> but I have lost
> one of the buttons on my jacket.

Children who notice the kinds of plots that Frog and Toad are involved in, their characteristic ways of talking, and the way the writer shows how they care about each other as friends are on the way to understanding texts as literature.

CRITIQUING

Readers learn to evaluate and critique texts. As adults, critical reading is important to us; we want to be informed consumers of written material and know how to judge it for accuracy and authenticity. We want to read financial or medical advice, for example, considering the qualifications of the writer and how the information fits with what we already know. We want to hear political speeches (which usually involve a person *reading* written text) with the appropriate skepticism.

Bringing judgment to the reading of a text begins by inviting and encouraging children's opinions. *Mom's Secret* (Costain 1997) [Level H] is a story in which a little girl tries to guess her mother's secret by asking questions. In the end, she guesses that the secret is "a new puppy" and is told that Mom is going to have a baby. When she asks whether it will be a boy or girl, the mother responds, "That's the baby's secret!" A group of first graders agreed that a baby could not really have a secret before it was born. They were acting on their own knowledge of the concept of secret and did not realize that the writer was using it metaphorically. They understood the idea better after discussion, but they were right to question the text. In reading *Nate the Great and the Missing Key* (Sharmat 1981) [Level K], one second grader suggested that she did not really like Nate very much because he was always "bragging" by saying, "I, Nate the Great." She did, however, go on to read several other Nate the Great books. In reading *Bats* (MacLulich 1996) [Level K], some readers questioned whether a bat could really be as big as a cat because nothing in their own experience suggested such a thing and the illustration did not really offer proof. They were prompted to seek confirming information. The fact that the author was connected with a museum provided some credibility for the author's statement, but the question remained open. As a foundation for later, more sophisticated, critical reading, we want readers to ask questions and form opinions as they read.

Summary

Using reading strategies is not a linear process, nor are strategies discrete entities. In this chapter, I defined strategies and separated them into categories to help us think more clearly about what readers do when they comprehend text. It is tempting to talk about teaching strategies one at a time. We can focus on any aspect of the reading process as we work with students while they read text; however, all texts require the integrated use of all strategies. We cannot talk about using one strategy for one text and another for the next. Certainly, we cannot identify a book to teach inferring and another to teach synthesizing. These strategies are employed constantly in a smooth and fluid way as readers process every text

they encounter. They may occasionally bring their thinking to conscious levels, thus increasing self-awareness. Indeed, you may promote this awareness through your teaching, with the goal of expanding readers' processing systems to think more about texts and better understand them. Largely, though, strategies are employed in an unconscious way; they all work together for the construction of meaning.

Ideas to Try

1. To understand what readers do, explore your own thinking while reading a text of your choice. Then talk with a friend about the experience. It might be fun to have a "read and talk" lunch with some of your colleagues. Or, for this experiment, you might want to read and talk with a friend who loves to read but is not a teacher. I recommend these wonderful works:

   - *East of the Mountains* by David Guterson (Harcourt, Brace & Co.). In this story, a retired heart surgeon with colon cancer sets out on his last hunt, walking across mountainous territory in central Washington State. He finds more than a place to die.
   - *The Bonesetter's Daughter* by Amy Tan (G.P. Putnam's Sons). This is the story of LuLing Young, who is searching for the name of her mother as she writes of her mysterious girlhood in China, and of her daughter Ruth, who learns by reading her mother's diary.
   - *The Last Time They Met* by Anita Shreve (Little, Brown and Company). This romantic and mysterious story begins when two former lovers meet after years apart and recall the affair that changed their lives. Keep reading to the final page for an interesting surprise.

2. If you like short stories, you might consider talking about one of the stories from:

   - *A View from Saturday* by E.L. Konigsburg (Atheneum)
   - *Every Living Thing* by Cynthia Rylant. Illustrated by S.D. Schindler (Bradbury/Simon & Schuster)

3. As you read, mark just one or two places that, *for any reason*, you want to talk about with your friend. Marking too many places will tend to interfere with your reading because you will start studying the text.

4. In your informal discussion, you might consider the following:

    - Talk about anything in the book that reminds you of your own life—characters, setting, feelings, events, and so on.
    - Consider what kind of background knowledge you brought to your reading. Had you visited, studied, or read about the setting for the story? Did you find yourself remembering events in history as you read?
    - How did reading this book affect your thinking? Did you expand your knowledge in any way? Did you enrich your understanding of people or the human condition?
    - What were the most important ideas in the story?
    - How did the writer make characters come alive for you?
    - What did you like (or not like) about the writer's style?
    - Talk about how (and where in the text) your thinking went beyond the literal meanings. Did you make assumptions or hypotheses? (You will be especially challenged by Shreve's book.)

5. In your discussion, you will find that you are talking about the process of your thinking, and you will actually probe the cognitive strategies that you want to help your students develop.

6. Choose a book that your students will be reading in guided reading sometime during the next week or so. With your colleagues, talk about the demands that even this simple text makes on readers.

    - Are they expected to make inferences, that is, to go beyond the text?
    - What background information will be required to understand the text?
    - Are there new words that they will be required to understand?
    - How do you expect their understandings to change (even slightly) as a result of reading this book?
    - How will it enhance the readers' enjoyment and understanding to make connections to their own lives?

This kind of thinking and talking about texts will help you make better decisions about your book introductions, as well as your interactions with readers, because you will always be thinking about comprehension.

CHAPTER 2

Teaching for Comprehension Across the Language and Literacy Framework

Gay Su Pinnell & Irene C. Fountas

No one instructional concept or approach can provide the support children need to be good comprehenders of written text. Comprehension is built through numerous and varied experiences with texts—hearing them read aloud, reading them independently, reading them with support and guidance, writing about them, and sharing the reading with others. Teaching for comprehension requires helping children construct meaning all the time, whenever they encounter texts.

By implementing a broad-based language and literacy framework, you can maximize your students' opportunities to construct meaning from text. In this chapter, we describe this framework; for each component, we describe the opportunities to teach for comprehending strategies.

Advantages of a Framework

Using a language/literacy framework has several advantages as you plan for literacy instruction. It can:

- provide a common language and vision that will facilitate grade-level discussions as well as planning across the grades. It makes it easier to articulate curriculum and develop a common set of practices. This common language also helps students because the more consistent the curriculum and management routines across the grades, the more predictable the environment. Students know what is expected of them in terms of productivity and routines; this predictability gives them more attention to devote to learning.
- support the efficient use of time. It provides for specific time allocations for reading, writing, and word study. By working with colleagues, you can reserve times schoolwide that are dedicated to literacy learning. Ideally, you would allocate 30 to 60 minutes for language and word study, an hour for reading, and an hour for writing. And you make connections across these three curriculum areas.
- make it possible to build routines for independent learning. As discussed in Chapter 13, the independent activities will change from kindergarten to second and third grade; however, the important thing is that students know they are expected to meet expectations for individual work.

- help you systematically plan for connections among different instructional contexts. Content areas can be integrated so that students are reading and writing about important topics or concepts.

Three Blocks of Time

In the past, we have presented the language/literary framework as a set of interrelated reading and writing contexts. Recently, however, we have focused on the management of instruction, and have found it useful to conceptualize the framework as three blocks of time: one for language/word study, one for reading, and one for writing. (See Figure 2-1.)

These blocks are helpful in managing time and planning for instruction. In addition, the intermediate framework that we use is also based on three blocks of time. This way of thinking promotes articulation between primary and intermediate instruction.

Block One: Language/Word Study

The focus of the language/word study block is to help children develop language knowledge and skills. This includes knowledge of how words *work* as well as investigation of the nature of language. A very important goal is to help children learn to notice, enjoy, and use language for many purposes.

In this component of the framework, children study words—their visual patterns as well as letter/sound relationships—so that they become good "word-solvers." They also explore high-quality literature and poetry so that they start to appreciate powerful and interesting language. The language/word study block provides some of the building blocks of comprehension—for example, the flexible word-solving that is basic to rapidly processing a text, leaving attention for meaning. At the same time, the language/word study block provides the opportunity to expand comprehending ability through books that are read aloud. Below, we define the components of the language/word study block.

INTERACTIVE READ-ALOUD

When you read aloud to students, you read the words for them and offer a demonstration of reading with phrasing and fluency. Freed from decoding, they can give their full attention to the meaning of the text. This creates an ideal situation for them to expand their comprehending strategies. When you read aloud, you are building up meaning and text resources that students can use throughout elementary school and beyond, perhaps throughout life.

A Language/Literacy Framework for Grades K–2

Children in primary grades are involved in a range of interrelated activities for learning about oral and written language, with emphasis on enjoyment, language play, and foundational concepts such as letters, sounds, and words. In many ways, they explore and learn about the relationships between oral and written language. The framework is implemented within an integrated two- and three-hour block of time.

BLOCK ONE: LANGUAGE/WORD STUDY

Interactive Read-Aloud	Students hear written language read aloud on a daily basis.
Shared Reading	Class engages in shared reading of enlarged texts to develop knowledge of early reading behaviors, high-frequency words, and letter-sound relationships.
Shared and Interactive Writing	Students participate in shared writing, interactive writing, and group instruction to learn how written language works, as well as to experience the writing process.
Word Study Mini-Lessons	Students participate in systematic study of letters, sounds, and words as part of each day's work.
Content Area Connections	Through discussion, reading aloud, and short lessons, students make connections to science, social studies, and other content areas.

BLOCK TWO: READING AND INDEPENDENT WORK

Guided Reading	Students read teacher-selected leveled texts in guided reading (small-group instruction within which teachers provided specific instruction on effective reading strategies).
Independent Language and Literacy Work	Students read independently to apply principles; active, systematic study of spelling principles (Buddy Study System activity and word study application activity); independent writing, listening, and projects related to content areas.
Group Share	Groups of students reflect on the quality of independent work.

BLOCK THREE: A WRITING WORKSHOP

Writing Mini-Lesson	Students hear written language read aloud on a daily basis.
Writing and Conferring	With the teacher, students write independently to apply principles.
Sharing	Class discusses and gives feedback on the application of principles to individual writing.

FIGURE 2-1

We often remember books that our teachers have read to us and use them to make connections between texts.

The wonderful text *Owl Moon* (Yolen 1987) tells the story of a little girl and her father who go out on a snowy winter evening to watch for owls. During an interactive read-aloud, some children commented that the little girl had waited a long time for her Pa to take her owling and that her brothers, who had been on the adventure years before, must have told her about it, based on the quote, "My brothers all said sometimes there's an owl and sometimes there isn't." This text also has beautiful language. With several rereadings, students will internalize language, such as:

> The moon made his face into a silver mask.
>
> The shadows were the blackest things I had ever seen. They stained the white snow.
>
> We watched silently with heat in our mouths, the heat of all those words we had not spoken.

Books such as *Owl Moon* provide literary resources for students as they write and read. The text is far beyond the reading competency of the first- or second-grade students who will hear the text read aloud, but they can understand the magic of the feeling between the father and the little girl, and can imagine the frozen, hushed setting in which owls are seen. Students thus learn to comprehend complex texts before they can read such texts for themselves, and they store up meaning and language knowledge for future reading.

SHARED READING

In the language/literacy block, you will be involving children in shared reading. They participate in the reading of a familiar text so they will know what it is like to be a reader. Through such participation, they develop knowledge of early reading behaviors and accumulate high-frequency words that they can recognize. While shared reading is often cited as a support for early strategies (word-by-word matching, locating words, using initial consonants, and so on), we can also make a case for its contribution to comprehension. As children process a text again and again, reading it with the support of their peers, they not only internalize the words but understand in deeper, more complex ways.

SHARED AND INTERACTIVE WRITING

Shared/interactive writing is a group writing context in which you have the opportunity to demonstrate the strategies and skills involved in writing. The structure of interactive writing, shown in Figure 2-2, mirrors the writing process. This structure is briefly described below.

- **Establishing a purpose for writing.** Interactive writing emerges from real experiences in the classroom that give rise to a need for writing. For example, one kindergarten teacher read a KEEP BOOK® (for additional information, see Appendix), *My Map*, and took the children for a walk around the school neighborhood. When they returned to the classroom, they decided to make their own map, which turned into a large mural. Writing emerged as a way to tell about their map, as they labeled the mural with sentences such as: "We made streets. We made houses." Another group of children enjoyed stories about the Little Red Hen. After hearing several versions many times, they decided to write their own story, with a twist. This time, the Little Red Hen would make a pizza. Their goal required them to think about the ingredients in a pizza and the steps in making one. At the same time, they had to think about the structure of this traditional tale and the language that characters use. These experiences gave rise to a reason to write.

- **Preparing to write.** In preparing to write, encourage children to think about a writing project based on their own experience. Then discuss the kind of text to write and the format you will use—perhaps a letter, a list, labels, or a story.

- **Composing the text.** As the discussion proceeds, guide the students to settle on the precise words for the text. They should relate these words to the meaning that they want to communicate.

Structure of Interactive Writing

- Establishing a purpose for writing
- Preparing to write
- Composing the text
- Constructing the text
- Extending the text

FIGURE 2-2

- **Constructing the text.** Constructing the text means to write (or encode) it. Once the text has been decided, students keep it in mind while they focus on the details of writing. To construct a text, students must think about the first word to write, then think about the first sound and the corresponding letter and write it, followed by the next sound, and so on. Patterns of letters are useful in the process. Competent writers enter into these operations automatically, without even thinking about them. For beginning writers, it is a challenge to concentrate on the letters and sounds necessary to construct a text while at the same time keeping the meaning of the whole text in mind.

- **Extending the text.** Once written, the text is a resource that students can return to again and again for many purposes. They might enjoy rereading it for shared reading; or they may use it as a resource for words that they want to write. The text will generally be more complex than the children could produce on their own, so it will serve as a model for language structures to draw on when students do their own writing.

In shared/interactive writing, children experience the composing and constructing of a text. You can demonstrate how different kinds of texts (letters, descriptions, stories, lists, reports) really work. In composing, students decide on an organizational structure, which is an important factor in understanding a text. Comprehension is not an issue here because the text arose in response to an authentic need and is related to their real experiences. They created the text together and participated in the details of writing it. Thus, when they reread it, they have extended experiences in reading with ease and understanding a text more complex than they can read for themselves.

WORD STUDY MINI-LESSONS

The ability to solve words is basic to processing a text in reading and constructing a text in writing. Phonics and spelling skills are developed across the many contexts of the language and literacy framework, but it's a good idea to set aside a time for direct attention to letters, sounds, and words. "The word study mini-lesson is a brief, powerful, direct piece of teaching that clearly demonstrates a principle of process to students. Mini-lessons are usually followed by an application activity that involves students in some kind of inquiry and then in sharing and discussion so that students can talk with one another about what they have discovered" (Lyons & Pinnell 2001, p. 131).

The Buddy Study System for Learning to Spell

ACTIVITY:	DESCRIPTION:	MATERIALS NEEDED:
DAY ONE Choose, Write, Build	The teacher provides a mini-lesson, making a chart of examples. Children choose words and write them on cards and the teacher checks. Children make words three times with magnetic letters.	• Easel and chart paper • Chart to post in room • Spelling card for each child • Magnetic letters
DAY TWO Look, Say, Cover, Write, Check	Children use a system for examining the word closely, covering it with a folder flap, writing it without the model, and then checking it letter by letter with accurate spelling. For each word, they repeat the process three times.	• File folders, with one side cut to make either three or four flaps • Sheets of paper with columns, with lines, to insert in folders so that children can write words
DAY THREE Buddy Check	Partners give each other a practice test. For words they miss, they try again and use a yellow highlighter to mark the parts they want to remember. Words they miss several times, they make with magnetic letters three times.	• Word cards for buddies to read • Paper and pencil for practice text • Yellow highlighters • Magnetic letters
DAY FOUR Making Connections	Children make connections between each of their spelling words and other words. They connect words by meaning, visual patterns, sound, and other ways.	• Forms for making connections, e.g., ____looks like ________ ____ sounds like ______ ____means same as ____
DAY FIVE Buddy Test	Partners give each other a test, written in a small booklet, and the teacher checks it later.	• Test booklets

The Buddy Study System is described in detail in Fountas & Pinnell (1996).

FIGURE 2-3

BUDDY STUDY SYSTEM

As children grow more sophisticated (perhaps toward the end of first grade or the beginning of second grade), a systematic spelling study system is implemented in addition to daily phonics. This "buddy study system" provides for five days of active exploration, with the goal of helping children to derive generative principles that they can apply to spelling many words in addition to the specific ones that they study. The daily system is outlined in Figure 2-3.

You may be wondering what spelling and word study have to do with comprehension. Of course, recognizing and rapidly solving words are part of keeping a basic reading process going; the less attention you must give to word-solving, the more attention you can devote to understanding and expanding meaning. Beyond word-solving, think about the connections between words that students make as part of the process. Making such connections is precisely the way vocabulary increases, and vocabulary is basic to comprehension. We cannot learn every one of the some 600,000 words in English (and we would assume about the same in other languages) as isolated units. Instead, we construct networks of understandings about words. Consider this set: *found, foundation, founder [become stuck], founder [person who establishes something], founding fathers, foundling, foundry, foundry proof, found money, foundation garment, foundational to*.... Thinking of "found" as a meaning base can lead you to understand all of these varied meanings, and to search for more examples. It is easy to become fascinated with words.

CONTENT AREA CONNECTIONS

Because you will usually meet with the entire class in the language/word study block, take the opportunity to make connections with areas of content study. After all, children must read and write about something of interest. Young children are a little more willing than adults to practice reading just to get better at it, but practice wears thin. All of us read to discover something interesting.

The books you read aloud to students can be connected to social studies, science, health, and other content areas. Doing this delivers texts to children that are beyond their present capabilities for independent reading—because you read the text to them, they can concentrate on the meaning. Through hearing stories read aloud, children learn that the expectation is that they will *think* about reading and learn from it. They also build vocabulary and language knowledge. When you read aloud in content areas, you build a foundation for later reading of informational texts.

Likewise, interactive/shared writing can focus on content areas. Anything children learn about can be the subject of interactive/shared writing. When children compose a text that restates what they have learned, their understanding deepens and they can later read and reread the piece of writing.

Block Two: Reading Workshop

The reading workshop block includes three interrelated components:

- Guided reading, during which you work with a small group of students to expand their reading strategies.
- Independent language and literacy work, which involves students in a variety of reading and writing activities.
- Sharing and reflection.

GUIDED READING

The goal of guided reading is comprehension of a text. In guided reading, you bring together a small group of children who have similar needs, introduce a new text to them, and support their reading. The structure of guided reading is outlined in Figure 2-4.

Structure of Guided Reading Lessons

Selecting the Text

Introducing the Text

Reading the Text

Revisiting and Discussing the Text

Teaching for Processing Strategies

Working With Words (optional)

Extending the Meaning of the Text (optional)

FIGURE 2-4

Grouping

Grouping for guided reading requires ongoing assessment of children's reading behaviors. You look for accurate reading, but reading *behavior* is actually more important. By examining students' reading, you gain insight into how they are constructing meaning from text. For example, look at Caroline's reading of *My Scrapbook* (Davidson 1998) [Level K], shown in Figure 2-5.

Caroline knew the words of this tricky book, which includes a variety of text—photographs and labels, nature collections with labels, notes, and journal entries. She had trouble, though, with the way language was used. One would not normally say, "smell spring" or "Hurry up, summer!" The author used figurative language, which seemed to make Caroline doubt her own word-solving. She was thinking literally and the figurative language structure was unfamiliar.

A conversation with her teacher after the reading helped Caroline and the rest of the reading group understand how you could imagine all the smells of spring. The little girl writing the journal wanted summer to "hurry," even though everyone knows the calendar can't be changed, just because she wanted so much to go to the farm. By the time they had this discussion, Caroline had read the rest of the text, which showed all of the fun the girl had at the farm in summer. The information from this text helped Caroline to build the meaning she needed to understand figurative language.

Every observation of children's reading behavior, along with your conversations with them about their reading, provides information that will help you assess their ability to read and comprehend texts. Grouping for guided reading is dynamic; young children change rapidly as they take on new skills in reading. Reassess often using running records and observation so that you can regroup the children. In selecting texts for guided reading, you will be considering the current strategies of your students and their needs for learning.

Caroline's Reading of *My Scrapbook* [Level K]

TEXT:	CAROLINE'S READING:	NOTES:
p. 2 Today I can smell spring.	✔ ✔ ✔ ✔ some | spr..A / spring | T	Shakes head. "Smell spring?"
p. 4 Grandpa sent me some	✔ ✔ ✔ ✔	
photos from the farm.	p- ph- ✔ / photos ✔ ✔ ✔	
Hurry up, summer!	✔ ✔ and "no" | come "no" s-A / summer	"This doesn't make sense."

KEY:

✔ = accurate reading of the word

Substitution = child's word / Text word

A = Appeal

T = Told

FIGURE 2-5

Selecting the Text

Prior to a guided reading lesson, select a text that will be *just right* for the group of readers. Text selection is a complex process. It is helpful to use a gradient of text that categorizes books as to what they demand of readers. Many different systems have been used to help teachers create leveled book collections that allow students to gradually increase their reading powers. Find a reliable leveling system and create a leveled collection for your own classroom, or create one to share with colleagues (an economical solution).

Introducing the Text

Introduce the text, taking into account the readers' strengths as well as text characteristics. The purpose of the introduction is to:

- provide a foundation for overall understanding of the text—the main idea.
- help students understand (and sometimes say) language patterns that they may find difficult.
- familiarize students with difficult concepts or ideas.
- draw attention to one or two words that students will need to solve within the context of reading continuous text.
- invite students to express their expectations of the text.

The introduction foregrounds comprehension. It sets readers up for the problem-solving they will need to do in a text that is a little bit more difficult than one they can process on their own. For example, in introducing *My Scrapbook*, the teacher could have chosen to emphasize the idea that you can *smell spring*, and children could talk about why you could use that expression and what smells would probably be involved. She might also say something such as this:

> "This little girl is really looking forward to going to her grandpa's farm in the summer.
> She wants summer to *hurry up*! Have you ever felt like that about something?
> *(Children might offer something such as their birthdays.)*
> You might want your birthday to hurry up just like this little girl wants summer to hurry up."

The introduction you provide is a scaffold. You want to create just enough support for students to read the text with understanding, but not so much that they will have no problem-solving to do. In this way, you make it possible for them to engage in the cognitive actions related to comprehension, and to learn from this process.

Reading the Text

After the introduction, each child reads the whole text (or a unified portion of it) softly or silently. This process is different from "round robin" reading, in which children take turns reading. Each student should process and understand the entire text. As they read, go around to each one and listen to a bit of oral reading. You may interact with children briefly to show them something specific about the reading, or to prompt for strategies that you have previously demonstrated.

Some prompts that are especially productive in helping readers attend to meaning are:

- Did that make sense?
- What would make sense there?
- What would make sense and look right?
- You are nearly right. What would make sense?
- That makes sense, but does it look right?
- It starts with that letter, but does it make sense?
- It looks right, but does it make sense?
- Try that again and think what would make sense.
- Try that again and think what would look right and make sense.
- Try that again and think what would sound right and make sense.
- Think of what would make sense and check the letters.
- Do you know something that would make sense and [starts like...ends like] that?
- What do you know that might help?
- Read from the beginning and try that again.
- How do you think your reading sounds? [for fluency]
- Make it sound like talking. [for fluency]

Prompts are effective only if you have previously demonstrated the expected behaviors and children have engaged in them. The precise language of the prompts should trigger an internal action that students have previously practiced.

Revisiting and Discussing the Text

After the reading, you have the opportunity to revisit the text to talk about the meaning. Collaborative discussion shores up comprehension because children's understandings are expanded by talking with others. For example, in the discussion after reading *My Scrapbook*, children talked about why they thought the little girl was so eager to get to the farm. One child mentioned swimming and took the group to page eight, where there was a photograph of swimming. Several children mentioned that they liked the new puppy Sam, that Grandpa gave the little girl, and they also loved the photograph of Jess, the horse, and her foal. This conversation helped them to understand the use of language they experienced earlier in the text.

Teaching for Processing Strategies

You can also teach for processing strategies of various kinds. Your teaching can touch on just about any opportunity the text offers. In this case, the teacher returned to the expression "I can smell spring." She had not focused on this sentence in the introduction, but thought it productive for Caroline to talk about what she had discovered, and to have students examine the meaning of this expression. She also took a look at the word "photos." Several children had substituted the word "pictures," which was meaningful; however, the teacher wanted them to notice letter clusters such as the "ph," which they knew very well.

Working With Words

After reading, you might engage students in word work. This involves taking a one- or two-minute look at words in isolation simply to discover something about spelling or phonics principles. The words have nothing to do with the text students have read; instead, they arise from your assessment of what students need to know. It might involve:

- Taking off first letters or letter clusters and substituting them with others.
- Changing the ending of words.
- Changing the middle of words.
- Adding prefixes or suffixes to words.

Word work should be brief and game-like, involving the use of magnetic letters or a white dry-erase board. It is especially helpful to children who need more experience in learning about words.

Extending the Meaning of the Text

Another option you have after the reading is to extend the text through writing, diagramming, drawing, or drama. In the case of *My Scrapbook*, because the scrapbook covers spring to winter, the teacher made a simple time line on a chart. The children placed important events, drawn from the diary, along the time line. They talked about how people keep journals and write down important things over time.

Comprehension—the Goal of All Reading

Every element of guided reading is connected to developing comprehension strategies in children.

- You select a text that is within readers' control; they will be solving problems against a backdrop of accurate reading. With supportive teaching, this text can be read with understanding and has opportunities for new learning.
- The introduction helps children think about the meaning of the text before they process it for themselves; the introduction emphasizes comprehension as the goal of reading.
- Children process the text for themselves, working for understanding with the teacher's occasional support and prompting.
- After reading, there is an opportunity to revisit the text to discuss the meaning.
- You teach for processing strategies; this process may involve explicit demonstrations of how to think about reading or searching for evidence in the text to support understanding.
- You may also involve students in word work or in extending their understanding of the text through additional activities, such as writing or diagramming.

Throughout the guided reading lesson, as shown in Figure 2-6, you can support comprehension in many different ways. The suggestions in this figure range

Supporting Children's Development of Comprehension Strategies

HIGH	Show, demonstrate, and explain effective behaviors related to comprehension.
	Share the task by giving readers opportunities to use strategies with teacher support.
	Prompt readers to engage in actions so that they use strategies for themselves.
	Reinforce effective behaviors by praising specific actions that children take.
LOW	Notice effective behaviors to inform teaching.

FIGURE 2-6

from low support to very high support, which involves explicit demonstrations. These demonstrations might include showing children how you figure out words and think about what they mean, or demonstrating your interpretations of texts so that they know what you mean. Such demonstrations can take place at any time during a guided reading lesson—before, during, or after the reading.

INDEPENDENT LANGUAGE AND LITERACY WORK

As you begin the reading workshop block, remind children of the expectations for independent work. The purpose of independent work is not simply to keep them busy while you work with small groups. While activities may vary, children should engage in activities that involve reading and writing. Some examples are as follows:

- Use *browsing boxes* for rereading familiar texts and easy texts. Create boxes for each reading group that have books they have read before, as well as books that you know will be easy for them. In this context, students will process texts with ease, fluency, and understanding.
- Have a word study application that follows the mini-lesson. This can involve making words with magnetic letters; sorting pictures, letters, or words; playing phonics games; or writing.
- Carry out the five-day steps of the Buddy Study System—one each day for about 10 minutes. (See page 41.)
- Use pocket charts for children to assemble sentence strips (shared reading of poetry and other texts) and then read them.
- Create personal poetry anthologies. Read poems in shared reading during the language/word study block; give children reproduced versions to glue into their own notebooks to read and illustrate.
- Have children listen to texts on a tape player and occasionally respond to those texts by drawing or writing.
- Ask children to read books from the classroom library.
- Create a writing center where children produce some of their own writing. You may structure the assignment (such as *weekend news* on Mondays) or leave the subject of writing up to the students.
- Have children engage in projects focused on content area study.

The expectation for independent work is that it will be quiet and productive. Children have the chance to try out reading and writing on their own, but their time is highly structured.

GROUP SHARE

Bring the group together at the end of the reading workshop block for a brief sharing period. Children can self-evaluate their use of independent work time, reflecting on whether they accomplished assigned tasks and sharing some of their discoveries (e.g., new insights relative to word work). They can talk about what they read, or you can return to your mini-lesson or something that you observed about reading that all members of the class can profit from, including comprehension strategies.

Block Three: Writing Workshop

The writing workshop involves a mini-lesson on some aspect of writing, having students engage in independent writing, and asking them to share and discuss their writing. (See Figure 2-7.)

One of the values of the language and literacy framework is the potential for connecting reading and writing. You may think that most instruction directed at comprehension takes place in the reading workshop, which is certainly a context for making the most of teaching. But writing contributes to the process in significant ways. Through writing, children:

- think about the way writers construct meaning.
- learn that writers are helping readers (audience) understand their meanings.
- learn that writers select words carefully to express meaning.
- become aware of how writers organize texts to present information clearly.
- learn what information to include and what to leave out so that the main idea is clearly revealed.

In a way, writing helps children *get inside* the process of constructing meaning.

Structure of Writing Workshop

- Mini-Lesson—Management, Convention, or Craft
- Writing and Conferring
- Sharing

FIGURE 2-7

Recent Books in First-Person Narrative

A Picnic in October by E. Bunting. Illustrated by Nancy Carpenter (Harcourt Brace).

Rudi's Pond by E. Bunting. Illustrated by Ronald Himler (Clarion).

My Dog, My Hero by B. Byars, B. Duffey, and L. Myers (Henry Holt).

26 Fairmont Avenue by T. dePaola (G. P. Putnam Sons).

Grandpa Never Lies by R. Fletcher. Illustrated by Harvey Stevenson (Clarion).

No Matter What by D. Gliori (Harcourt Brace).

I Look Like a Girl by S. Hamanaka (Morrow).

My Bear and Me by B. Maitland. Illustrated by Lisa Flather (Simon & Schuster).

I, Crocodile by F. Marcellino (HarperCollins).

I'm Taking a Trip on My Train by S. Neitzel. Illustrated by Nancy Winslow Parker (Greenwillow).

In My Momma's Kitchen by J. Nolen. Illustrated by Colin Bootman (Lothrop, Lee & Shepard).

Don't Make Me Laugh by J. Stevenson (Farrar, Straus and Giroux).

Zachary's Ball by M. Tavares (Candlewick).

Compiled by Patricia L. Scharer

FIGURE 2-8

Reading aloud to children is a key part of helping them to expand their writing powers and to develop important concepts about understanding texts. In the language/word study block, you will build up a large repertoire of high-quality texts, such as *Owl Moon*, from which children can draw as they become increasingly sophisticated in their own writing. One second-grader we remember started her story with this phrase:

> The cat headed North.

What a suspenseful and articulate beginning for a story! She accessed the kind of language she had heard as her teacher read aloud. Your selections for read-alouds are excellent examples to bring into mini-lessons on how writers construct texts. A list of recent works of children's literature, written in first-person narrative, is included in Figure 2-8.

WRITING MINI-LESSON

Begin the writing workshop block with a mini-lesson on any aspect of writing. There are three kinds of mini-lessons:

- **Management mini-lessons** acquaint students with the procedures for writing workshop. They help students learn how to find materials, where to place their drafts, how to ask for a conference, and so on. The complexity of routines you use will be related to the level of students you teach. Provide very explicit demonstrations of exactly what you want students to do. The better your students understand routines, the more attention you will be able to give to helping them develop their writing strategies.

- **Conventions mini-lessons** help students expand their control of the mechanical aspects of writing—those rules that have been established because they help readers to access writers' messages. These rules of writing are *standard* or *conventional* so that all readers can use them. You may focus on such aspects as page layout, spelling, punctuation, grammar, or word choice. After you provide a mini-lesson on conventions, ask students to be especially watchful as they write, and check to see whether they observe the convention.

- **Craft mini-lessons** help students improve the quality of their writing by learning what good writers do. Craft mini-lessons are directly related to comprehending text because they concern the way writers communicate meaning. Using children's literature that you have read aloud to students, help them think about how writers choose words, make comparisons, provide descriptive detail, start a piece of writing in an interesting way, or use exciting language. This kind of reflection helps students notice how texts are structured.

Mini-lessons provide direct instruction. Work hard to be clear, using examples and visual representations to make points. Texts that students have heard read aloud (some many times) are extremely valuable in illustrating points. You will find detailed descriptions and examples of all three kinds of mini-lessons in *Guiding Readers and Writers, Grades 3-6: Teaching Comprehension, Genre, and Content Literacy* (Fountas & Pinnell 2001).

Writing and Conferring

After the mini-lesson, students engage in their own independent writing. For beginners, this may involve simply producing some approximation of any kind of writing they want to do. As children become more sophisticated, they can work on the same piece of writing over several days.

As they work, circulate and confer with individuals. Many teachers keep records and notes of their conferences with children. Conferences serve the purposes of:

- ensuring that you confer with all children within the space of a week.
- recording significant writing behaviors.
- recording significant conversations that help you know children's conceptualizations of writing.
- helping you think across the group to inform mini-lessons.
- helping children to move forward in their production of a piece of writing.
- offering helpful suggestions to expand children's knowledge of the writing process.
- expanding your own knowledge of how children learn to write.

Sharing

Hold a brief sharing period during which children talk about their own writing. Obviously, it will not be possible for all children to share their writing each day, but you can select a few pieces for examination. Your conferences will provide some information that will be helpful in guiding the sharing session. Also, you will want to return to your mini-lesson to help children reflect on how they used the information.

Summary

In this chapter, we explored a comprehensive language and literacy framework for conceptualizing and organizing instruction. Comprehension is not built in a few lessons or in any single component of a literacy program. Comprehension is truly *thinking*, and it must be developed at every moment of our time with students. The broad-based language and literacy framework described here offers students opportunities to expand their ability to think about the concepts and ideas in texts.

Ideas to Try

1. Meet with grade-level colleagues and take a look at the demands for comprehension (and opportunities to expand strategies) across your reading/language arts curriculum. Concentrate on one day of learning. You may want to set the date beforehand and plan for a full range of activities. You can choose one reading group or consider all that you taught during the day.

   - **Kindergarten and first grade.** Bring the books you read aloud, texts used for shared reading, books used for guided reading, several of the books children read for independent reading, the text you and the children wrote during interactive writing, and any text referred to during writing workshop or language/word study mini-lessons.
   - **Second and third grade.** Bring the books you read aloud, texts used for shared reading, poetry read aloud or shared, books used for guided reading, several of the books children read for independent reading, the text you and the children wrote during interactive writing, and any text referred to during writing workshop or language/word study mini-lessons.

2. Lay out the array of texts from each classroom and look across them. Work together to make a list of what each text demands of readers. Ask:

   - What background information will be required for children to understand the text?
   - What words will they need to know the meaning of?
   - What personal connections will be possible for readers?

- Will they be able to connect this text to others they have read or written?
- What necessity (or opportunity) is there for readers to think beyond the text?
- What opportunity does this text give children to learn about the purpose or style of writing?

3. After you have made your list, compare it to the categories of comprehending strategies in Chapter 1. Discuss the opportunities to teach for comprehension you have in a single day. Note that each text provides opportunities for the reader to utilize a wide range of strategies. Ask:

- How can the text base for my teaching be made even richer?
- How can I increase my attention to supporting comprehension across my day?
- How can I make connections across the texts my students write and read?

Authors' note: For their work on conceptualizing the three-block and transitional framework, we are indebted to Lesley University faculty members Diane Powell, Sandra Lowry, and Patricia Starnes.

CHAPTER 3

The Role of Emotion in Memory and Comprehension

Carol A. Lyons

The goal of all reading instruction is to develop children's capacity to read independently increasingly more complex texts with ease and understanding. We want them to take charge of their learning and to develop self-extending systems, or strategies to improve and expand literate behaviors through successful reading. When that happens, we know that individuals have become self-regulated. They are experiencing success as readers and writers—success which has both cognitive and emotional significance.

Research on brain functioning shows that cognition and emotion are closely linked through experience. The meaning we take from all experiences has power, not only because we are taking on new information, but perhaps even more because of the emotional responses experiences trigger. The same is true for reading.

This chapter explores the role of emotions in an individual's ability to think and remember, as well as how emotions are critical in a student's ability to engage in self-regulating behaviors. I will make the case that the meaning children bring to and take from their experiences in learning to read, and their ability to search for and gain meaning while reading, are related to their ability to invest positive emotions while reading.

I focus on children who are struggling in reading and draw on my own experiences as a Reading Recovery teacher. Reading Recovery is a short-term (12-20 weeks, 30 minutes per day), one-on-one early intervention for the lowest achieving first-grade students. Unfortunately, when it comes to reading, many children have high levels of negative emotions. Skilled teaching, supportive relationships, and the experience of success can turn this situation around. These are lessons that can help all of us become better reading teachers.

A Russian psychologist, Lev Vygotsky, developed a theory of self-regulation (Vygotsky 1978). According to Vygotsky, self-regulation is encouraged by a specific type of interaction children have with a caregiver or teacher, one that actively engages the child as a collaborative partner in problem-solving activities just beyond the child's independent capacity. This zone represents what the child can nearly do. With adult support, the child can experience success with the task, creating positive emotions in the process.

Self-Regulation: Will and Skill

Self-regulation is defined as the child's capacity to plan, guide, and monitor his or her behavior from within and the flexibility to adjust according to changing circumstances (Diaz, Neal, & Amaya-Williams 1990).

There are two properties associated with the term "capacity:" will and skill. Will means choosing to act, a desire, controlling your own actions, volunteering to participate. Will is associated with pleasure, energy, and enthusiasm, representing the affective side of human development. From a neurophysiological perspective, these properties reside in brain structures that are associated with emotional development.

Skill, on the other hand, represents expertise that comes from instruction, training, acquired ability, or proficiency. Skill is the development of knowledge, understanding, and judgment, and represents the cognitive side of human development. These properties reside in brain structures that are associated with cognitive development.

What does this have to do with reading comprehension? Just about everything. To expand their strategies, readers are required to solve problems. But, the problems should not be so great (e.g., too many hard words) that they cannot attend to meaning. Ideally, every experience a child has in reading should be successful and full of meaning.

The teacher's job is to figure out the child's plan for problem-solving because it drives what the child does at time of difficulty. A plan might refer to any kind of problem-solving. It is a repertoire of possible actions. Consider a simple example: when a child comes to a word he or she doesn't know, the plan is a series of actions to be tried. Included in the plan might be actions categorized as *plans to abandon efforts*, as well as actions categorized as *plans to attempt*.

Plans to abandon efforts indicate little will to attempt to solve a problem. They include:

- Looking to you for help. You certainly have experienced this behavior: the child's head swivels toward you in appeal.
- Creating a diversion by claiming a need to go to the bathroom, blow the nose, take a break. One child we know claimed to be having a heart attack.
- Looking into the air or at the ceiling. One child said he was praying to Monica (a character in the TV show *Touched by an Angel*).
- Crying. We hope that this does not happen, but sometimes when children face difficulty, emotions can reach this level.
- Quitting. One child commented, "I can't think any more, I'm too upset." Another said, "I am having a bad hair day."

Plans to attempt include:

- Examining the print and illustrations on a page.
- Rereading.
- Looking at the first letter.
- Looking at the picture.
- Looking at the end of the word.
- Looking at the word parts or chunks of letters.
- Trying a word that makes sense.
- Thinking of a known word that looks like the word in the text.

Any of these plans to attempt will be inefficient if it is the only weapon in the reader's arsenal. To read and comprehend texts, children must have a range of problem-solving strategies, not just for word-solving but for all reading strategies. The plan the child uses, revealed through his or her behaviors, will help you interpret his or her capacity (both will and skill). For example, the five plans to abandon efforts are not only ineffective but charged with emotion. They represent little will to try, perhaps because the child does not have the tools for success.

Helping children develop various ways to problem-solve will result in flexible, broad-based plans to resolve problems. You teach for strategies that develop the skill component of self-regulation, but that also have implications for the will component. If a child shows you he is using only one plan (reread and look at the first letter), he is on shaky ground. That plan will not serve him well, especially when the texts are more challenging. That child will not succeed, and he will know it. And when the child encounters failure over and over again, the will to continue is jeopardized.

In his book *The Emotional Brain*, Joseph LeDoux (1996) suggests that continued emotional distress can create deficits in a child's intellectual abilities, crippling the capacity to learn. What does this mean for us as teachers? We must do powerful teaching of the skill component while at the same time attending to will. It is so important to look for and support the child's approximations or partially correct responses and then show how to complete the processing. In any new learning, all of us need encouragement to take risks and approximate. Without will, the child will not learn to read and write.

When you teach children how to use multiple strategies for reading and writing text and see to it that they are successful in their attempts, they learn how to learn. The *will* to learn is *charged*, something like charging your cell phone for longer, more effective use. Success builds emotional support, confidence, and the willingness to try—a *can do* attitude.

That attitude motivates children to continue to work with you, and in the process they become self-regulated as their circumstances change. How do you know if children are developing self-regulatory strategies? One way is to observe what they do at a time of difficulty. For each child, you may be thinking, What is the child's plan? Are there multiple plans? Do different plans guide and monitor behavior flexibility when circumstances change?

David: From Learning Disabled to Successful Reader

Let's look at an example drawn from one child I taught who was having severe difficulty in reading. David was classified as learning disabled (LD) in kindergarten and first grade by two separate teams of professionals. David had all the behaviors and supporting tests needed to be classified as LD. His brother and father had been classified and placed in learning disability classrooms in the primary grades, so it was assumed that his dyslexia ran in the family. When David experienced difficulty learning letters in preschool and did not make much improvement after five months in kindergarten, his well-intentioned parents wanted to get help immediately. In February of David's kindergarten year, he was classified as LD at Children's Hospital. Later, he was one of the first children tested by the school psychologist for a learning disability in the fall of first grade.

The results of David's tests by the school psychologist and doctors at Children's Hospital indicated that David was language delayed and LD with attention deficit hyperactivity disorder (ADHD). It was recommended that he attend speech and language classes three times a week and be placed on the waiting list for the primary learning disability room. While waiting for space in a primary special education classroom, David was placed in a regular education first-grade classroom. I began working with David because I had specifically asked to teach Reading Recovery students classified as LD.

David's scores on *An Observation Survey of Early Literacy Achievement* (Clay 1993) revealed that he was the lowest-achieving student in the class. David could identify 37 of 52 letters by name; he could not identify F/f, G/g, Y/y, P/p, W/w, M/m, or U/u. He did not read 1 of 10 words on the Ohio Word Test, but he did look at the first letter to attempt several words; he read "two" for "the" and "there," "dad" for "did" and "down," and "you" for "yes." David knew 5 of 24 Concepts About Print, indicating an understanding of the front of the book and the bottom of a picture, the concept of one and two letters, and the meaning of a question mark and capital letter. Although David could not write one word, he did write the first letter of his first and last name, but he wrote the letter D backward. The dictation test revealed that when asked to write the sentence, "The bus is coming it will stop here to let me get on," David heard 4 of 37 phonemes. The text reading score

Weekly Record of Book Level

RECORD OF BOOK LEVEL

Name: David K
RR Teacher: Carol Lyons

○—○—○—○ 90% accuracy or above
●—●—●—● below 90% accuracy

Week	Date	Title & accuracy	# of Lessons
1	9/26	In the Mirror	
2	10/1	Dan the Flying Man	
3	10/8	Look for Me	
4	10/18	Dave's Tricks	
5	10/25	Lazy Mary	
6	10/31	The Chick & the Duckling	
7	11/7	The Grumpy Elephant	
8	11/14	Excuses, Excuses	
9	11/20	Mrs. Wishy-Washy	
10	11/30	Rosie's Walk	
11	12/8	Kipper's Birthday	
12	12/16	Dear Zoo	
13	12/21	Dad's Headache	
14	1/6	Saturday Morning	
15	1/13	Blackbird's Nest	
16	1/26	Titch	
17	2/4	Rosie at the Zoo	
18	2/10	The Flood	
19	2/15	Gumby Shop	
20	2/20	There's a Nightmare in my Closet	
21	2/28	Little Gorilla	
22			
23			
24			
25			

Level: 1–20

FIGURE 3-1

placed David at Level B, indicating that he could point and read the words "No, no, no" when reading "Where's Spot?" (Hill 1980).

David entered Reading Recovery on September 26 and exited the program February 28. He was in the program 21 weeks and had 99 sessions. His reading growth is shown in Figure 3-1.

David entered the Reading Recovery program reading text Level 1 and exited the program reading text Level 16, equivalent to the end of first-grade basal reading material. He could also write 66 words in 10 minutes and could hear and record 37 phonemes when asked to write, "The boy is riding his bike. He can go very fast on it." At the end of the year, David read at text Level 22 (with 94 percent accuracy), which is equivalent to third-grade basal reading material. David's total reading score on a standardized test placed him in the 99th percentile for first-grade students. David also exited the Reading Recovery program without three labels—LD, ADHD, and language delayed.

CLASSROOM TEACHER'S PERSPECTIVE

His classroom teacher commented that David was a completely different child at the end of the school year than he had been at the beginning. In October, she said that his attention span was about four minutes long. He showed little interested in any classroom activities. He appeared disinterested in the books she read to the class. When she read to the children, David had a difficult time sitting still, and he either stared into space or looked out the window. When she asked him how he enjoyed a story, he would say, "It was OK." But when asked what he thought was the best part of the story, he did not know. During the first month of school, David consistently drew pictures rather than attempt to write anything.

David's speech teacher had similar concerns regarding his attitude, behavior, and interactions with his friends or herself in speech class. She had a difficult time getting him to attend to any of the hands-on activities she organized. He volunteered little information about himself. He had a lisp and difficulty pronouncing some letters. For example, he would say "tick" for "sick," "tool" for "school," "pease" for "please," and "wif" for "with."

On the playground he seemed to have little difficulty talking to his friends, suggesting that his speech did not get in the way of communication. He seemed to have fun and to enjoy his many friends. How could this good social behavior manifest itself in instructional contexts?

SHIFTS IN BEHAVIOR

After about four weeks in Reading Recovery tutoring, David's classroom and speech teachers noticed a major shift in his behavior. This once fidgety, overactive, disengaged child, who seemed reluctant to talk in class, was beginning to settle down and become more task-oriented and communicative with his teachers and classmates. He listened to the stories and willingly discussed why he liked or did not like them. He also wanted to share and write about personal experiences. He would tell a story about a picture the children were discussing in speech class and became involved in activities. His parents even noticed a positive change in his attitude about going to school, and that he seemed to pay more attention when he was read to before bed.

FACTORS CONTRIBUTING TO CHANGE

What caused this sudden change of behavior? The classroom and speech teachers believed it was the individualized attention he received during the first four weeks of Reading Recovery that made such a dramatic difference and contributed to David's success in the classroom and in speech class. But I wanted to further analyze how individualized instruction helped to change David's attitude, motivation, and engagement.

Recently, I reanalyzed videotapes of David's Reading Recovery lessons with a new set of eyes. I was looking for evidence of David's emotional response to our interactions and sought to discover the impact that this response might have had on his thinking and subsequent behavior. As I analyzed the tapes, I noticed that more was going on than teaching for cognitive strategies. David and I were establishing a relationship that was having an impact on emotional learning. Below I share three insights that emerged from this analysis—insights which suggest ways that you can positively impact children's emotional and cognitive development.

1. Show through your actions that you are genuinely interested in what children think and do.

How do you do this? By engaging in genuine, relevant conversation focused on their interests. Have real conversations with the child. In this case, David and I talked as we walked to and from the lesson. We discussed what he was doing and/or interested in at home and in school. I got to know him as a person. If your own experience with such conversations is initially one-sided, keep trying—it will pay off in the long run.

A major breakthrough came for me when I asked David for advice about what to get my son for his birthday. He had several ideas, but the best gift he could think of was a puppy. The most important thing was that I wanted his opinion, and he knew it. He acted surprised that I had asked for advice. David offered many reasons why a puppy was the best present of all: puppies are alive and always happy. They do not grumble and are always willing to play. We kept this conversation going for weeks. He said, "I thought of the best reason why your son should get a dog. They don't crab at you or get mad when you make a mistake." That comment certainly revealed something about this child's own experiences.

These conversations were pivotal to David's change in attitude, his increased interest in reading, and his feelings about working with me. I valued his opinion and cared about him as a person, and he sensed it.

2. Select books and generate sentences that reflect children's interests.

Carefully selecting texts that are *just right* for children (that is, are within the child's instructional level) helps to ensure success in processing them. You also should consider their interests and show that you really care about what they like. Using the children's own interests to guide your selection makes it much easier for them to read the text and comprehend it. David's interest in puppies was evident in his writing. For many weeks, he wrote about how to take care of a puppy—how often to feed it, how to train it, the kinds of things you can teach a puppy, where you can take it for a walk, and the games you can play with it. David was successful and he knew it. Every little success motivated him to continue to engage in reading and writing. He had recaptured the will to continue learning.

3. Prevent inappropriate behavior from occurring.

Sometimes children must unlearn behaviors that are getting in the way. It is not always easy to help children unlearn inappropriate behaviors without causing emotional stress. You must know the child well and anticipate moves that signal the onset of an inappropriate behavior. The goal is to prevent a habituated pattern of behavior from occurring and engage the child in a new pattern of behavior to replace it.

For example, David routinely wrote the capital *D* in his name backward. I would watch him closely and as soon as I saw that he was going to start writing the *D* backward, I intervened by taking his arm and hand through the appropriate movements while verbally describing the movement. I prevented the inappropriate behavior from occurring until he could manage without guidance.

This support was matter-of-fact rather than critical or punitive and it was very important. Why? Because the more an inappropriate response is repeated (in David's case making a backward *D*), the more the neural linkages in the brain are strengthened and the more difficult it becomes to unlearn what has been regularly done. David was a quick responder, labeled impulsive by the school psychologist and classroom teacher; that behavior needed to change. The backward *D* was only one example of many.

If I did not catch him in time to stop his movement, he would become upset and frustrated, so frustrated that he would make holes in the paper with his pencil. This action caused a downward spiral; he became angry and mad at himself for not remembering. His emotions took over and he was unable to use what he knew. Instruction stopped. His anger was an emotional response to a mistake, but it was so strong that he had difficulty regrouping and attending to the rest of the lesson. Research reported by Greenspan (1997) shows that, for some children, getting off course causes a downward spiral which often is very hard to stop and reverse.

The bottom line is to recognize a student's feelings; talking is not sufficient for boosting problem solving and getting the learner back on track. Saying, "You can do it" is not enough. The solution for a learning problem is not to attend to cognition alone, but to address the inseparable fusion of emotions and cognition. Telling the child he is smart will not solve the problem; chances are, a child like David will not believe you anyway. David had to learn to act as a reader and writer, as one who had mastered part of the process. The changes in his actions also changed what he thought and how he felt.

Thinking About Cognition and Emotion

Neuroscientists now know that there are multiple memory systems in the brain, each devoted to different memory functions. The brain system that allowed David to make a capital letter *D* quickly and accurately is different from the one that allowed him to learn how to form the letter, and different still from the system that made him tense and anxious when he wrote the *D* backward. Though these are each forms of long-term memory (memory that can last for a lifetime), they are mediated by different neural networks.

Antonio Damasio (1994), a neurologist, has uncovered convincing evidence of neural networks in the brain. These networks support and provide the foundation for cognitive processing and are also associated with emotions. The connections between cognitive processing and emotions emerge from the unique experiences of individuals.

When there is an upset to one's routines, for example, such as getting lost while driving to a destination, the emotional responses—often unconscious, automatic, and involuntary—are activated in various parts of the brain. This activation is actually a full-body activation of the endocrine system, which includes the heart, blood pressure, and other regulations of the body that affect cognition and emotion. This evidence indicates that it is not simply the brain, but the totality of the mind and body that makes up the unified whole of thinking.

Furthermore, because the emotional system can act independently of the neocortex (cognitive system), emotional reactions and emotional memories can be formed without

conscious, cognitive participation at all. You remember most clearly those times when you were scared or when you experienced a psychological response. In the past, educators have thought about learning at the cognitive level. Now we need to broaden our understanding of learning and to remember that there is an inseparable relationship between emotion and cognition. In order to understand this relationship, we will look at the neural networks that integrate emotions and cognition.

NEURONS

Recent pediatric research (Damasio 1994; Greenspan 1997) has concluded that infants' and young children's learning involves emotional, social, and cognitive functions that are not *hierarchical.* They are not acquired in sequence, nor is one function more important than the others. Instead, emotional, social, and cognitive functions are *synergistic*; they are a combined and correlated force of united action. This synergy is the building block of all learning from birth and throughout life.

A mother cannot see what is going on inside a newborn's brain. She cannot observe the electrical activity as a neuron in the infant's retina makes a connection to a neuron in the visual cortex in his brain; but when this happens, her face becomes an enduring memory in the infant's mind that will last for a lifetime. She cannot observe the release of a chemical substance called a neurotransmitter as a neuron in the baby's ear, carrying the electrically encoded sound of "*Mom*," connects to a neuron in the auditory cortex of his brain. But when this happens, the sound of "*Mom*" creates a cluster of neuronal cells in the baby's brain that will respond to no other sound but his mother's voice for the rest of his life (Bagley 1997).

The child's brain continues to form microscopic connections every day, connections that are responsible for feeling, learning, and remembering. The brain is hard wired from birth to direct everything it is supposed to do (e.g., walk, talk, think, reason, remember) without actually knowing how to do it. Neuroscientists are now realizing that experiences after birth, rather than something innate, determine the actual wiring of the human brain. This means that early childhood experiences exert a dramatic impact on a child's development, physically determining how the intricate neural circuits of the brain are wired. These early experiences influence the very structure and organization of the brain itself (Bagley 1997).

We know that in order for the necessary connections to be made—allowing a child to register his mother's face so that he can distinguish her from every other female he encounters, and to recognize the sound of her voice so that he can distinguish it from every other voice he hears—the child must be attending. The attentional system regulates all incoming sensory information. When a child is not attending, he will not learn. When tasks are too difficult, learners do not attend. We all experience positive and negative synergy while learning something new. We cannot prevent this from happening, because it occurs within our brains as neurons communicate with each other.

An Example of Learning

A clear memory for me is the negative emotion connected to learning trigonometry in high school. My teacher would routinely ask every student to come to the blackboard to work out trigonometry problems, which she orally gave to the class. There were only 16 students in the class, so there was plenty of room for all of us to have a place at the board. We had to write out all of the steps in the process we used to solve the problem. I dreaded going to the board because I usually did not get the problem right. The teacher, Sister Agatha, would ask the class to look at my work and identify where I had made the mistake.

I always prayed that I would get the problem right, and that if I were wrong, she would not single out my work for everyone to examine. When she did, I was embarrassed because my errors seemed so obvious to my classmates. I was too emotionally involved to listen to the teacher while she explained the steps for getting the correct solution. I dreaded going to class for the first month. Finally, I asked my father for help.

Dad watched me working on several different types of equations, and then asked me to talk about what I was doing. He pointed out an error in my reasoning that was causing me to consistently make similar mistakes. My teacher had probably explained my pattern of errors the same way Dad explained it to me, but at the time I was so upset and embarrassed that I did not listen. My lack of attention made it hard for me to understand and remember what she was saying. Through my father's interest and help, a negative experience became positive, and I could continue to increase my understanding of trigonometry. Without his support I do not know what would have happened.

The negative experience that occurred during the first few weeks of class triggered a stress response as soon as the teacher said, "Let's all go to the board." As soon as she said those words, I felt myself flush, my stomach started to churn, my heart beat faster, and I started to sweat. In other words, physiological changes in my body took place. These physiological changes occurred because previous experiences going to the board to solve trigonometry problems had not been positive; stress interfered. I remember this high school experience vividly, which is not surprising because emotional memory takes precedence over every other type of memory. And emotional response interferes with thinking. The structure of the brain helps us understand how this works.

Structures of the Brain

The cortex is the outer layer of the brain. The inner layers of the cortex contain neural structures essential to learning and memory. Incoming information is processed through the reticular activating system (RAS), which is located at the top of the brain stem. (See Figure 3-2.) The RAS sends messages coming from the five senses to the thalamus, which sorts the information and sends it to the three organs or lobes of the brain: the temporal lobe, which processes auditory information; the occipital lobe, which processes visual information; and the parietal lobe, which processes sensing and motor information. The information is processed in the manner described below.

SHORT-TERM MEMORY

Incoming information first goes to *short-term memory*. Short-term memory lasts only for 15 to 30 seconds. Some researchers say that you have limited space for short-term memory; the older you are, the more space you have for short-term memory. You can generally hold up to seven items in short-term memory before those items go to *working memory*.

WORKING MEMORY

Working memory is located in the prefrontal cortex. It can be used for hours, and it gives you the ability to form more lasting, *long-term memories*. We have all used our working memory to cram for a test. We study really hard the night before, and this information is stored in working memory long enough to take the test, but forgotten after we take the test. In fact, we would have a difficult time recalling the information the following week. If information is not meaningful or allowed to form patterns in the brain, it will be lost. Short-term memory and working memory represent only temporary storage.

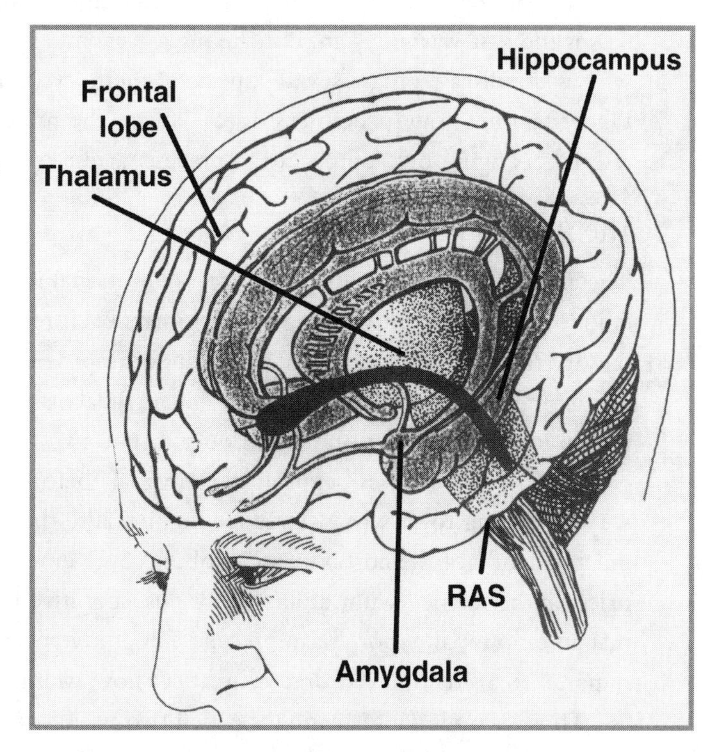

FIGURE 3-2 Structures of the Limbic System in the Brain
Adapted from Vander, Sherman & Luciana (1990) Human Physiology

LONG-TERM MEMORY

After moving through working memory, information is sent to the frontal lobes, where it is decided whether it will be stored in long-term memory. Information sent to long-term memory is sorted and sent to two different structures critical to learning and memory: the hippocampus and the amygdala. These structures are found deep inside the medial part of the temporal lobe. The amygdala lies adjacent to and underneath the hippocampus.

The Hippocampus

The hippocampus catalogues, files, and stores factual information and communicates this information back to the surrounding regions of the brain. To maintain the stored information for a few years, the components of this system must also store the memory trace, which is maintained by interactions between the temporal lobe system and the frontal lobes. Gradually, over years, the hippocampus relinquishes its control over the memory and the memory appears to remain as long as it is a memory, which may be for a lifetime.

This model of memory has helped physicians and neuroscientists better understand what occurs in a mind afflicted with Alzheimer's disease. The disease begins its attack on the brain in the temporal lobe, particularly in the hippocampus, thus explaining why forgetfulness is the first warning sign. But the disease eventually creeps into the cortex, suggesting why, as the disease progresses, all aspects of memory (old and new) are compromised. Understanding how Alzheimer's disease affects the mind and brain in tandem is helping researchers figure out approaches to prevent, arrest, or reverse the disease.

The Amygdala

The amygdala catalogues, files, and stores emotional information and determines if it is emotionally important for long-term storage. Each route that leads to the amygdala—sensory thalamus, sensory cortex, and hippocampus—delivers unique information to the organ. According to LeDoux (1996), the amygdala is a critical site of learning because of its central location between input and output stations.

Emotional responses begin in the amygdala before we completely recognize what it is we are reacting to or what we are feeling. Because the neural emotional system can act independently of the cortex (frontal lobes), some emotional reactions and emotional memories can be formed without any conscious, cognitive participation at all. What this means is that an emotional response can precede a cognitive perception and response. The amygdala's response to a situation can drastically affect how well it is remembered.

Thus, incoming information is coded two ways: emotionally and cognitively (Greenspan 1997). It is coded in two different regions of the brain, each specifically designed and responsible for learning and memory. The hippocampus files, catalogues, and stores *factual* information; the amygdala files, catalogues, and stores *emotional* information. The hippo campus is responsible for planning, problem-solving, and reasoning related to factual information; the amygdala is responsible for telling us how we feel about that information, which is then stored in our emotional memory. Emotional and cognitive memories are stored and retrieved in parallel, and their activities are joined seamlessly in our conscience experience (LeDoux 1996).

LEARNING—EMOTIONAL AND COGNITIVE

LeDoux (1996) suggests that neural pathways are set so that a learning situation may evoke either an emotional response that may be helpful, or a rapid, negative emotional response that can impair learning, memory, and thinking even before engaging cognition.

Understanding how the hippocampus and amygdala function in learning and memory may provide an explanation for what happened in my high school trigonometry class. I could not think because I was worried that I would get the problem wrong again and Sister Agatha would ask the rest of the class to examine my work. I could not hide the steps I took to resolve the problems because they were written on the board for everyone to see. As soon as Sister Agatha said, "Everyone to the board," I panicked. Her words were sent immediately to the amygdala (seat of the emotional brain), bypassing the thalamus, which would have sent it to the frontal lobes to examine the situation. When this occurred, neurotransmitters (chemical signals) were released and my body started to prepare for flight. My heart raced faster to get my blood flowing quickly. This stress response was triggered by a few words from the teacher, words that I associated with embarrassment and failure. The stress response can save your life or it can cause you great embarrassment, which it did in my case.

Likewise, David's emotional reaction to instruction in reading and writing, with which he was seldom successful, may have had a physiological root. *Remember that the emotional memory takes precedence over cognitive memory. The brain always gives priority to emotions.*

THE NATURE OF LONG-TERM MEMORY

Long-term memory consists of information stored for an indefinite period of time. Five different but interrelated facets of long-term memory are critical to learning and comprehension: procedural, automatic, episodic, semantic, and emotional memory are all used to access and store information.

Procedural Memory

Procedural memory is located in the cerebellum. It includes sequences that are consistently repeated until they become automatic routines. That means you can execute these sequences without thinking about what you are doing. Consider such automatic behaviors as riding a bike, driving a car, or running your finger along a line of print. Procedural memory allows you do two things at once; for example, driving a car and listening to a book on tape. It allows you to divide your attention. When reading, you simultaneously recognize visual symbols and imagine what characters in a novel look like and feel.

Automatic Memory

Automatic memory resides in the cerebellum. Certain stimuli evoke a conditioned-response memory automatically. After you hear the first few words of a song from years past, you might remember all the words of that song. Other things you have stored in automatic memory include letter names, letter sounds, multiplication tables, high-frequency words, and so on.

Episodic Memory

Episodic memory is located in the hippocampus. Episodic memory may be triggered by your automatic memory. For example, you sing a song from your youth and just a few words from the song trigger a memory of the circumstances in which you heard the words for the first time. You remember where you were and who you were with when you first heard it. The words of *Camelot* may trigger a memory of President Kennedy; then you may remember where you were when you heard that he had been assassinated. Some children will remember when a teacher showed irritation or anger when they could not remember how to make a letter or the letter sound after it had been taught to the class. Your responses to children's inability to recall information may impact their memory more than you will ever know.

Semantic Memory

Semantic memory, located in the hippocampus, holds information learned in words. Most of our educational experiences involve semantic memory. When we receive new information, it may be connected to previously learned information and sent to working memory. Working memory will continue to sift and sort the old and new information. Through prior knowledge and interest, the new information will be added to the old information to form more long-term memories. This process can be called *synthesis*. Synthesis will be

repeated several times before long-term memories are formed. Semantic memory is stimulated by associations, comparisons, and similarities; building semantic memory is the heart of the comprehension processes.

Emotional Memory

Emotional memory exerts a powerful influence on thought processes. Emotional memory registers and retains positive and negative responses, and brings up these responses if circumstances are repeated (as the trigonometry experiences were). If the child repeatedly reads or senses disapproval in the teacher's response to an error, he will be reluctant to put himself in that circumstance again. He won't take the risk; he may think, "I can't learn how to read." The will to learn is gone. Embarrassment and fear of making a mistake may prevent the child from trying again. All of us remember our mistakes. You can give an hour-long talk that was perfect for 59 minutes, but the one minute you forgot what to say and fumbled the words may never be forgotten. For some individuals, that one minute of fumbling prevents them from ever speaking in front of a group again.

Emotions affect short-term, working, and long-term memory. Negative emotions can impair the activity of the prefrontal cortex, the area involved in working memory. This interference offers a reason why, when we are emotionally upset, we cannot think straight. It also explains why continued emotional upset can cripple the capacity to learn. Positive emotions, on the other hand, can facilitate working memory that is critical to long-term memory and thus basic to comprehending strategies. All of this means that children's capacity to think and problem-solve is heavily dependent on positive affective experiences.

Social Forces Are Critical to Learning and Memory

Experience is a major factor in the development of an infant's ability to reason and make sense of what she hears and sees in the environment. Social interaction, through language, is the means through which this cognitive ability is developed. Language researchers, such as Bruner (1983) and Lindfors (1999), have shown that a toddler's vocabulary is strongly correlated to how much the mother talks to the child. Furthermore, only a *live* voice, not the electronically-produced voices of television, increases a child's vocabulary and language structure because language must be used in relation to an ongoing event. Otherwise, the sounds are just noise.

Language is embedded in an emotional context that seems to stimulate neural circuitry more powerfully than information alone. The child will more readily learn the concept of

the word "more" if it refers to the happy prospect of more milk, or the concept of "later" if it is attached to a frustrating wait for a trip to the playground. Or she may understand the word "again" when it is associated with the happy experience of rolling the ball to Mom again. Happy and sad emotions contribute to vocabulary development and memory. If abstract words such as "more," "later," and "again" were presented outside of a meaningful context, in isolation from things the baby cares about and wants to know about or do, they would not be remembered. In this way feelings, concepts, and language begin to be linked to form memories, even as early as seven months (Gopnik, Meltzoff, & Kuhl 1999).

The infant cannot tell you about what she has learned because she does not have control of the necessary language to do so. But she has a memory of what she has learned, and so can show you that she knows. Especially when they are hungry, children know what they want to eat and what they do not want to eat. Parents read the intonation of the child's voice and interpret the child's wishes. I remember giving our son a pickle, and he hated the taste of it. From that day on, whenever I put the pickle jar on the table he became upset.

We continue to form memories in a similar way throughout life. Adults form memories much more readily if the new information is accompanied by emotional content. Most adults can easily recall happy occurrences, such as their wedding day or the birth of a child, and tragedies, such as the death of a parent or child, or the day the space shuttle carrying Christa McAuliffe exploded.

If my father had not stepped in to help me with trigonometry, I probably would have dropped the class. Who knows how that negative experience would have changed my educational life? If David had not successfully learned how to read, he would probably have been labeled LD and ADHD for the remainder of his school years. This designation may have had an impact on his progress throughout his schooling, even throughout his life. Instead, David had a good academic record in school and is now a freshman in college.

Summary

The brain strengthens frequently-used neuronal connections by pruning connections that are not used. Experience determines which connections will be strengthened and which will be pruned. Connections that are activated most frequently are preserved and stored in long-term memory. Emotion, the brain's primary architect, facilitates this process. Learning depends on memory, and the most powerful learning takes place if multiple memory areas (procedural, automatic, emotional, semantic, and episodic) are involved.

The brain at a young age is flexible, like plastic. The plasticity of the brain enables students such as David, who once had difficulty learning, to reorganize the brain's activity. In his case, he became a good reader and writer. The downside of the brain's great flexibility is that it is acutely vulnerable to stress and trauma. Experience may alter the behavior of an adult, which was apparent in my experience in trigonometry class, but it literally provides the organizational framework for the brain of the child—the brain's organization reflects its experience. If a child experiences fear and stress, then the neurochemical responses to these emotions become powerful architects of how that child's brain is organized. If a child has experiences that are emotionally overwhelming, and has them again and again, the structure of his brain is changed (Greenspan 1997).

We cannot prevent or stop the synergy among the emotional, cognitive, and social forces that influence children during learning. What we say and do, and how we say and do it, makes a difference. It is therefore important that we remember to:

1. Show through your actions that you are genuinely interested in children, in what they think and what they do.
2. Select books and generate sentences that reflect children's interests.
3. Prevent inappropriate behavior from occurring.

Ideas to Try

1. Have fun probing your own memories and emotions. With a group of friends, think of at least one of the following:

    - A song that immediately comes to mind when you think about high school or college.
    - An object that you treasure even though it has little monetary value.
    - A time you love to remember because you were so happy.

2. Share your memories and the emotions connected with them. Now think of something that you found very hard to learn, e.g., skiing, public speaking, playing the piano, or learning calculus. Share the emotions connected with your struggle.

    - Did emotions ever get in the way?
    - Did you abandon the effort or keep struggling until you learned?
    - How did you deal with your feelings? What helped you?

3. Now think about one or two struggling students in your class. Plan to observe these students carefully over several days to determine when emotions are working *for* them in terms of learning and how their emotions might be working *against* them.

4. If possible, have a colleague observe you as you work with these students (e.g., in guided reading). You want students to work so that they will learn, but not to *struggle* so much that they experience negative emotions. Becoming sensitive to negative emotions will help you sense when to give a little extra help or more demonstration and explanation.

CHAPTER 4

From Primary to Intermediate Grades: How Do Children Change as Readers?

Gay Su Pinnell & Irene C. Fountas

One of the greatest challenges for us as teachers is shifting our instruction in response to children's learning. Sometimes it seems that this process changes every day, but certainly it changes profoundly over a school year and across the elementary grades. To every grade level, children bring expanded sets of knowledge and new needs. The first chapters of this book describe the sophisticated range of comprehending strategies that young readers develop throughout the elementary school years. To develop these strategies, children need extensive engaged time for reading, writing, and word study to support their learning. Across the instructional contexts of the framework, we must constantly up the ante, so to speak, by supporting more complex learning. Consequently, we need to understand the transitions that occur in learners between the end of first grade and the beginning of third grade.

The time of significant change that this chapter focuses on is the period somewhere between the middle of second grade and the beginning of third grade. Identifying just *when* to make shifts in your teaching is a decision that you make based on the knowledge and skills evidenced in the behavior of the children you teach. This chapter specifically describes second graders, because most children demonstrate these important shifts in learning between the end of first grade and the beginning of third grade. While we recognize that first-grade and third-grade teachers also will have many children exhibiting these changes, we focus on second graders to illustrate the continuum of change across the primary grades.

How Are Second Graders Changing as Readers and Writers?

Second graders experience significant changes in their literacy learning. Some examples of these changes are shown in Figure 4-1. Any class of children will have a wide range of experiential backgrounds, so we cannot precisely define any specific second grader. The descriptions in Figure 4-1 represent a continuum of change over time; you will observe these changes in some students before seeing them in others. For most children, as we have said, these changes will occur sometime between the end of first grade and the beginning of third grade.

CHANGES IN READING BEHAVIOR

Second graders are growing rapidly in their ability to read longer, more complex narrative texts over several days as opposed to short, straightforward texts, which can often be read in 20-30 minutes. Literary elements such as character, setting, and plot become more important to understanding these longer stories. In simple stories, characters may encounter some surprises or learn something, but there are usually only one or two such episodes. In longer texts, some with several chapters, characters change and develop through their experiences. The reader has more opportunity to think about how characters feel and their motivations for doing what they do.

Good examples of easy chapter books are those in the *Henry and Mudge* series by Cynthia Rylant. These books center around the adventures of a little boy named Henry and his huge dog Mudge. These Level J books have about 50 to 60 pages, organized in 8 to 10 short chapters. Chapters present different episodes, which are linked together as the plot develops. These books are easy to read: They have a great many easy high-frequency words, sentences are generally simple, and the layout is friendly to the young reader. Sentences usually start on the left margin and there is plenty of space between words and between lines. Settings for the stories are the home and neighborhood; Henry has the kinds of everyday problems that are close to most children's own experiences.

All of these factors support readers, but *Henry and Mudge* books also give them plenty to think about while reading. Rylant's language exquisitely communicates simple but powerful emotions as Henry experiences loneliness and fear. In *Henry and Mudge: The First Book* (Rylant 1987), for example, she describes Henry's imagined fears as he walked to school alone, thinking about tornadoes, bullies, biting dogs, and ghosts. "He walked as fast as he could...He never looked back" (p. 15). With his big dog Mudge at his side, though, Henry thought good thoughts—about rocks, vanilla ice cream, and rain. "He walked to

Transitions in Second Grade

FROM:	TO:
Reading simple narrative texts with straight-forward plots.	Reading narrative texts that have more complex plots.
Reading shorter texts that can be read in one sitting or one language/literacy block.	Sustaining reading over several days or even more than one week on a single text.
Reading mostly narrative texts.	Expanding to read more expository texts.
Beginning to build the background students need to read and understand informational texts.	Applying background to read simple informational texts.
Reading informational texts that are organized much like narratives.	Learning to read informational texts with several different organizational patterns.
Understanding the information in pictures with some labels.	Understanding the information in pictures and simple graphics with labels, legends, and some other print information.
Reading orally.	Reading silently.
Writing mostly short pieces that can be finished in one or two days.	Sustaining writing over several days.
Correcting errors while writing texts; seldom creating pieces for publishing.	Learning to proofread and revise some pieces of writing; publishing a few pieces.
Writing simple texts relating personal experiences.	Still describing personal experiences but producing longer texts with more detail.
Writing expressively, as ideas come to mind.	Varying writing according to purpose; e.g., sometimes incorporating notes, lists, or directions within personal experience writing.
Reading and writing a large number of easier, high-frequency words quickly and automatically.	Rapidly expanding the number of easy and harder high-frequency words that can be automatically read and written.
Understanding how to take words apart and to write words by using letter-sound relationships, letter clusters, and word parts.	Understanding how to take apart and to spell longer, multisyllable words by using a range of word-solving strategies.
Working independently in active exploration centers with low talking.	Sustaining independent work for longer periods of time and longer periods of silent, individual work.

FIGURE 4-1

school, but not too fast. He walked to school and sometimes backward" (p. 16). In another book (*Henry and Mudge Get the Cold Shivers*, Rylant 1989), Mudge gets sick and has to go to the vet. Henry is worried but takes good care of Mudge.

As they read these beginning chapter books, second graders have opportunities to expand their ability to solve words and process text, but they will also make connections across texts, make inferences about characters' feelings and motivations, and predict solutions to problems.

Another change that is important for most children between the last months of first grade and the middle of second grade is the switch from more oral to more silent reading. While there are always reasons to read aloud (reading stories and books to children and adults, reading scripts of various kinds, reading poetry for the pleasure of the sound, and so on), reading is, in general, a silent activity. As soon as children have a basic reading process that they can employ automatically, we want them to move into silent reading. As they grow in fluent processing, they read very softly and often begin to read parts without voicing the text.

It is not necessary to force children suddenly to read silently. Some readers spontaneously begin to move to silent reading of easy texts because they find they can read faster; others need to be to encouraged to try *reading with their eyes*. As they try out the process, check on understanding and talk with them about the fact that they are actually reading but not saying the words out loud. The transition may take several months for some children and happen much more quickly for others. They may read some texts aloud and others silently, depending on the kind of text, the difficulty level, and the purpose for reading.

The best way to check on how children are processing print still is to sample oral reading as part of daily guided reading lessons. Frequent conversations with students about the texts they read will demonstrate their ways of thinking about reading that go beyond the literal text. It is good to keep in mind, though, that the transition to silent reading is an essential one for students to make. Silent reading makes a higher level of comprehension possible, along with much greater speed in reading because you simply do not have to take the time to pronounce each word.

Gay recently worked with a group of children who were reading *The Stories Julian Tells* (Cameron 1981). They read the text silently and accurately; four of the six read fluently and two were fluent for the most part. The teacher's observation of their behavior and Gay's assessment of the quality of their processing went beyond those limited observations. This text consists of a series of short stories about family life (cooking pudding, creating a garden, etc.) told by Julian, who is about eight years old. His stories, however, are from throughout his life, so they show him and his younger brother Huey at different ages. Like any children,

Julian and Huey get into trouble, tell tall tales, and build relationships with their family and neighbors.

This Level N text is appropriate for most children at about the beginning of third grade. The writer, Ann Cameron, introduces some challenges even for students who are processing it with high accuracy. One example of her language is as follows:

> My father is a big man with wild black hair.
> When he laughs, the sun laughs in the window-panes.
> When he thinks, you can almost see his thoughts sitting
> on all the tables and chairs. (p. 2)

The text requires that readers understand and, hopefully, enjoy, the use of figurative language, because it makes the family relationships more meaningful and helps readers to understand Dad's way of working with the boys. In this text, students are required to understand new meanings for words for which they might have only one meaning in their oral vocabularies (e.g., *beating the pudding*). The text also requires readers to make inferences as to Julian's feelings (based on his behavior) and the underlying reasons for his likes, dislikes, and actions.

When Irene worked with Jeremy, Brittany, Jazmyne, Nora, Amber, Tiara, and Maya, she pointed out the interesting language to them, read it to them, and asked them to think about what it might mean. They were just beginning to encounter books in guided reading that had these complexities, and the first thing for them to learn was that the writer is not necessarily using language literally. Irene wanted them to say some of the language. They puzzled over the words *whipping* and *beating*. These words already had one meaning for them, but as many children have little experience with cooking, they were not as familiar with the author's intended meaning.

In addition, Cameron used the terms to play out the plot of the story. When the boys eat the pudding (which was to be saved for Mom), their father teasingly says, "There is going to be some beating, here now! There is going to be some whipping!" The *double meaning* made the boys scared, but the story turned out fine, because Dad had them whip up another pudding for Mom. During the discussion after reading, Brittany said that she had not been sure what kind of *whipping* was going to happen, and then two other children volunteered that they had also been uncertain. They were able to discuss the meaning of these words and Dad's sense of humor. Understanding these nuances was vital to their understanding of the text.

CHANGES IN WRITING BEHAVIOR

In second grade, writers greatly increase the number of words they can write quickly and automatically, and expand their spelling skills as well. The Buddy Study System (described in Pinnell & Fountas 1999; see also Chapters 2 and 13), helps them to learn generative principles that they can apply to the spelling of many words. The motor skills involved in writing become more fluid; everything is faster and easier, allowing students to focus more on the messages they want to communicate. They can produce longer, more complex pieces of text. As in kindergarten and first grade, students are still writing from their own experiences. Indeed, this will be true through most of the elementary grades because that is how writers learn. But second-grade students will be developing their topics more deeply and engaging in more revision of their first drafts.

First-grade students reread their work to keep the meaning of the piece in mind and make some corrections to their to writing, occasionally even copying important pieces over. But they do not spend a great deal of time on editing and revision. Second graders are often in the process of learning simple proofreading skills to help them spell known words accurately and use capitalization and punctuation correctly. They also may be making greater use of technology to support their writing.

CHANGES IN LEARNING ABOUT THE LINGUISTIC SYSTEM

Most second graders know how written language works; they can spell many words conventionally and understand some basic spelling principles. They are still expanding their knowledge of the ways words work and are encountering greater complexity. For example, they might make collections of examples that help them understand larger categories of words, such as words that sound like they end in "t" when "ed" is added. They might understand simple contractions, as well as the principle that the apostrophe replaces a letter or letters, and they might expand that knowledge to harder contractions such as *should've* or irregular ones such as *won't*. But they still need explicit teaching and to engage in active, systematic word study.

CHANGES IN INDEPENDENT WORK

Second graders are able (and should be expected) to sustain independent reading and writing for increasingly longer periods of time. They therefore do not need as many different activities during independent work time. They often enjoy listening to longer books on tape and are more capable of using writing to respond to books they have read or heard. Of course, like all students, if they have to complete a writing assignment every time they read, then the result will be not much reading and a lot of tedious, empty writing. But, in general, second graders expect to do more reflection on what they read, and some of that reflection may include writing on their own. We describe the growth of independence, as well as the introduction of reading response journals and Think Books more fully in Chapter 13. A reading response journal is a special notebook in which students record titles of books they read and also write letters to the teacher that reflect their thinking. A Think Book is a notebook to record, with teacher guidance, a wide variety of writing: note-taking, making lists, responding to a read-aloud, and so on. It is exciting to see young students begin to immerse themselves in books for much longer periods of time, and to notice how they are increasingly able to respond both orally and in writing to the texts they hear read aloud and those they read for themselves.

What Do These Changes Mean?

All of these important internal changes, signaled by students' overt behaviors, mean that students are processing and comprehending texts at a deeper level. They are using the whole range of strategies described in Chapter 2, and they are beginning to apply them to longer and more complex texts. As readers, they are still beginners, and we should not forget that. They still need strong support in comprehending more complex texts.

These students can also be seen as beginning writers because they have only recently acquired a body of words that they can write quickly and automatically, and they should be adding to this repertoire daily. Their word-solving skills make it possible to write a great many more words, but their spelling will not be completely conventional. As teachers, we want them to experiment with words, as well as to write conventionally all of the words they know. An important change is that these students can use writing more rapidly and easily, and so it is more available to us as part of instruction.

Figure 4-2 lists several implications of the profound changes seen during the second-grade year. In a sense, these implications reveal our expectations of students at this time. Some will take on the new behaviors later and need much more support and explicit demonstration. Others will forge ahead easily, becoming independent with seemingly little effort.

The ability to sustain the reading of a longer text over several days and to read silently for longer periods of time makes a qualitative difference in the educational program for these students. For example, instead of moving through several independent activities and reading several short books, you might see students becoming more deliberate about choosing texts and reading them independently. Their knowledge of texts (built both from

hearing you read aloud *and* from reading for themselves) is much richer, and they have a repertoire of language, assumptions about the way texts work, vocabulary, types of characters, plots, and so on, that they can bring to all of their reading and writing. They know a core of words that they can write quickly and automatically and can solve many more with their growing phonics and spelling strategies. Finally, they can sustain independent behavior, working alone and silently, for longer periods of time.

Summary

These attributes of readers and writers raise our expectations and call for shifts in both teaching and management. Second grade is an exciting time, and it must be both successful and challenging for our young students. Close observation helps us to detect evidence of those important changes. Observation also provides insight into the kind of teaching that will be needed to support these important changes in students' behaviors.

Implications of Shifts in Behavior, Grades 1 to 3

Students will:

- be engaged in reading silently for longer periods of time.
- become more flexible in the kinds of texts they can read.
- make connections between texts because their repertoire will have expanded.
- go beyond the texts they read to make inferences and synthesize information.
- have greater capability to sustain writing over longer periods of time.
- begin to use writing to document reading as well as to record their responses.
- employ a wider range of word-solving strategies because they are building networks of understanding about how words work.
- be able to work independently without talking to others for designated periods of time.
- reflect on and self-evaluate to a greater degree their reading, writing, and independent work.

FIGURE 4-2

Ideas to Try

1. Meet with colleagues who teach children in grades kindergarten through third grade. Make your goal to expand your understanding of the transitions students make between first and third grade.

2. Ask teachers to bring some materials to examine.

   - Ask first-grade teachers to bring student writing samples saved from the end of first grade; ask second-grade teachers to bring samples from the beginning, middle, and end of second grade; and ask third-grade teachers to bring samples from the beginning and middle of third grade.

   - Ask all teachers to bring samples of texts that their students would read in guided reading at the beginning, middle, and end of the year. Kindergarten teachers may wish to bring samples from March to June only.

3. Compare the writing samples and make a list of the important changes you notice over time.

4. Compare the reading texts and discuss the changing demands on readers that you notice. You may want to make some notes on a chart to capture the important new challenges at each level. (Save these reading texts and any lists you make if you plan to discuss Chapter 6 of this book.)

5. Laying out the writing samples and reading texts in order of complexity will give you and your group a visual picture of the changes to expect. Then discuss how to shift your teaching to support students as they change over time.

Part II

Teaching for Comprehension as Students Engage With Text

Part II provides information about and examples that illustrate how teaching supports students in developing and using comprehension strategies. The first six chapters focus on guided reading as a context for expanding processing strategies. Chapter 5 explores the literary path to comprehension and presents the idea that responding to the literary quality of texts encountered in guided reading will enhance readers' appreciation, understanding, and enjoyment of texts. Chapters 6 and 7 provide suggestions and examples from lesson components in guided reading. Chapter 8 focuses on the development of fluency and phrasing, both important influences on comprehension. Chapter 9 offers suggestions for comprehension instruction in guided and independent reading. In Chapter 10, you will find suggestions for extending students' understanding of texts after reading, and in Chapter 11, interactive read-aloud is described as a way to further develop students' comprehension strategies.

CHAPTER 5

The Literary Path to Comprehension: Writer's Craft and Guided Reading

Patricia L. Scharer

As we select books for guided reading lessons, we often focus on the accessibility of the text. How difficult will this book be for a given group of children as they read? Will it be just a bit more challenging than the last book, so that they can experience success and some reading challenges as well? Are there unknown words that children might be able to read independently with their current strategies or others that may require a bit more support during the introduction? Which words might I want to discuss and locate in the text before reading? Attending to words is important. Understanding new stories, however, goes well beyond reading new and familiar words.

In this chapter I will explore the ways that thinking about the writer's craft and the techniques of the illustrator can influence many of the instructional decisions we make regarding book selection, the introduction, the conversation after the reading, and teaching points in guided reading. These factors are also important in selecting, reading, and discussing books during interactive read-aloud.

Exploring the Craft of Writers and Illustrators

The authors of *Children's Literature in the Elementary School* (Huck, Hepler, Hickman, & Kiefer 2001) argue that although children are not born with literary insights in a conventional sense, their natural responses to books should be valued and encouraged because they are an important start in developing an awareness of the writer's craft. Teachers "need to help children discover what practiced readers look for in a well-written book" (p. 13) through purposeful literary study across genres beginning with the very youngest of readers. Writers use many tools while crafting their work (see Figure 5-1), and it's our job to help students to understand these tools.

- **Plot.** Often, the plot in books for children is told in a sequential, step-by-step manner as the writer describes what happens to the story's characters. For example, the plot may build toward a problem of some kind that is then resolved. The way the writer creates the plot is well worth exploring with young readers because it fosters greater

understanding of writing styles and expands comprehension. Laura Joffe Numeroff, for example, employs a cyclical device in *If You Give a Mouse a Cookie* (1985). The story ends where it began, with the same problem at the end as at the beginning. The plot of Pat Hutchins's *The Wind Blew* (1974) is cumulative as the belongings of more and more people are tossed about by the wind. The plot winds down and is resolved as the hats, scarves, newspapers, and other items are returned to the ground and the wind blows off to sea. In other stories, such as Mem Fox's *Shoes from Grandpa* (1990) or her more recent *Harriet, You'll Drive Me Wild* (2000), repeated phrases help children anticipate changes in the plot, participate in the story, and support their understanding of the story line. A story's plot should keep the reader's interest throughout the action, challenges, and resolution of the story.

Discussing how writers achieve successful plots helps children understand the artistic devices writers use. Linda Aufdencamp's second graders, for example, discussed how Eve Bunting let the reader know that Timothy's Gram in *Sunshine Home* (1994) was joking when she described another resident of the nursing home by saying, "That Charlie Lutz is my destruction…he's a terrible driver. Always bumping me with his wheelchair. He shouldn't be allowed on the road." It was important that the readers did not read this comment literally, as Gram's playful attitude toward Charlie was an important element in the story's plot.

Literary Elements and Definitions

PLOT	What happens to the characters
SETTING	When and where the story takes place
MOOD	How the story makes the reader feel
THEME	What the story is really about
CHARACTERIZATION	How the reader understands the characters' thoughts, feelings, and actions
POINT OF VIEW	Who is telling the story

FIGURE 5-1

Setting. The setting of a story is often described through both text and illustrations. In *Owl Moon* (1987), for example, Jane Yolen's opening text combines with John Schoenherr's watercolor and ink drawings to create a quiet, peaceful nighttime setting as the child and father leave the house to go owling.

> It was late one winter night,
> long past my bedtime,
> when Pa and I went owling.
> There was no wind.
> The trees stood still
> as giant statues.
> And the moon was so bright
> the sky seemed to shine.

Questions to Explore the Writer's Craft

PLOT	What did you notice about the way the writer told the story? Tell me about the problem in the story. How was the problem fixed?
SETTING	Where does this story take place? How do you know?
MOOD	How does this story make you feel? What does the author do to make you feel like that? Did your feelings change during the story? If so, how?
THEME	What is this story really about? What did the characters learn in the story? What can we learn from the story?
CHARACTERIZATION	What do you know about the characters in the story? How did you learn about them?
POINT OF VIEW	Who is telling this story? How do you know?

FIGURE 5-2

- **Mood.** The writer and illustrator's use of poetic text and calm shades of blue and evening black contribute to the story's mood as the father and child experience both the search and the discovery of a Great Horned Owl.
- **Theme.** The theme of a story moves readers beyond a literal understanding to consider something even larger than the plot itself. The theme of the folktale *Little Red Riding Hood* suggests that children should never talk to strangers, while the benefits of working together is the theme in a folktale such as *The Great Big Enormous Turnip*. Other themes common to children's books include growing up, overcoming fears, the importance of being a friend, and the cycle of life. Discussions identifying themes move readers' understanding beyond the literal meaning of the text and into interpretations of the text by asking, "What is this story *really* about?"
- **Characterization.** Readers learn about the author's use of characterization by discussing how the text develops the qualities of each character. Teachers can begin exploring characterization by asking questions such as "How do you know that the wolf in this story is bad?" The discussion in response might center on things the wolf says, what the pigs say about the wolf, the size of the words on the page, or the menacing

Questions to Explore the Illustrator's Technique

MEDIA	How did the artist make the pictures? What materials were used? Why do you think those materials were chosen?
FORMAT	What is special about the shape of this book or the ways the pictures are placed on the page? How do these pictures help readers understand the story?
USE OF COLOR	Why did the artist use certain colors in the pictures?
MOOD	How do the colors make you feel?
POINT OF VIEW	Where are you in the story? In front of the pictures? Above? Up close? Far away? How do the pictures change? Why does this artist do that?

FIGURE 5-3

style of illustrations emphasizing the wolf's teeth, drooling jaws, or dangerous size. The changes in and growth of a character are also important to discuss. For example, readers should consider how being saved by her little sister when Sheila was lost affected both characters in Kevin Henkes's *Sheila Rae, The Brave* (1987).

- **Point of View.** It is important to discuss a story's point of view from both the writer's and illustrator's perspectives. A narrator describes the daily, troublesome activities of a little cat in Cindy Ward's *Cookie's Week* (1988). Tomie dePaola's illustrations emphasize the naughtiness of the kitten by placing the reader very close to the action. Readers are sometimes so close to Cookie's activities through the illustrations that only part of Cookie's body is visible as the kitten runs away from the destruction it has wrought. All of the consequences of falling into the toilet, knocking over a plant, upsetting the trash, and climbing into the kitchen drawer and closet are clearly portrayed. In contrast, the story of *Uncle Jed's Barbershop* (Mitchell 1993) is told in first person through the voice and perspective of a young girl. She narrates her story of how her Uncle Jed used the money he had saved to open a barbershop on a lifesaving operation for her, instead.
- **Style.** Finally, discussing the style of illustrations and characteristics of each book's format supports young readers' understanding of the book's meaning. Why are there holes and various sizes of pages in Eric Carle's *The Very Hungry Caterpillar* (1969)? Why do the illustrations and white space change in size in Sendak's *Where the Wild Things Are* (1963)? Why are Janet Stevens's illustrations placed sideways in *Tops and Bottoms* (1995)? All of these questions will help children to study the intentional decisions authors and illustrators make as they create meaning through the marriage of text and pictures.

It is not necessary to use sophisticated, technical language while studying the writer's craft or illustrator's technique with young children. Rather, the questions in Figures 5-2 and 5-3 can help children to think about complex ideas without complicated language.

Studying Craft: Why Bother?

Sometimes, it seems you have enough of a challenge in just helping young readers to successfully read the words of increasingly more difficult texts. Planning book introductions and teaching points following the lesson to learn about letters, sounds, and words can consume instructional time. You may ask yourself, "Why should I talk about craft with young children? The books we read are simple texts without a lot of fancy literary notions. I will help them learn to read; teachers in the upper grades can help them study the literary qualities of books. I do not have the time."

Decisions about the use of instruction time often hinge on the value placed on the activity. If having children read books from their browsing boxes is important, there will be time for independent reading. If reading in small groups is important, there will be time for guided reading and literature discussions. The same is true for studying craft—if it is important, there will be time. So, what are the values of studying craft—why bother? Studying craft:

- **increases enjoyment.** Certainly many of the books the youngest readers find in guided reading lessons are simple, accessible texts. These texts, however, are not without literary merit. Efforts by publishers to provide interesting books for early readers have resulted in quality writing with fascinating characters, suspenseful plots, and illustrations worth exploring. In addition, lists of quality children's trade books are leveled in both *Guided Reading* (Fountas & Pinnell 1996) and *Matching Books to Readers* (Fountas & Pinnell 1999) to support the acquisition of high-quality children's literature in paperbacks quite suitable for guided reading instruction. The quality of these books provides rich opportunities for readers of all ages to heighten their enjoyment of reading by looking carefully at the techniques used by both the writer and the illustrator.
- **encourages higher-level thinking.** Inviting children to respond to their reading, valuing their responses, and offering interpretive questions to support further conversation ensures that children will continue to think about their reading in similarly complex ways. The discussion resulting from such instruction not only encourages higher-level thinking, but also benefits children as they listen to the comments and questions of the other readers in the group.
- **helps children see connections across texts.** Discussing texts encourages children to think deeply as they read so they can talk about other stories that come to mind and how their knowledge of that story connects with the book they are reading. Children who first meet Joy Cowley's Greedy Cat, for example, in *Greedy Cat Is Hungry* (1988) will

We study the writer's craft to:

- increase enjoyment.
- encourage higher-level thinking.
- help children see connections across texts.
- support personal writing.

easily apply what they learned about the cat's personality to the more difficult text, *Greedy Cat* (1983), as Mum teaches the cat an important lesson with a pot of pepper!

- **supports personal writing.** As children openly and thoughtfully discuss the decisions writers make in their stories, the lessons may influence their own writing as they try using the writers' techniques. The connections with their reading may range from the use of quotation marks and exclamation points in *Mrs. Wishy-Washy* (Cowley 1998) to the repetitive sequencing found in *Ox-Cart Man* (Hall 1979). Trinity's (age 7) written response to listening to the repetitive language in *Pigs in the Mud in the Middle of the Rud* (Plourde 1997) began with a style of writing reflecting a similar kind of repetition as she wrote:

  Pigs were in the mud and the brothers said, "I'll get them."
  Then the hen was in the mud and the sister said, "I'll get them."

Her independent work appeared to be influenced by listening to and discussing the book her teacher read aloud.

Studying Craft During Guided Reading

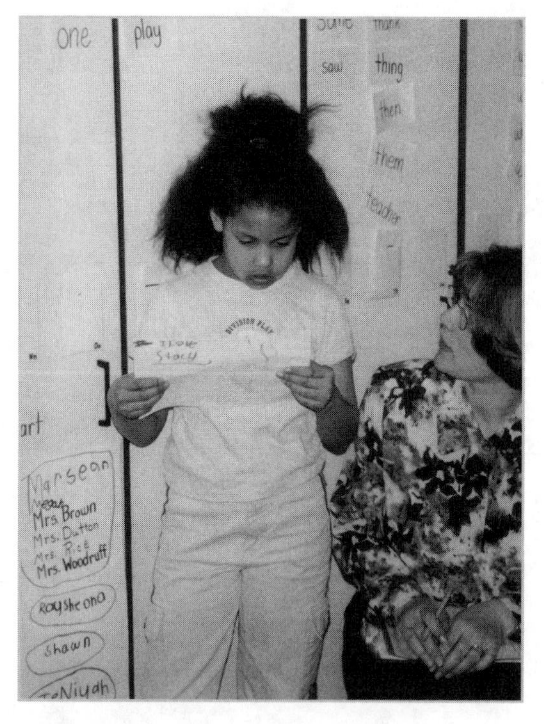

Trinity shares her story.

The instructional context of guided reading offers rich opportunities for calling attention to the craft of writers and illustrators. During your introduction of a new book, invite children to share their initial responses to the style of the illustrator or the topic of the book. Point out unique features of the book that readers should be thinking about while they are reading. During Nikki Woodruff's introduction to *Trash or Treasure* (Clyne & Griffiths 1999) [Level H], Trinity, one of the first graders in the group, looked closely at the pictures and noticed the dust Mom created while cleaning house to find things to donate to the school fair. Trinity spontaneously read the speech bubble showing the little girl, Jess, saying, "Achoo." This action led to more discussion of how the dust and Mom's cleaning efforts were important parts of the story's plot, and it helped

prepare the young readers for the surprise ending as Jess bought all of Mom's donations the next day at the fair.

You can plan for such introductions by thinking about the craft of the writer and illustrator and deciding on a point or two that will facilitate children's understanding while they are reading. For example, when introducing *Dad Didn't Mind at All* (Naden 1989) [Level F] to her first graders, Sue Brown discussed the author's use of the days of the week on most of the pages as a way to describe the family's week of vacation camping at the lake. The children also talked about the author's repeated use of the refrain, "Dad didn't mind at all," by linking it with the title. The special qualities of books representing a variety of levels are shown in Figure 5-4 as examples of ideas to incorporate literary notions into book introductions.

Sharing ideas during a book introduction.

After the reading, you have another opportunity to talk with students about literary concepts. First, go back to what you discussed during the introduction to see if children have further insights into how the story developed, the contribution of the illustrations, or the particular quality readers were to look for during their reading. Then, open invitations can encourage children to share their initial responses. In contrast to asking children if they liked the story or other questions that inspire brief yes/no responses, these invitations are broad. You can extend open invitations with questions such as:

- What part did you like best?
- What special part do you want to talk about now?
- What did you notice about the pictures while you were reading?
- What other books did you think of while reading?
- How does this story compare with other books by ________?

The intent behind such open invitations is to establish the expectation that children's thoughts and feelings about what they read are important and should be shared with the group. Often, young readers' insights into texts and illustrations represent fresh, new approaches that adults have never considered. Your role at that point is to encourage open response and follow the lead of the children— supporting, encouraging, and valuing each contribution. These conversations, however, are also rich opportunities for you to extend

Learning About Craft During Book Introductions

TITLE, AUTHOR, LEVEL:	TEACHER'S QUESTIONS OR PROMPTS:	CRAFT LESSON:
The Little Red Hen, Cowley, Level B	"Be looking for changes in the pig, cat, and dog."	• Plot changes • Use of dialogue
My Bike, Martin, Level D	"Watch for words the author repeats to help us understand when the story takes place."	• Days of the week to indicate sequence and time
Sam's Mask, Cachemaille, Level E	"Look for how the author and photographer explain the steps Sam used to make his mask."	• Links between the text and illustrations • Plot sequence
Each Peach Pear Plum, Ahlberg and Ahlberg, Level G	"What storybook characters do you notice in the illustrations?"	• Intertextual links in both the illustrations and the text
The Enormous Watermelon, Parkes and Smith, Level H	"Notice the different sizes of pages. Why do you think the illustrator did that? Be ready to talk about the pictures after you read."	• Contribution of the format of the book to meaning
Do Like Kyla, Johnson, Level I	"Think about the repetition of the title throughout the story. What makes this a good title?"	• Repeated refrain linking the plot together
Frog and Toad Are Friends, Lobel, Level K	"There is a problem in each of the five chapters of this book. Read to learn more about the characters as each of the problems is solved."	• Plot development and resolution • Characterization
George Washington's Mother, Fritz, Level M	"George Washington and his mother are the two main characters in this story. Be thinking about how they are alike and different."	• Character development • Compare/contrast writing style

FIGURE 5-4

the literary awareness of young readers by "shooting literary arrows" (Peterson & Eeds 1990) with a well-crafted question or comment directing readers to a particular quality of the writing or characteristic of the illustrations.

Talking about Why Elephants Have Long Noses

After her students read *Why Elephants Have Long Noses* (Bacon 1989) [Level G], Sue Brown asked them to think about this story's explanation of why elephants have long noses and the usefulness of having a long nose if they were an elephant. This conversation led to considering other animals in a similar way as they thought about why a tiger has stripes or a bat has wings. Later, the readers selected their favorite animal and wrote an explanation for one of the animal's physical features. Figure 5-5 offers ideas for questions or prompts that can help children explore the literary qualities of the books they read by studying the decisions authors and illustrators make as they create the story.

Linking Interactive Read-Alouds and Guided Reading

Yet another way to help young children understand the creative process is to continue the conversation about literary elements during interactive read-aloud sessions. These instructional times are called interactive because children are invited to respond to the story while it is read and are expected to offer comments and questions reflecting their thoughts during the reading. You might start the session with a discussion of what students can learn about the main character by looking at the cover or endpapers. During the reading, stop as children offer their spontaneous responses or ask an interpretive question or comment on something you want to share. This pausing is in stark contrast to a read-aloud time, when the children are expected to be quiet until the end of the book. By reading the book interactively, you encourage language development and capture the thoughts and feelings of the children as they listen. Thus, the conversations with the children before and during an interactive read-aloud provide learning opportunities similar to those described previously in this chapter.

Learning About Craft After the Reading

TITLE, AUTHOR, LEVEL:	TEACHER'S QUESTIONS OR PROMPTS:	CRAFT LESSON:
Splish Splash!, Cowley, Level B	"Let's talk about the sounds the words make when you say, 'Splish Splash!' What other words can describe what the children did with water in this story?"	❁ Onomatopoeia, words that sound like what they describe
It Looked Like Spilt Milk, Shaw, Level E	"What do you notice about the pictures in this book? What was special about the ending?"	❁ Use of collage ❁ Surprise ending
The Lion and the Rabbit, Randell, Level F	"What did the lion learn from his experience?"	❁ Theme: appreciating what you have
Greedy Cat, Cowley, Level G	"Look back through the pictures and see if you can find messages created by the illustrator. How is this book like the other stories you have read about Greedy Cat?"	❁ Linking with styles found in other books by the same author or illustrator
Emma's Problem, Parker, Level H	"How do the author and illustrator tell readers about when the story takes place? Why can Emma touch the branch now, but she couldn't at the beginning of the story?"	❁ Subtle use of the seasons and inference that Emma grew taller over time
Amazing Grace, Hoffman, Level L	"What stories did you think about while you were reading? What did Grace learn about herself?"	❁ Intertextual connections ❁ Theme of achieving success with self-confidence
Anansi and the Moss-covered Rock, Kimmel, Level M	"How did you learn about what Anansi is like? How would you describe him? What do you learn through the pictures? How Anansi talks? How the other animals talk?"	❁ Character development through dialogue, illustration, and narration

FIGURE 5-5

Studying Craft During Interactive Read-Alouds

Figure 5-6 lists recent picture books that offer many opportunities to think about craft. This list was created by a group of teachers as they explored the unique characteristics of each book and considered the "literary arrows" they might use as they read each book aloud to their students. Those literary arrows, listed as questions, invite children to go back into the text and examine illustrations to develop new, deeper insights into the meaning of the story.

An added benefit of interactive read-aloud is the fact that the discussions are likely to link with similar talk during the other components of the language/literacy framework. For example, children who are already familiar with nursery rhymes, having fully explored Mother Goose collections such as *Here Comes Mother Goose* (1999) by Iona Opie, will be able to read nursery rhymes on chart paper during shared reading with greater ease. Discussions can focus on the interpretations of the nursery rhymes as reflected in the large, colorful illustrations by Rosemary Wells compared with illustrations students make of the rhymes for their poetry notebooks. Similarly, familiarity with folktales such as Janet Stevens's *The Three Billy Goats Gruff* (1987) or Paul Galdone's *The Three Little Pigs* (1970) will support children's readings of easier variations of such stories often found in publishers' collections of little books for guided reading. More specifically, introducing literary aspects of writing or illustrating during an interactive read-aloud can heighten the quality of the conversation during guided reading and deepen readers' understanding of both the craft and the story itself. Figure 5-7 contains suggestions of recent trade books and questions you might ask inviting discussion of the literary merits of each book, and includes titles of books commonly found in guided reading collections with similar literary qualities.

Recent Books to Read Aloud and Discuss

Book		
Quack and Count, Baker	**SETTING:** How do you know about where the ducks live? **MOOD:** How does this story make you feel? What makes you feel that way—words, illustrations?	**WRITING STYLE:** What is special about the words the author uses? **ILLUSTRATIONS:** How did the artist make the pictures? What about the colors—what did you notice?
Wolf!, Bloom	**THEME:** What message does the writer want to share with readers? **CHARACTERIZATION:** How did you learn about the characters through the words and pictures? Let's think about what the animals say to each other. What do you learn about each of them?	**POINT OF VIEW:** Who is telling this story? How might it be different if the wolf or one of the other animals told the story?
Red-Eyed Tree Frog, Cowley	**SETTING:** How do you learn about where the tree frog lives? **WRITING STYLE:** How did the author tell the story of the tree frog?	**ILLUSTRATIONS:** Let's look at the colors in the photos. What do you notice? What about the photos themselves?
Tessa's Tip-Tapping Toes, Crimi	**CHARACTERIZATION:** How are Tess and Oscar different from other mice and cats?	**WRITING STYLE:** What words does the author use to describe the music and movement in the story?
The Hatseller and the Monkeys, Diakite	**PLOT:** Does this story remind you of any other story? Why? **SETTING:** What do you know about where the story takes place? Look closely at the pictures. What do you notice about the setting?	**ILLUSTRATIONS:** What do you notice about the pictures? Let's talk about how the white lines are made (discuss batik). How do the borders, small illustrations, and full-page illustrations work together?
Cow, Doyle	**WRITING STYLE:** What words does the author use to describe the cow? How do the words paint a picture of the cow's day?	**ILLUSTRATIONS:** Think about the close-up pictures. How do they make you feel as a reader?
Eight Animals Bake a Cake, Elya	**WRITING STYLE:** What do you notice about the words on each page?	**ILLUSTRATIONS:** How do the illustrations help you understand the English and Spanish words?
Nonsense! He Yelled, Eschbacher	**WRITING STYLE:** What do you notice about the children in this book? How does the author tell about each of them?	**FORMAT:** How do the size and positions of the words help you understand each character?
Muncha! Muncha! Muncha!, Fleming	**WRITING STYLE:** What other stories did you think of that are like this one? **ILLUSTRATIONS:** How do the colors change between day and night?	**PLOT:** What surprises happened at the end of the book? How did the author and illustrator tell you about those surprises?

Laugh-eteria, Florian	**MOOD:** How do these pictures make you feel? What did the author do to make you feel like that? **WRITING STYLE:** What do you notice about the words the poet uses?	**POINT OF VIEW:** Who is telling these poems? **ILLUSTRATIONS:** How do the pictures help you think about the poem?
One Rainy Day, Gorbachev	**SETTING:** How do you learn about the two places where this story takes place?	**ILLUSTRATIONS:** How do the illustrations help you to see what happens in the woods and at the goat's house?
I Stink!, McMullan and McMullan	**ILLUSTRATIONS:** How do the end-papers help you think about the story? **WRITING STYLE:** How does the author express loud, noisy sounds?	**THEME:** What big ideas do you learn about by reading this book?
Here Comes Mother Goose, Opie	**WRITING STYLE:** What do you notice about the words in the nursery rhymes? **ILLUSTRATIONS:** Do you see any characters from other books illustrated by Rosemary Wells?	**FORMAT:** What do you notice about the ways the author and illustrator have put the words and pictures on each page?
One Duck Stuck, Root	**SETTING:** What helps you understand where the story takes place? **FORMAT:** Think about the shape of the book and the way the pictures and words are placed on each page. What do you notice?	**WRITING STYLE:** Let's think about the words the writer uses. What do you notice? (words representing sounds, rhyming, repetition, varying words for each animal)
Epossumondas, Salley	**WRITING STYLE:** This is a noodlehead story. Why do you think it's called that?	**ILLUSTRATIONS:** How do the illustrations add to the silliness and humor of the story?
The Adventures of a Nose, Schwarz	**THEME:** What message does the author share with readers? What can readers learn from this book?	**ILLUSTRATIONS:** Look closely at the pictures. What do you notice about the nose and object around the nose?
Bertie Was a Watchdog, Walton	**CHARACTERIZATION:** How do you get to know Bertie? How is Bertie different from the robber?	**FORMAT:** What do you notice about the shape of the book and illustrations? How does the format add to the story?
So Many Bunnies, Walton	**WRITING STYLE:** What can you learn from this book? (numbers, rhyming words, ABCs) Does it remind you of another nursery rhyme? What is the same? What is different?	**ILLUSTRATIONS:** How did the artist make the pictures? What do you notice about the boxes where you find the words?

FIGURE 5-6

Making Connections During Interactive Read Aloud and Guided Reading

TRADE BOOK:	CRAFT QUESTIONS ABOUT THE BOOK:	CONNECTIONS TO GUIDED READING BOOKS:
A Beasty Story, Martin	**MOOD:** How does this story make you feel? Why do you feel like that? **WRITING STYLE:** Let's talk about the two kinds of words in this story—some tell the story and others are in speech bubbles. **POINT OF VIEW:** Who is telling the story? **FORMAT:** Let's think about the cover and the endpapers. How do they help us understand the story?	*Goodbye Lucy*, Cowley, Level D *Roll Over*, Skelly, Level D *Dad Didn't Mind at All*, Naden, Level F
Open Wide: Tooth School Inside, Keller	**THEME:** What does the writer want readers to know? **WRITING STYLE:** What is special about the way the writer tells this story? **ILLUSTRATIONS:** What did you notice about the pictures? How do they help readers think about the story? **FORMAT:** Think about how the book is put together. What do you notice about the cover? Endpapers? Title page? Different pages?	*The Wobbly Tooth*, Jordan, Level D *Too Many Bones and a Toothbrush Tale*, O'Connell, Level G
You'll Soon Grow Into Them, Titch, Hutchins	**ILLUSTRATIONS:** How did the pictures show you that there was a long time between the beginning and the end of the story?	*Emma's Problem*, Parker, Level H
The Seals on the Bus, Hort	**PLOT:** Does this story make you think of another one? Why? What's the same? What's different? **CHARACTERIZATION:** How do you get to know the characters: What do you learn through words? Through the pictures? **WRITING STYLE:** What is special about the way the author tells the story? What kinds of words does he use? **ILLUSTRATIONS:** How did the artist create the pictures? What do you notice about the words where are they placed?	*Wheels on the Bus*, Kovalski, Level I
Cook-A-Doodle-Doo, Stevens *The Little Red Hen Makes a Pizza*, Sturges	**PLOT:** Does this story make you think of another one? Why? What's the same? What's different? **THEME:** What is the author trying to tell readers? What can we learn from this story? **FORMAT:** Let's go back and read the sidebars in *Cook-A-Doodle-Doo*. How do they connect with the story? **ILLUSTRATIONS:** What do you notice about the pictures in *The Little Red Hen Makes a Pizza*? How did the illustrator make them? (notice 3-D effect, depth, labeling, colors, layout)	*The Little Red Hen*, Galdone, Level J

FIGURE 5-7

Summary

Studying the writer's craft should be a natural, enjoyable shared experience between readers. At times, children may take the lead based on their personal responses to a text or something special they have noticed in it; other times, you may purposefully shoot literary arrows to stretch the thinking of the group. I am not implying that you should think of literary elements such as mood, plot, and characterization as items to "cover" in the curriculum during certain grading periods or with certain texts. Rather, literary devices are tools to help readers more fully explore the meaning of texts by studying the unique characteristics of each author or illustrator. Consider this work as a way to foster both a love of books and an appreciation for the choices writers and illustrators make, while also having fun talking about books and their creation with your students.

In a recent speech, Lucy Calkins was concerned about the child who read Jane Yolen's *Owl Moon* straight through and simply closed the book as if to say, "I'm done. What's next?" She argued passionately that children need the influence of talented writers such as Yolen, and need to approach these writers' texts with the following question in mind: "What am I dying to talk about?" Reading is much more than getting through the book, closing it, and asking, "What's next?" You can make sure that a celebration of wonderful words, delicious sentences, and amazing art is what's next—and that children approach their reading knowing that this celebration is coming.

Ideas to Try

1. Meet with other teachers to read copies of your favorite guided reading books and discuss the literary arrows inspired by the text and illustrations.

2. Review the books in your book room to see if there are collections of leveled texts in need of a higher quality of writing. Discard books with limited interest for children or poorly written text and replace with paperback collections of quality children's literature.

3. Create a school-wide chart in your book room of quality books to read aloud that are particularly good examples of literary elements such as plot, theme, mood, characterization, setting, format, or point of view. Maintain a lending collection of those books in the book room for all of the teaching staff to use.

4. Create a book group of other teachers interested in reading new books for children and talking about their literary and artistic merits. Write a grant for funds to provide your group with new copies of children's literature for your enjoyment, professional growth, and classroom use.

Author's note: Special thanks go to the literacy coordinators from Marion City Schools, Marion, Ohio, for many helpful suggestions for this chapter and to the 2000-2001 literacy coordinators training with The Ohio State University's Team Gray who contributed to the list of questions for the interactive read-alouds. The first graders of Sue Brown and Nicole Woodruff from Glenwood Elementary School, Marion City Schools, Marion, Ohio, also contributed to this book through their lively discussions during guided reading and their willingness to be photographed.

CHAPTER 6

Scaffolding the First Reading of a Book for Children Who Are Learning to Read

Mary Fried

As we consider introducing a new book or story to children, most of us draw on a wealth of experience—we have introduced hundreds, even thousands, of books to students. In this chapter, I invite you to examine some important understandings that underlie the practice of introducing stories to young readers. A book introduction can be a powerful tool that scaffolds their first reading of a new and more challenging text. The support in an introduction takes many forms and can focus on just about any aspect of reading, but the ultimate goal is to help students expand their comprehending strategies. I begin by discussing the traditional method of introducing texts and then focus on some new and different concepts to consider when introducing new books to young readers in guided reading.

Building on Our Past Experiences as Teachers

The practice of introducing a text should not be daunting, because it is not entirely new. Like me, you may have experience using a basal reading system. If so, you probably are able to call up an educational "tape," or set of responses that are embedded in your repertoire of teaching practices. These practiced responses have served us well over the years. The tape, or traditional framework for introducing a story using a basal reading system approach, would usually begin with building interest for reading the story. For example:

Teacher: We are going to read a funny story called *The Smoke Detector*.

Linking the concepts of the story to the students' own background of experience is the next step. Some of the children might be asked to share their own experiences that relate to the story:

Teacher: Do you know what a smoke detector is?
First Student: We have one in our house and you have to push this little red button to see if it is working and it goes BEEP real loud.

Second Student: Yeah, our smoke alarm went off one time when Daddy was cooking bacon. Oooo, it was loud.

Teacher: So everyone knows what a smoke detector is?

If any of the concepts in the story are unfamiliar to the children, you would take time to introduce and explain the concept:

Teacher: Do you know what a smoke detector is?

Students: (*No response.*)

Teacher: Well, a smoke detector is a small plastic box in the ceiling or on the wall that is like the fire alarm you hear at school when we have a fire drill. It makes a loud noise when it detects smoke, so it warns everyone to get out of the house because there might be a fire.

The next component of the traditional introduction might be to look at some of the pictures and predict what is going to happen in the story. Often, only the picture on the cover or those on the first few pages will be used. Many times you might not refer to any other pictures and would end the discussion of the major concept of the story with a question or a statement to establish the purpose for reading the story:

Teacher: Read this story, *The Smoke Detector*, to find out what happens when Rayshawn and Grandpa hear the smoke detector go off.

This traditional book introduction will vary slightly based on your teaching style and your students, but the basic components will remain fairly consistent. (See Figure 6-1.)

For many years, I used this format for introducing basal stories to students in my fourth- and fifth-grade classrooms. If you have worked using a basal series, this format is familiar to you. The knowledge you have

Traditional Framework for Introducing Storybooks

- Select next story in basal.
- Engage students' interest.
- Introduce new concepts.
- Look at the pictures.
- Predict what might happen.
- Establish a purpose for reading.

FIGURE 6-1

provides a valuable base for explaining some new ways of introducing texts. My focus in this chapter is not on introducing stories to students who know how to read, such as the fourth and fifth graders I taught. Instead, the focus is on the emergent readers who may be learning that it is the print we read, not the pictures, and on the early readers who are learning to bring together multiple sources of information as they problem solve unfamiliar words during reading. A different kind of introduction is also needed for transitional readers who understand many of the basic concepts of how the printed language works, but are not yet comfortable and independent in reading books with more complex vocabulary and unfamiliar concepts. All of these beginning readers need a different kind of introduction, one that will support them in such a way that they will be successful in becoming literate. For beginning readers, the meaning of the story is supported by the introduction.

Scaffolding: A Concept for Thinking About Book Introductions

Consider what Marie Clay (1991) says about introducing new books to young readers in guided reading:

> As the child approaches a new text he is entitled to an introduction so that when he reads, the gist of the whole or partly revealed story can provide some guide for a fluent reading. (p. 335)

The word *entitled* should be stressed because it is critical for young, beginning readers to have a great deal of support as they begin the complex journey of becoming literate. The established, basal format is a good background for beginning, but we want to move away from the traditional introduction in some important ways. The kind of support I will describe can be thought of as "building a scaffold" for a successful first reading of a new book.

WHAT IS A SCAFFOLD?

What is the origin of the concept of *scaffolding*? The dictionary defines "scaffold" as a temporary platform for supporting workers. The key word in that definition is "support." The word "temporary" should also be noted, as it implies that the need for support will change over time. As students learn more and more about how to read, they need less support for reading at an easy or instructional level or for a familiar kind of text. The term scaffolding used in an educational sense was introduced in an article written by Wood, Bruner, and Ross (1976). They described scaffolding as "a process that enables a…novice to solve a problem, carry out a task, or achieve a goal which would be beyond his unassisted efforts" (p. 90).

The scaffold you build makes it possible for the student to carry out the task of reading the new book independently or with very little assistance from the teacher. The scaffold makes it possible for them to read the hard or challenging book. The scaffold is considered selective assistance, a concept explored by Tharp and Gallimore (1988):

> Scaffolding, however, does not involve simplifying the task; it holds the task difficulty constant, while simplifying the child's role by means of graduated assistance from the adult/expert. (p. 33)

If the appropriate level of difficulty is considered when selecting a book for emergent, early, or transitional readers, then your job is not to simplify the book or rewrite the story. Your job is to focus the children's attention on critical aspects of reading the story by highlighting what they need to take into account and learn about before they begin to read. Building a scaffold for the successful reading of a new book is a critical skill for teachers of beginning readers. As Wood (1988) states: "Built well, such scaffolds help children learn how to achieve heights that they cannot scale alone" (p. 80).

LETTING GO OF OLD CONCEPTS

Working with primary teachers for many years, I have seen how difficult it is to "eject" the old tape for introducing books. Letting go of old concepts and taking on new ones takes a great deal of persistence, but the process of revising our responses is worthwhile. Our goal is to work more effectively with young, beginning readers, and the first step is understanding that there is a difference between our previous practice and the new way of thinking. The next step is learning to build the scaffold.

Characteristics of Readers Along a Continuum of Development

As a foundation for building the scaffold to prepare children effectively for a new story, understanding the terms "emergent," "early," and "transitional" readers will be helpful. Fountas and Pinnell (1996) provide detailed discussions and charts to clarify characteristics of readers and their behaviors along a broad continuum of development. I will highlight key concepts to differentiate these three achievement levels of beginning readers.

CHARACTERISTICS OF EMERGENT READERS

Emergent readers refers to children who are just acquiring very early concepts of literacy. An emergent reader may be a child who only looks at the pictures and is not yet aware that we read the print. It is wonderful when young children at home (or in preschool or beginning kindergarten) pick up a book and pretend to read by saying a story as they look at the pictures. In order to become readers, eventually these children will need to learn to attend to the details of print and understand how print operates. Emergent readers may know some words (for example, their names in all capital letters, *mom*, *dad*, or a sibling's name) as well as some letters, but they do not yet understand how the letters go together to make words, that we are reading those words when we read books.

As teachers, it is our job to build a foundation by selecting appropriate books for emergent readers to read during guided reading. Select from books that have the following characteristics:

- Familiar concepts.
- A small amount of easy-to-see print.
- Appropriate font and spacing between the words.
- Print that is clearly separated from the pictures.
- Pictures that clearly illustrate the text message.

The page layout from *Zoo Animals* (Fried 1999) [Level A] illustrates the simplicity of books that are appropriate for use with emergent readers. (See Figure 6-2.)

Building a Scaffold for Emergent Readers

As in the traditional approach to introducing new books, it is important to tap into the children's background experiences that relate to the story. In the case of *Zoo Animals*, the teacher, Judy, builds a scaffold for her students before they begin to read the story:

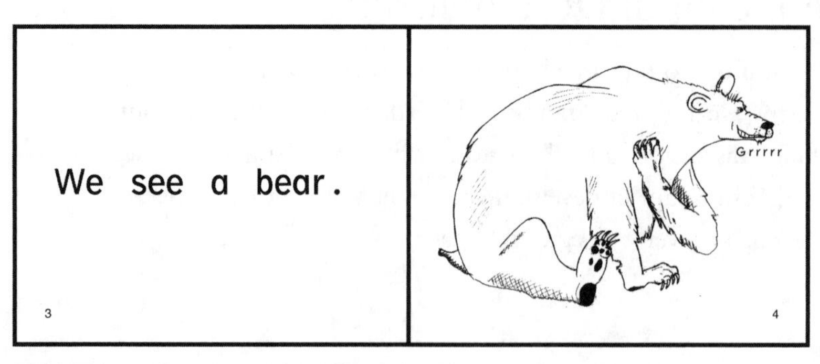

FIGURE 6-2 Page layout from *Zoo Animals*

Judy: Have you ever gone to a zoo? Talk to a partner, someone sitting close to you, about going to the zoo.

Students: (*Students turn and talk to each other about any zoo experiences they might have had, or anything about a zoo or zoo animals. The conversation buzzes.*)

As Judy listens in, she can determine the extent of the children's zoo experiences while the children talk to each other instead of responding to the teacher's questions. Some students may be asked to share what their friend said, or they might share an idea of their own. This brief activity is different from the traditional approach in which the teacher poses the discussion questions, then calls on individual children to respond by taking turns. When building a scaffold for reading the story, all children have the opportunity to talk and share experiences. Using oral language to relate personal experiences to new learning is the basis of comprehension.

The introduction continues:

Judy: Here is the title of our story (*pointing to each word to help focus the children's attention*): Zoo Animals.

William: That is the word "zoo!"

Markesia: Z Z Z!

Judy: That's right. That is the word "Zoo" and there's the Z.

FIGURE 6-3 Cover of *Zoo Animals*

This primitive print connection is reinforced and praised by Judy. With the background experiences related to the story and some of the words used to focus on the print, she will now tell the children what the story is about. She shows the cover of the book. (See Figure 6-3.)

Judy provides the main idea of the story and is careful to use some of the language structures of the book. Next, she and her students do a thorough review of the book as she highlights some of the important sources of information the children should use as they read the book independently:

Judy: This story tells us about the different animals we see at the zoo. Look at the pictures on the front cover. Think about what zoo animals might be in our story.

William: I like the monkeys. They are funny hanging around.

Judy: *(She turns to the book's first page.)* Oh, look we see a tiger. Say that word tiger. See him in the picture. The tiger goes: Roar-r-r-r! Let's all roar like a tiger. Softly. Roar – r-r-r.

Students: Roar-r-r-r (*all join in roaring*).

Judy: Now let's all say: We see a tiger.

Students: We see a tiger.

Judy: These are the words that say (*she points and reads*) "We see a tiger." (*She focuses the children on the print.*) Here is the word "we." See the big *W*. It's like in William's name. Everyone say "we" as I point to it. And here is the word "tiger." See the "t" for "tiger." Watch while I point and read the words: "We see a tiger."

(Judy provides a clear demonstration of pointing with her index finger under the words.)

Turn the page. Now we see…what?

Students: A bear…a bear!

Shawn: He's scratching himself. He's got fleas.

Judy: Yes, we see a bear. And, Shawn says he has fleas. What do you think?

Tina: No, he's just itching, I think. Like I itch and I don't have fleas.

Shawn: He's got an itchy flea.

Judy: Now what do we see?

Students: Monkeys!

Judy: Yes, monkeys. We see monkeys. Let's think about the word "monkeys." Say "monkeys" slowly.

Students: M o n k e y s.

Judy: "Monkeys" starts like somebody's name. "Monkeys" starts like Mark and Markesia.

Markesia: M M M!

Judy: That's right, "monkey" and "Mark" and "Markesia" all start with M. Let's look on this page (page 5) and find the word "monkeys" that starts with *m*. (See Figure 6-4.)

(Some children now confuse uppercase W with M, and some go easily to the lowercase m for monkeys. To sort out the confusion and reinforce the m for monkey, the teacher points and says...)

Judy: Everyone point to the word "monkeys." See the m. Yes. We see monkeys... *(She turns the page) ...everywhere!* Do you see monkeys everywhere? I'll pass the books around and you look at the last picture to see how many monkeys we can see. Count how many monkeys you see.

Students: (*The students begin to count and squeal out how many monkeys they see.*)

Judy: OK. Lots of monkeys *everywhere*. This is the word "everywhere." Everyone point to that word. *Everywhere!* This story was not about the bear and his itching. This was about what zoo animals we see. And what animals did we see everywhere?

Students: Monkeys! Monkeys everywhere.

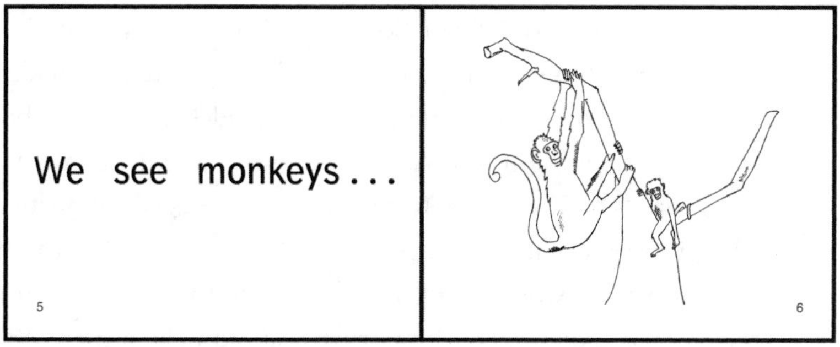

We see monkeys . . .

5

6

FIGURE 6-4 Page layout from *Zoo Animals*

In this introduction to *Zoo Animals*, Judy wove pictures, words, letters, sounds of letters, book language structures, and the excitement and fun of the story into a scaffold for the children's first reading. She provided clear demonstrations; tried to sort out confusion; introduced important concepts of how our printed language operates at the letter, sound, word, and sentence level; and encouraged the joy of literacy as the children prepared to read the book. As this example shows, Judy's introduction varied greatly from the traditional new book introduction.

Judy's introduction was also more in-depth than and different from a "picture walk," which has had a surge of use in recent years. We do not use the term "picture walk," because it is somewhat misleading both for teachers and children. Yes, the pictures are discussed, but the language structure of the book also is shared and some of the words and letters are highlighted. Any part of the book's format may also be clarified as the children and the teacher look through the book together for the first time.

Building a scaffold of information to use while reading the book is certainly more than a labeling of the pictures. Clay (1998) reminds us that "...although the interaction flows like a conversation and leaves room for the child's input to inform the teacher, it [the introduction] also includes deliberate teaching moves" (p. 175). In the example described above, both the conversational flow and the deliberate teaching moves are apparent. These types of demonstrations are critical when providing an introduction to children who are just beginning to learn how to use the print to read the message of the book.

For text introductions in the first guided reading lessons for emergent readers, many teachers like to hold the book so that all the children focus on the right page, word, or picture as the teacher points things out. As children learn the routines of guided reading, they also learn how to hold and use books independently during the introduction.

In summary, pictures are only a part of the focus and interaction when building a scaffold for a successful, independent reading of a story during guided reading. Instead of using only the pictures to predict what might happen in the story, you can skillfully help emergent readers (who may still be sorting out that it is the print we read, not the pictures) focus on a variety of information sources: their background knowledge, oral language structures, the print itself, and the pictures. This distinguishes building a scaffold for reading a story from the traditional introduction, and includes more than the term picture walk implies.

As you might imagine, when the group of emergent readers are turned loose to read *Zoo Animals* on their own, it will continue to need supportive instruction, help, and individual guidance. Without a supportive scaffold for the first reading, the children possibly would be at a loss and would most likely continue to make up a story or invent text to go with the comical pictures. The supportive scaffold helped them begin to use the print as they enjoy reading a wonderful little story.

Summary of Key Concepts in Building a Scaffold for Emergent Readers

In introducing texts to emergent readers, be aware of general characteristics of learners at this level. Consider the particular behaviors and strengths of the children you teach, as well as the characteristics of the text you are introducing. Some key concepts in building a scaffold for emergent readers are:

- Introduce the concept of the story to support comprehension.
- Encourage the children to talk to each other about the topic/concept.
- Share some of the comments/personal information.
- State the main idea of the story. Tell what the story is about.
- Discuss the story using the pictures, the language structures, the words, and the meaning of the story.
- Engage the children in looking at important aspects of the print (letters, words, punctuation, where to start, which way to go, etc.).
- Clarify any confusion.
- Provide clear demonstrations.

CHARACTERISTICS OF EARLY READERS

What are the characteristics of early readers? What are their strengths? What distinguishes them from emergent readers? (See also Fountas & Pinnell 1996.)

Early readers have gained basic understandings of how print operates in the English language; that is, where to start, which way to move across a line of print, return sweep, and the basic concepts of letters and words. They use pictures as a source of meaning and have become adept at surveying the pictures before they read a book or page. Pictures are not the only information they use, however. At difficulty, early readers may quickly check the picture, but usually rely less on illustrations than emergent readers do. Early readers use more information from the print.

Most early readers have control of several high-frequency words and read familiar stories with phrasing and fluency. They often use the visual information of the print—what the letters and words look like—in combination with meaning and syntactic information to notice when they have made an error. They tend to work to integrate sources of information (meaning, language, and visual information from print), making them match in order to read accurately. Often, early readers can self-correct the errors they notice; self-correction is more frequent and more independent than for emergent readers. (Note: Expect to see some early evidence of self-correction even at the emergent level.)

Building a Scaffold for Early Readers

Early readers have more experience in reading printed language and bring a wider range of strategies to processing texts, but they are still learning how to read and need the support of a well-built scaffold from you. Vary the amount and type of support you provide based on the familiarity of the story concepts and/or the difficulty of the level of the text. An easy version of *The Three Little Pigs* (Francis 1995) [Level E], for example, might need only a brief overview and a focus on one or two particular words before the children begin to read:

Judy: At our read-aloud time, you have listened to me read three different versions of *The Three Little Pigs*. Now you get to read a different version of the same story. Talk to your neighbor about what you remember about the three pigs stories.

Students: (*Students are quickly engaged in animated conversations of their favorite parts of the three pigs and big bad wolf stories.*)

Judy: Wow! You know a lot about the three pigs. Look through the pictures in this book and think about the story. You can talk with a friend quietly as you look at the pictures.

Let's look at page six. What is the wolf doing?

Ronnie: He huffed and puffed and huffed and puffed and blowed the house way up in the sky.

FIGURE 6-5 Page Layout from *The Three Little Pigs*

Terry: He made a tornado!

Judy: In our story it says, "The wolf blew down the house of straw." Can you find the word that says "blew?"

Students: (*Some point to the word "blew" while others are pointing to the word "down."*)

Judy: (*She writes the word "blew" on a whiteboard and talks a bit about the letter b.*) This is the word "blew." See the *b*. This is different from how you write the color blue. (*She writes the word "blue" under the word "blew."*)

They both have a *b* first but this one is the one in our story. The wolf blew down the house of straw.

Good, everyone found the word "blew." Turn to page one. This story starts just like our first story of the three pigs: "Once upon a time." Everyone point and read that part with me: *Once upon a time*.

(*Judy needs to help two of the students match up the tricky book language with their pointing. Others use this opportunity to begin reading.*)

Because the children all had extensive, prior knowledge about this familiar tale, the introduction focused on drawing their attention to the visual information along with the language structures on just two pages. The teacher provided a visual model of the irregular word "blew" and helped the children sort out what might have been a confusion about the homophone "blue/blew."

It is important to provide a concrete example when helping children to focus on the analysis of the print. In this example, the focus was on the positive similarities, i.e., both words have a *b* as the first letter. (You should avoid having children compare very similar and easily confused first letters such as the *b* and *d* of "blew" and "down.") Writing on the whiteboard provides a concrete example on which to focus the students' attention. Talking about the complexities of our language without a clear model (writing down text or pointing to print in the text) has the potential of creating confusion for children who are still at the early level of using the details of print as they read.

A book at the same level of difficulty but with unfamiliar concepts, *Growing a Pumpkin* (McCarrier 1995) [Level E], might require a more thorough introduction before reading. Here, the introduction should help students to explore and develop the unfamiliar concepts of the life cycle of a pumpkin plant:

Judy:	Our new book is called *Growing a Pumpkin*. If you were going to grow a pumpkin, what would you do first?
Students:	(*Several students shout out*) Buy a pumpkin!
Judy:	Look at the cover of the book. In this story the little girl and her grandma want to *grow* a pumpkin. Why do they have shovels?
Students:	(*Most students do not respond. Judy hears one student ask, "What's a shovel?"*)

Based on the students' responses, Judy quickly shifted her book introduction to a more detailed survey of the pictures and a discussion of the concepts around the life cycle of a pumpkin plant from the seeds, to the need for water, to the growth of little plants, and the blossoming of the flowers before the pumpkin makes its first, tiny appearance on the vine. Interwoven with this discussion of growing a pumpkin plant was a focus on some key words and how they look in the text, including "seeds," "dirt," and "poured water."

Early readers are actively engaged in learning how to read, how to make sense of the abstract symbols of our printed language, as well as learning more about the many concepts in the day-to-day world of living and learning. Compared to emergent readers, they do not need as much protection from concepts that are a little more distant from their direct experience, but you should still provide as much of a scaffold as needed for successful reading and comprehension.

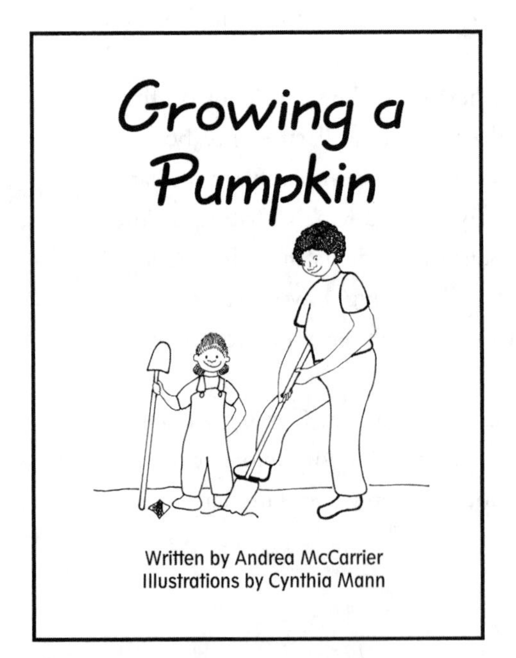

FIGURE 6-6 Cover of *Growing a Pumpkin*

It is common for young children not to have a great deal of background to bring to their reading. Teachers have long been aware that informational books are usually more difficult for children to read than story narratives. When a lack of experience or knowledge base is noted, strengthen the support you give in your introduction so that students are actively engaged and learning at complex levels as they prepare to read the book. Another way to think about providing a scaffold is to weigh the concept level of a new book and estimate how to increase the support and teaching in the event the children do not have enough understanding of their own to plunge in and start reading independently. As Clay (1998) reminds us, "Book introductions enlarge the range of what children can do with whole stories at a first reading" (p. 175).

Summary of Key Concepts in Building a Scaffold for Early Readers

As with emergent readers, preparing and providing an introduction for early readers is a complex process, one which requires you to consider the readers' strengths and needs as well as the features of the text. Some key concepts in building a scaffold for early readers are:

- Weigh up the concept load when selecting a book.
- Prepare contingency plans to strengthen the introduction if prior knowledge needs to be supported before reading.
- Encourage the children to talk to each other about the topic/content.
- Allow children to share knowledge or engage in building knowledge if concepts are unfamiliar to all or some of them.
- Take an active role in building concepts; if they are unfamiliar, use more pictures and explanations as needed.
- Engage the children in looking at important aspects of the print (letters, endings, word parts, specialized vocabulary).
- Clarify confusions and build concepts.
- Provide concrete examples (written examples in the text or out of the text).

CHARACTERISTICS OF TRANSITIONAL READERS

Transitional readers have made a definite shift to relying more on print as a major source of information while reading. The transition here is from the kinds of overt and sometimes sequential ways children attend to pictures and print to a smoothly-operating process, in which the reader uses multiple sources of information simultaneously to problem solve and make meaning while reading continuous text. Emergent and early readers are learning to integrate the various sources of information available to them; their behaviors are overt and we can almost see them checking their information. For transitional readers, the process of reading is more automatic. They now control all of the basic concepts of print and are flexible enough in their knowledge to adjust to more unusual formats and layouts of the text.

Transitional readers have built up a large core of sight words that are frequently used in our language. This achievement means that they are required to give less attention to word-solving. Rapid recognition of most words in a text helps them read in a fluent, phrased manner and to bring more expression to their oral reading. Transitional readers can search for and use all sources of cues in an integrated way as they read, and can solve words "on the run," with greater efficiency and independence. Because they are reading longer, more complex texts that contain more multisyllable words, irregular words, and descriptive adjectives and adverbs, transitional readers still need supportive teaching so that they can expand their word-solving strategies.

Providing a strong scaffold in the new book introduction is still an important aspect of guided reading instruction for transitional readers. You can help them bring the whole process together; the scaffold is temporary but important. As always when providing a scaffold, you are giving students the support that they need to move to the next level in their developing abilities. These transitional readers are moving toward silent reading. Soon, their reading processes will have become *learning systems* which enable them to expand their skills continually as they read a wider variety of increasingly more difficult texts. As this occurs, they will become what Clay calls *self-extending* readers (Clay 2001).

Sometime toward the end of second grade or the middle of third grade, we can expect students to become self-extending readers. Of course, because we are always dealing with individual children, we understand the wide range of differences and time requirements that exist among them as they become self-extending readers. Some children learn rapidly and develop early, sprouting with seemingly little cultivation from the teacher. Others need a longer time and more instruction before bearing fruit.

Building a Scaffold for Transitional Readers

A book introduction for a guided reading group of transitional readers would be similar to the components and the weighing-up of concepts discussed above for early readers. Take into account the concept level and demands of the text in relation to the experiences and learning of your students. The most important shift in planning the introduction of a new book is for you to be aware of the increasing demands and complexity of the text. When there is a definite shift in the complexity of the language structures, your scaffold should be prepared to support this heavier load. Figure 6-7 provides examples of typical texts at the three different levels.

The differences between these three texts are obvious. The text for transitional readers makes more demands on readers. By analyzing it, you can determine the areas needing support or consideration for support. Questions you may raise about the text example are:

- Are my students familiar with the concepts of "windowsill" and "bird feeder?"
- Should I call attention to the phrase "brightly colored birds" and/or "twitches his tail"?

It is impossible to predict whether the concepts of *windowsill* and *bird feeder* will be problematic for any one group of transitional readers. But, in general, modifying phrases that precede the noun can be a tricky business. Also, a word such as *twitches* might benefit from a closer examination of the two parts, even if the phrase is introduced as an unusual language structure.

Examples of Texts at Three Different Levels

EMERGENT: We see a cat.

EARLY: We could not find the cat.
It ran under the steps.

TRANSITIONAL: In the afternoon Mugs sits on the
windowsill and watches the brightly
colored birds flying in and out of the bird feeder.
He twitches his tail.
Then he takes a nap in the warm,
afternoon sun.

FIGURE 6-7

Below are excerpts from a new book introduction for transitional readers:

Judy:	In this story Mugs does whatever he wants to do. He always goes around twitching his tail. What does that mean?
Students:	He moves his tail back and forth.
Judy:	Look on page four. Can you find the word "twitching" or "twitches"?
Students:	(*Students locate twitches in print and verify the ending.*)
Judy:	Yes, sometimes we add *-s* to the end of words and sometimes we need *-es*. Ronnie, at the end of reading group today could you please add that word to our chart of words we are collecting is the *-es* category? Thank you. Look at this picture of Mugs.
Sam:	He's looking at the birds. He's going to eat one of them.
Judy:	Yes, he is looking at the birds, but in this story the author uses some words to describe the birds. She says "brightly colored birds." I'll write the word bright on the chart paper. Who could come up to add something to the end to make it say "brightly"?
Zetta:	(*Zetta adds le to the end of "bright."*)
Judy:	OK. It sounds like it might be *-le* but it's *-ly*. Can you fix that, Zetta? Good. We are going to be looking for more words that have *-ly* on the end of them. I think we can start another chart of all the *-ly* words we find. That should help us in our spelling also. Let's find and read that part on page four about the birds. Now look through the book before you start to read to help you think about the story and what old Mugs does all day long. Remember to read silently to yourself. I'll be around to listen to you read part of the story.

Judy did the problem solving and planning to prepare an introduction to *Mugs* (Pinnell 1996) [Level H] for her transitional-level guided reading group. She helped them to advance their analysis of the increasingly complex visual information they would need in order to read this book successfully, and also to expand their strategies for word analysis in general so that they can apply them to other texts.

Her concern was not to have children learn the particular words "twitches" or "brightly" in order to read *this* text accurately, although she certainly values accurate (although not

perfect) reading. Judy supported children's learning of *how* these words and similar words *work* across many different and increasingly more difficult texts. Her work on word analysis will strengthen skills and understandings as students write independently and use word-solving strategies in spelling.

Judy has mastered the concept of building a scaffold as a means of introducing a new story to beginning readers. Her skills and understanding can be used for any appropriate book or story (including stories in a basal series). She is able to adapt the scaffold of support based on her understanding of the different achievement levels of readers in her classroom. She demonstrates flexibility in her understanding by being able to shift the introduction once she observes an area of immediate concern. Her introductions are planned ahead of time to fit the instructional needs of her students, but she remains observant and alert for new possibilities.

Introducing New Stories: A Decision-Making Process

Building a scaffold of support for reading a new story is a decision-making process based on careful observation of the children and an analysis of the text. (See Figure 6-8.) As a teacher, you are the decision-maker who determines how strong the scaffold needs to be for any unique group of children. Planning a new book introduction becomes a challenge to customize the support you give your students based on their needs instead of a routine delivered the same way, time after time, for every group. Clay (1998) describes a

Building a Scaffold for Successful Reading of a New Book: Introductions in Guided Reading

- Select books based on children's knowledge of literacy concepts.
- Tell what the story is about.
- Connect to students' background experiences by inviting them to talk to each other (engagement and conversations).
- Review the book, highlighting multiple sources of information in the text (meaning/structure/visual information).
- Focus attention on some aspects of the print, using what children already know to connect to new learning.
- Gradually increase the difficulty of the text.
- Build a temporary scaffold, but remain flexible to increase the strength of the support when appropriate.

FIGURE 6-8

book introduction as "a process of drawing the children into the activity before passing control to the children and pushing them gently towards problem-solving the whole first reading of the story for themselves" (p. 172). In guided reading, there is the expectation that teaching and prompting for strategies is provided during the first reading of the book. However, it is the intent of the book introduction to prepare each child in the group to read and problem solve difficulties during the first reading as independently as possible, with only a limited amount of help. For emergent and early readers, comprehension is supported by the introduction of the story. Only after children have learned basic reading skills are they asked to read and comprehend stories more independently. When concepts are unfamiliar, however, you must provide additional support.

Summary

Becoming an expert at introducing stories to children in guided reading is a learning process that takes time. It may be helpful to audiotape your book introductions over several days or weeks. Then you can analyze them on your own or work with a colleague to evaluate your effectiveness, asking whether you provided the appropriate level and kind of support for children to process the text successfully. Remember that processing a text successfully does not mean reading every word accurately. We want children to meet and solve problems, because that is how they expand their reading strategies. The planning guide (Figure 6-9) at the end of this chapter was designed to help you analyze your work with emergent, early, and transitional readers.

Planning Guide for Scaffolding Book Introductions

DATE ____________ TEACHER ____________ GRADE ____________

READING ACHIEVEMENT LEVEL: ❑ EMERGENT ❑ EARLY ❑ TRANSITIONAL

BOOK/STORY TITLE ____________

Key concepts to consider when planning book introductions for beginning readers:

MEANING

- ❑ Tell what the story is about / provide the main idea
- ❑ Draw upon students' experiences and knowledge by engaging them in discussions with each other / share some of their ideas
- ❑ Help students understand unfamiliar concepts
- ❑ Discuss pictures to build a framework of meaning and to spark interest and involvement in the story (more pictures for emergent / less for transitional)

STRUCTURE

- ❑ Introduce and let the students practice language patterns / character names / unfamiliar book language

VISUAL

- ❑ Point out any unusual aspects of text layout / unfamiliar punctuation marks
- ❑ Draw attention to some new and/or important words in the story
- ❑ Provide concrete examples to demonstrate how visual information is analyzed (letter, letter cluster, endings, syllables, irregular spelling patterns)

NOTES

FIGURE 6-9

Ideas to Try

1. Meet with kindergarten, first-, second-, and third-grade teachers. Work with the sample texts that you used in your discussion following Chapter 4. [If you did not discuss that chapter, collect sample texts that teachers use in guided reading in all the primary grades (about four per grade)] .Discuss the important new requirements for each level of text and list them.

2. Working in cross-grade level groups, plan an introduction for at least two texts per grade level. Assume that you are working with a group of children who can read the text with 90 to 95 percent accuracy. For each text, you can consult the teacher at the appropriate level and use a group of children from that classroom as the focus for planning. Think about:
   - the supports that are in the text.
   - the particular demands of this text.
   - concepts, language structures, or tricky words that you might bring to students' attention during the introduction.
   - what you might want them to figure out on their own.

3. Bring the whole group together for a discussion. Discuss:
   - What is the role of the introduction in helping students read more challenging texts?
   - How does the introduction change as the texts become more challenging over time?

4. Leave the meeting with the goal of thinking about your text introductions over the next two weeks.

5. If you can, audiotape or videotape several of your introductions for texts at different levels.

6. Meet again with a partner to review your tapes and reflect on the quality and effectiveness of your introductions.

Author's note: The texts presented in this chapter are KEEP BOOKS®, inexpensive books for children to read at school and take home to keep. See the appendix for additional information.

CHAPTER 7

Teaching Versus Prompting: Supporting Comprehension in Guided Reading

Lynda Hamilton Mudre

Kecia was helping a small group of her kindergarten students learn how to use one-to-one matching. She was also encouraging them to use some of the words they knew as guideposts in making their oral reading correspond with the text. After prompting them to use their "good pointing" and "the words you know," she noticed during the guided reading lesson that several children seemed confused about how to use their pointing finger and known words to help them with their reading. After talking with her literacy coach and asking her to observe a lesson, Kecia decided to provide the children with direct modeling and assisted practice before prompting them. In the next lesson, she introduced the children to *Cat on the Mat* (Wildsmith 1982) [Level B]—to everyone's delight. Before the children began to read independently, Kecia demonstrated one-to-one matching with known words as anchors for self-monitoring.

In the example shown in Figure 7-1, Kecia provided a firm foundation for comprehension. She helped her students develop some early strategies that will serve them well as they read new books. Over time, they will acquire a whole "self-extending" system (Clay 1991) of strategies that will help them understand and enjoy many texts.

Kecia models voice-print match.

Demonstrating Reading and Pointing

Kecia: You're going to see some words you know, and you're going to be using your pointing finger, and this is what I want to see you do. (*She holds the book up close to the children, reads, and points slowly and deliberately under each word.*) *The cat sat on the mat.* (*She locates the word "on."*) And when you're saying this word "on" we know—watch my finger—*The cat sat on* (*stops with her finger under "on"*). Where's my finger pointing when I'm saying the word "on"?

Children: On.

Kecia: It's under the word "on," isn't it? That's what I'm going to need you to watch for to make sure the word coming out of your mouth is the word you're pointing to. (*She demonstrates again.*) What is the word I'm pointing under now?

Children: The.

Kecia: Go ahead and start reading now.

(*They start guided practice, with children reading the story and Kecia observing closely. On one page Madison stops, noticing that her finger is not matching the word she is reading. She rereads with correct one-to-one correspondence.*)

Kecia: Madison, when you went back, did your finger match what you were saying? Were you right?

Madison: Yes.

(*The children and Kecia have a conversation about the story when everyone has finished.*)

Kecia: I was so happy to see that you were using your pointing fingers. And Madison, I was so proud of you. You were on this page where the goat is (*holds book up*), and you were working on making your voice match where your finger was, and you got a little bit ahead of yourself (*demonstrates*) and you read, "The goat sat on the" (*pointing to "on"*), and it was because of your good pointing that you knew that word wasn't "*the*." What was it?

Children: On.

Kecia: And she decided to go back and fix it because that's what good readers do. So let's read this together. I'll do the pointing, and you read it. (*Children read.*) See how my finger matched what you were reading?

FIGURE 7-1

Meaning-Making: A Complex Process

We sometimes hear "meaning-making" spoken of as if it were separate from the network of word-solving, fluency, and correcting strategies that students are building within the beginning reading process. In fact, all systems of strategies within reading make up one interwoven, inseparable process (Hiebert, et al. 1998). By helping students internalize ways of using visual, contextual, and meaning-based sources in the text, you can enhance their ability to understand and interpret what they are reading. One way to foster this independent strategic action during the guided reading lesson is to understand the difference between *prompting* and *teaching*, and be able to determine when each can help your readers construct meaning from text.

Teaching and Prompting

The aim of guided reading is independence. We want our students to command a well-balanced repertoire of reading operations and be able to choose specific actions that are well suited to the problem at hand. More important, we want readers to take the initiative in using them (Askew & Fountas 1998). Active processing comes when children know *when* and *how* to use their own plans for problem-solving. Many children internalize these strategies implicitly, often through interactions with experienced literacy mentors in a rich literate environment. Other students seem to need a more direct approach. If we ask these children to use strategies that are not within their control, our prompting may cause confusion. In this case, we are often guilty of using language that is not clear or accessible to these young readers. What is often needed is the use of very specific language to model the task you want the children to perform (Flippo 1999). As Kecia's interaction with her kindergartners illustrates, you sometimes need to show students *how* the process works and guide them until they can make it their own. In other words, you need to *teach* before you *prompt*. Figure 7-2 illustrates the difference between these two types of instruction.

When teaching, you model the reading behavior that will be helpful to students in understanding the text, such as solving new words, checking and correcting predictions, or maintaining fluent, phrased reading. When prompting, you are fairly confident that the children understand and can perform the strategic action you are asking of them. Your prompts will be most effective following a demonstration and guided practice of the desired behavior. If you notice that students do not seem to understand the language or action you request, this confusion is a sure signal that teaching is necessary. Finally, it is important to

understand that prompting is a temporary support system for the internalized, independent strategies that you want the children to initiate and use quickly and flexibly.

This chapter illustrates how you can provide the clear demonstrations that are often needed before supporting a child's responding through prompts. (See Chapter 12 in Fountas & Pinnell's *Guided Reading* for further information.) As you read these examples, notice how the teachers clearly model the strategic behavior they want their students to adopt, and how they explain the action in concise, well-chosen language.

Teaching and Prompting

TEACHING: Showing How	PROMPTING: Asking for a Specific Action or Response
Watch my finger and see how I point under each word. (*demonstrates in the text*) I made my finger match each word. Now you try it.	Did it match?
This is what you can try next time you come to a tricky word. (*rereads the sentence and verbalizes the first part of the unknown word*)	Reread that again and start the word.
I'm thinking about the picture to see what might make sense here. (*points to the picture and thinks aloud*) I'm going to read this again, and I'm thinking, "What would sound right?" (*rereads and pauses before the unknown word*) "Ride" would make sense here, and I can check the word like this. (*slides finger slowly under the word and reads it*) That lets me know it looks right too.	What can you try?
Listen to how I put the words together to make it sound like __________ is talking (or to make it sound like a story).	Put your words together to make it sound like talking.

FIGURE 7-2

Emergent Readers: Using Early Strategies

During guided reading, Judy noticed that the children in her kindergarten group were beginning to attempt some useful strategies for solving unknown words. She wanted the children to understand that readers can draw from several options to solve a new word. The children had completed *Out in the Weather* (Giles 1996) [Level B], a story about children playing in different kinds of weather. They discussed possible reasons for the characters' dialogue. Judy then decided to demonstrate three of the strategies the children were using during the first reading of the text. She had observed that the children were attempting to solve words in multiple ways, and wanted to bring this effective and flexible processing to their attention by using their own reading behaviors. (See Figure 7-3.)

With Cody's help, Judy showed the children how the first letter of a word can be a useful clue in predicting an unknown word. Tanya and Josh had used rereading to gather context clues for their predictions. Judy modeled the precise course of action that Tanya had followed by locating the "tricky" word and rereading, as Tanya had. When demonstrating the third strategy (using the picture to think about what would make sense in the story), Judy pointed to the picture Brian had noticed to help him solve the new word. She was modeling three useful problem-solving actions, fostering flexibility of choice, and giving the children opportunities to internalize their actions.

Judy helps children recall useful strategies.

Teaching Early Reading Strategies

Judy: I noticed some good things you were doing to figure out words. Cody, when you got to this page (*points and holds up page*), and you stopped right here (*points under the word "frosty"*), what did you do?

Cody: F–f–f.

Judy: Yes, you were sounding the first letter, like "Franklin" on the name chart. You used a word you knew to help you remember how that sounded, and then you thought of "frosty." (*Judy had used this word in the introductory conversation with the children about the story.*)

Tanya, what were you trying? On the very first page (*holding up first page*) you were reading and got stuck right here (*pointing to the unknown word*), and what did you do?

Tanya: I went back.

(*Judy rereads the sentence up to point of unknown word and allows children to read the word.*)

Judy: And Josh, what did you do?

Josh: I went back.

Judy: So there are two things you can do when you get stuck. You can go back and you can use...

Children: The first letter.

Judy: You know what? I watched Brian, and he got stuck on this page. (*She rereads, stops at the word, and points to the picture.*) And he glanced over here. So what did he see to help him think about the story?

Tanya: The picture.

Judy: So there are really three things here. Wow! There are lots of things you can do to help yourself when you get stuck. You can...

Josh and Conner: Go back.

Cody: Use the first letter.

Tanya: Look at the picture.

Judy: And you can try these things when you get stuck in other books, too!

FIGURE 7-3

Early Readers: Working From What You Know

Good readers often use what they know to get to something that is new. They might use a word or word part that is familiar to solve a word that is not familiar. Supporting students in this kind of linking, or use of analogy, not only makes it possible for them to take on many new words, but also helps them develop a powerful strategy for word-solving every time they read or write. The next example shows how Lynn demonstrated the use of analogy. She gave students opportunities to apply what they already know to solve new words in the text.

Five of Lynn's first graders had just finished their first reading of *Tabby in the Tree* (Randell 1996) [Level F]. After talking with students about the story, Lynn used her whiteboard to demonstrate how a known word-part can be useful. She learned from observation that several of the students hesitated or needed support in solving the word "stayed." She knew that as these readers read more difficult texts, they would encounter words with multiple parts or syllables. One strategy they would need to acquire would be taking words apart quickly, so that meaning is not lost. This strategy is made easier if the reader recognizes some of the parts.

In the example shown in Figure 7-4, Lynn first modeled with a known word and then guided the children's responses as they practiced applying the principle. Finally, she took the children back to the text and to the meaning of the word they had solved. Later, Roshon demonstrated that he had generalized the strategy independently by generating yet another word, away.

Guiding the Reading Process During Individual Conferences

During the conference in Figure 7-5, Tina was also teaching how to use analogy and how to combine some known word-parts to form a word. She listened to Conner read a soccer story orally after observing in guided reading that he tended not to initiate strategies for word-solving. Although he was a beginning second grader, he was having difficulty getting beyond saying the first letter and looking at the picture. During the reading of the soccer story, Tina provided several words after Conner tried the first letter-sound and waited. As he turned the page, he encountered the word "last." Their interaction is shown in Figure 7-5.

Using What Students Know

Lynn:	Here's something you already know. (*She writes "day."*)
Children:	Day.
Lynn:	We could break that into some parts. We could do it this way. (*She writes d ay.*) And we could use this *ay* part to make a new word. Can anyone think of a word you know with that part, like day?
Brian:	P-l-a-y.
Lynn:	All right, if we took this part (*writes pl and leaves space*), let's say this part...
Children:	Pl-
Lynn:	And we took this part (*points to ay*), and we put them together... (*She erases pl and writes word in normal fashion.*)
Children:	(*Slowly, as Lynn runs her finger under the word*) Play.
Lynn:	Now let's look at this. (*She writes st beside ay with no space.*)
Children:	Stay.
Lynn:	Now we're going to put a part on the end (*writes ed*), and we're going to have...
Children:	(*At different times, one or two say hesitantly*) Stayed.
Lynn:	Is that right? Let's check it. (*She slides finger slowly under the word as children read it.*) Now let's look in our story on page 10 and find that word. Can you point to it?
Children:	I found it. Here it is.
Lynn:	Why do we have that word on this page?
Megan:	Because Tabby stayed up in the tree and wouldn't come down.
Lynn:	Let's read this page together.

FIGURE 7-4

Word-Solving Beyond the First Letter

Conner: L-l-l... (*pause*) l-l-l-

Tina: I like the way you are trying to figure that out. What did you try so far?

Conner: I thought it was "lets," but it's not.

Tina: All right, so get your finger in there and see if you can find a chunk at the end that you already know. (*Conner points to "st."*) What does that remind you of? (*Long pause.*) Does it remind you of the word "stop" you know? All right, put it with the first part.

(*She demonstrates by saying "la-" and fading as they both read "-st."*)

(*Conner rereads "Last Saturday" and reads to the end of the page.*)

Tina: Wait a minute. What did you do to figure that out? (*points to "last"*) You learned a new trick.

Conner: Well, you say the first part "la-" and then you add that "st" and you get "last."

Tina: And it becomes a word you know, right? Let's see if you come across another word you need to figure out, you could try that new trick.

(*On the next page Conner stops before isn't.*)

Conner: Now that's "is." It's kinda like "is not," but it's not.

Tina: Okay, now start here with "is-" and add the other sounds. (*Conner tries "is-" and pauses.*) Make the n sound (*Conner tries "n"*), and now the t (*Conner tries the "t"*).

Conner: Isn't.

Tina: Did that sound like a word you know, isn't?

Conner: Yeah.

Tina: Now read it in the sentence to see if it will make sense or sound right to you.

FIGURE 7-5

In this example, Tina thought about the level of support she would need to give Conner in word-solving. She modeled how to look for a known part in a word and combine it with other parts. She then supported Conner's attempts to solve "isn't" through very clear, concise language until he had accomplished the action she had modeled. Tina was ready to step in and demonstrate further if necessary, but not until waiting to see what Conner would try. By observing his attempts, she was able to adjust the level of support to the cutting edge, so to speak, of his responses.

Self-Extending Readers: Word Meaning in *Cam Jansen*

Understanding how words are meaningfully related provides strong support for comprehension. Melissa's second-grade group had reached a stopping point in *Cam Jansen and the Chocolate Fudge Mystery* (Adler 1993) [Level L]. She wanted to show them how knowing the meaning of a root word in a story could help them understand the meanings of other words containing the root. She also wanted them to notice the visual similarities. (See Figure 7-6.)

Melissa asked the children to notice both visual and meaning similarities in the words they were constructing. This word study was an appropriate part of the guided reading lesson because words built from the root occurred frequently in the story. Students had an opportunity to learn about a specific group of related words. In addition, they learned a principle: It helps to know that if words look alike, they may have similar meanings.

Melissa helps students notice visual and meaning similarities.

Making Meaningful Connections

Melissa:	Look right up here on the whiteboard. (*She writes "mystery."*) What does this word say?
Children:	"Mystery."
Melissa:	I want to show you something about this word "mystery." You are reading a...
Children:	Mystery, *Cam Jansen and the Chocolate Fudge Mystery*.
Melissa:	Look at this word. (*She writes "mysteries," and the children read it.*) Do you see the word "*mystery*" in this one? (*Some children come up to point.*)
Beth:	If you put a "y" right there, it would be "mystery."
Melissa:	Yes we've changed the "*y*" to "*i*" to make "mysteries." Did we do the same thing here? (*She writes mysterious.*)
Robert:	Yeah, if people act mysterious usually there's a mystery involved.
Melissa:	That's right. What would it say if we took this word "mysterious" and added an "ly"? (She writes *mysteriously*.)
Cameron:	Mysteriously.
Melissa:	Do you think he's right? Adam, would it say "mysteriously"? (*She runs her finger slowly under the word.*)
Adam:	Yes.
Melissa:	Good job. Now there's a mystery here, and the mysterious woman is acting mysteriously. She has given Cam the idea that there is a mystery.

FIGURE 7-6

Teaching for Prediction Strategies

A final teaching example focuses on prediction strategies. As readers, we constantly make and confirm or discount guesses about what we think will unfold in the text. We use context clues, world knowledge, and knowledge of language, along with ways of solving words visually (i.e., breaking words into parts) to form hypotheses as we read. We ask ourselves questions, visualize, sort out main ideas from supporting details, summarize, and synthesize (Keene & Zimmerman 1997). A monitoring process (metacognition) mediates our understanding as we ask ourselves, "Am I understanding? What am I understanding?"

Michelle worked with a group of passive second-grade readers to help them take some definite actions to monitor their understandings and check their predictions. They took turns discussing and summarizing what happened in the first chapter of a baseball story. (See Figure 7-7.)

Michelle's teaching helped students to state and reflect on their predictions. In a very clear and simple way, she explicitly demonstrated the actions Charles took to discount his prediction. Reading aloud the pertinent portion of text supported his logic and provided a memorable example of an important comprehension strategy for students who had not previously initiated a definite plan of action. Michelle showed her students exactly how to search for evidence to check their assumptions.

Michelle demonstrates how students can check their predictions.

Reading to Monitor Comprehension

Michelle: What do you think is going to happen in the next chapter?

(*Each child makes a prediction. There is discussion about why students think their predictions might be correct.*)

Michelle: I like the way you are thinking about what's happening in the story to make your predictions. You've all made predictions; now let's read to see if they were right. Remember, if something is not making sense, you need to go back and reread.

(*Michelle listens to one or two students read orally as others read silently. When students have completed their reading, she asks,*)
Charles, was your prediction right?

Charles: No, because he only met one friend.

(*Charles had thought the main character, Martin, would make many friends in this chapter.*)

Michelle: Where in the story would it show us that he only met one friend?

(*Charles locates the page and reads the passage that discounted his prediction, with other members of the group being asked to follow along.*)

(*Michelle asks other children if their predictions were correct and has them locate and read portions of the text that support their thinking. To complete the teaching sequence, she decides to model what Charles did.*)

Michelle: Sometimes it is important to go back and reread in the story the way Charles did. (*She locates the passage Charles has used and holds up the book.*)

He found the place to help him see if his prediction was right. He found the place that told him Martin only found one friend. (*Michelle points and reads.*)

"The tall boy laughed in a friendly way." Does that mean only one boy?

(The class discusses.) Yes. I bet Barry is going to be important to Martin...

FIGURE 7-7

Teacher Support

Clay (1991) writes, "I regard meaning as the 'given' in all reading—the source of anticipation, the guide to being on track, and the outcome and reward of the effort." She points out that, in addition to bringing prior knowledge to the text, the reader "carries out reading work in order to make sense of what he is reading and uses meaning as the ultimate check that all is well" (p. 292). While creating a context for this "reading work" during guided reading, you make decisions about the amount of support you need to give to a particular child or group of children. (See Figure 7-8.)

You can match the level of support you give your students and what form it will take with where the students are in the construction of a strategy network. If they need to know *how* to take strategic action that will help them ultimately to reach the meaning of what is being read, consider teaching before prompting.

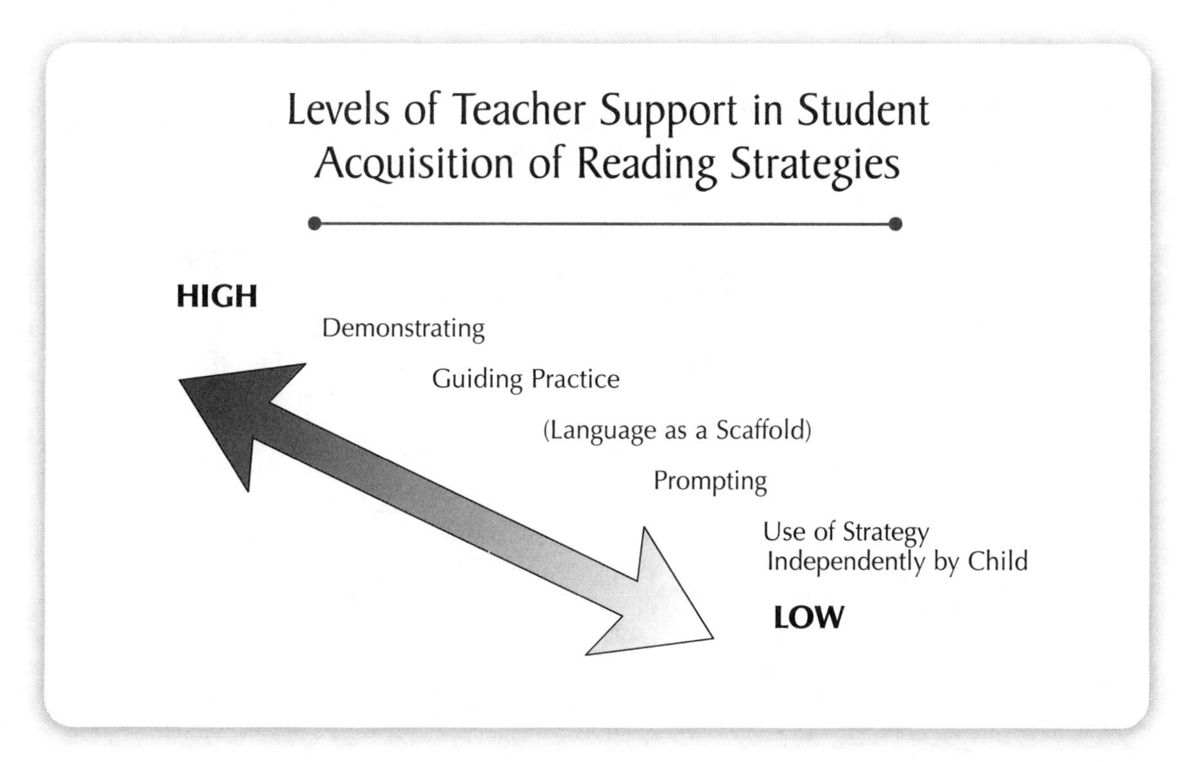

FIGURE 7-8

Ideas to Try

1. Check to see if materials for demonstrating (whiteboard, pens, eraser, MagnaDoodle®, chart paper, etc.) are at your fingertips in the guided reading area.

2. Resources such as the word wall, name chart, alphabet linking chart, and word study charts often provide valuable connections from *known* to *new* for students and are, therefore, productive examples for teaching. If these resources are not visually accessible to the children during guided reading, consider moving the guided reading area or duplicating the resources in some way.

3. Examine recent running records of your students. Consider demonstrating strategies for students who have received a number of "tolds" (teacher providing the word if student is unable), have not made an attempt, have initiated a very limited or unproductive try, or have appealed for help consistently.

CHAPTER 8

Teaching for Phrasing and Fluency: Connections to Comprehension

Andrea McCarrier

When good readers process print aloud, the way they sound provides a window into how they are constructing meaning. They pause to set off parenthetical expressions, use falling tones at periods, let their voices rise for questions, and get slightly louder for emphasis at exclamation points. They set off dialogue and make it sound like talking. They divide language into phrases that indicate their interpretation of the author's intended meaning. Good readers also process text with momentum—at a rate that allows listeners to make sense of the language. Good readers are not simply fast; phrasing, pauses, and inflection also figure strongly into the quality of their reading.

When individuals read silently, we assume that they are also processing the text fluently and, at some level, getting a sense of phrase units even though they may not be consciously aware of the process. They are accessing the meaning of the text, or comprehending. As Fountas and Pinnell (1996) stated, "Reading is the construction of meaning. Comprehending is not a product of reading; it is the process" (p. 156).

There is a deep relationship between what the reader does to comprehend and what the reader does to sustain fluency and phrasing. As a teacher, I find that it is important to notice and encourage fluency and phrasing as a way of supporting children as they make sense of reading, even when they are just beginning.

This chapter examines the relationship between comprehending and phrased, fluent reading. First, I provide evidence indicating that a deep relationship does exist between comprehending and phrased, fluent reading. Then I share ways that other teachers and I have taught for phrasing, fluency, and expression in reading. Finally, I summarize the importance of explicitly teaching for phrasing and fluency.

Evidence of the Relationship Between Fluency and Reading Comprehension

My own experience indicates that when students read with phrasing and fluency, their comprehension increases. Evidence from research supports this assumption.

Data from the National Assessment of Educational Progress (NAEP) (Pinnell, et al. 1995), the Literacy Collaborative 2000 Research Report (Williams, Scharer, & Pinnell 2000), Rasinski (2000), and Blevins (2000) all demonstrate a relationship between fluent reading and comprehending text. While all four studies also indicate that fluency is not the only factor affecting comprehension, they provide evidence that an intricate relationship exists between fluency and comprehension.

Research sponsored by the Educational Testing Service (Pinnell, et al. 1995) focused on the relationship between characteristics of students' oral reading and their comprehension. They measured oral reading of fourth-grade students in terms of fluency, reading rate, and accuracy. They also gathered information on the amount and kind of reading that students engaged in outside of the school setting. Results of the study revealed that students with higher fluency ratings tended to engage in more extracurricular reading than students with lower fluency ratings. Students who read more fluently had higher average scores on the NAEP test of comprehension. For a more complete description of the fluency rubric used in this study, see Fountas and Pinnell (1996, p. 81).

Williams, Scharer, and Pinnell (2000) conducted correlation analyses on data collected from 2,474 second-grade students. The analyses revealed that fluency ratings on the books children read predicted about 50 percent of the variance in comprehension scores as measured by the Gates MacGinitie Reading Test. In other words, fluent reading of benchmark books was a good predictor of performance on a standardized reading test.

Based on his research, Rasinski (2000) suggested that slow, disfluent readers tend to have lower comprehension than faster, more fluent readers do. Finally, Blevins (2000) led an action research project with second-grade teachers. They investigated the relationships between comprehension, as measured by the Developmental Reading Assessment (DRA); fluency ratings, using the NAEP fluency rubric; and accurate reading. They found that phrased, fluent reading was a more powerful predictor of a child's ability to comprehend text as measured by the DRA than fluent reading alone.

Factors That Contribute to Fluent Reading

As an adult, I am a fluent reader, but at times I still become disfluent. Take a moment and think about yourself as a reader. Consider these two sets of directions:

1. Directions for making oatmeal cookies.
2. Directions for changing oil in your car.

Which set of directions would be easier for you to read with fluency and understanding?

Reading a recipe is much easier for me because I know the format and vocabulary. Usually there is a list of ingredients followed by a set of step-by-step directions for combining ingredients. I can process the directions quickly because my years of experience in reading recipes helps me know what to expect when I read this sort of text. Also, I am familiar with the terms used in cooking. I do not need to ask someone what to do when the recipe reads, "Sift the dry ingredients."

On the other hand, following the directions for changing oil in my car is much harder for me. I lack the prior knowledge about changing oil that would help me anticipate what should come next. I falter over unfamiliar vocabulary. My reading slows down because I have difficulty making sense of the directions. Comprehension eludes me! To read the directions with greater understanding I need an orientation to the material—an overview of what happens in an oil change, for example, or a brief explanation of some unfamiliar terms.

Let's look at another example. Why do I find it easier to read a novel such as *The Notebook* (Sparks 1999) than to read an article from a research journal such as *Reading Research Quarterly*? First, I love romantic novels. I get all wrapped up in the plot and easily identify with the characters. I relate my life to the book and the book to my life. Second, predicting what will happen is easy because I have read so many romantic novels and seen so many romantic movies. I am familiar with how a romantic novel works. If the author has a beautiful young woman from a wealthy family fall in love with a rugged young man with no money, I can readily predict what might happen. The reading flows easily.

Reading a research article is an entirely different experience. I am much less familiar with its format, content, and vocabulary. I sometimes find it hard to understand the structure of the research design. Because my classes in statistics were so long ago, I often have trouble remembering how to read the tables. Comprehension eludes me—just as it did when I tried to follow the directions for changing oil in my car.

Readers are more likely to understand an author's message if they have some background knowledge of the topic. It also helps to know how different genres of literature are organized; cookie recipes, research reports, and romance novels all have different organizational structures.

Knowing the content of a text and how it is organized allows us to predict what we will be reading. (See Figure 8-1.) When the text does not match our expectations, a red flag goes up and prompts problem-solving behavior such as rereading a phrase, a line, or even an entire paragraph. As proficient readers, we are constantly monitoring whether we understand what we are reading and whether we need to search for more information. We fix errors and clear up confusion using all sources of information available to us. Background knowledge and awareness of text structure help us gather this information more quickly and precisely.

Good readers are both accurate and fluent. The problem-solving mentioned above takes place against a backdrop of accurate reading. When good readers do make errors in reading, they distinguish between the errors that change the meaning of a passage and those that do not. They monitor their reading for meaning-changing errors and self-correct them, while ignoring the unimportant errors. In terms of Clay's definition of reading, highly fluent readers seem to be able to extract the author's message from the text through effective problem-solving of errors that can cause breakdowns in meaning for less fluent readers. This entire discussion assumes that there is a match between the text being read and the reader's instructional level. If the book is too hard, the reader will have to spend so much time in problem-solving at the text's word level that it will be difficult for him to fully comprehend the text.

I am not implying that fluency results in comprehension or vice versa. Comprehension and fluency may be an example of a *chicken and egg* relationship. It does seem clear, though, that knowledge of the topic, text structure, language structures, and vocabulary

Factors Related to Sustaining Fluency and Phrasing

- Recognizing and solving words in a quick, automatic way.
- Recognizing phrase units.
- Being aware of and using punctuation.
- Activating and using background knowledge.
- Understanding and using the organizational structure of the text.
- Using meaning and language structure to monitor reading (making sure reading makes sense and sounds right).
- Predicting at the word, phrase, and text level.

FIGURE 8-1

all aid the reader in constructing meaning in a smooth process. These kinds of knowledge also aid the reader in predicting and confirming his reading more quickly, because he can use everything he knows about the topic to read in an efficient and flexible way.

Teaching for Phrasing and Fluency in Reading Across Instructional Contexts

If we value phrased, fluent reading, then we need to teach for it. Children will not automatically develop a sense of phrasing and fluency. We have found that you can teach for phrasing and fluency across every element of the comprehensive language and literacy framework. (See Chapter 2.) Figure 8-2 lists four instructional contexts that are components of the comprehensive framework for teaching language and literacy. This section provides a brief

Teaching for Phrasing and Fluency Across the Language and Literacy Framework

Framework Element:	Value in Supporting Teaching for Fluency and Phrasing:
Interactive Read-Aloud	• Demonstrate phrased, fluent reading. • Talk aloud about reading to show how it works.
Shared Reading	• Demonstrate phrased, fluent reading. • Have children participate in phrased, fluent reading. • Demonstrate how to use the organizational features of text. • Teach children to read with their eyes.
Guided Reading	• Give an overview of the story for children to use as they construct meaning when they read the text. • Introduce new text structures or unusual language to support meaning-making during reading. • Demonstrate phrased, fluent reading by reading a page or two of text with the children.
Independent Reading Mini-Lessons	• Focus attention on a particular aspect of text that can support students' fluent reading. • Explicitly demonstrate using text layout, punctuation, or phrase units. • Have children practice using text layout, punctuation, or phrase units.

FIGURE 8-2

overview of these four contexts, all of which are productive for supporting the development of phrased, fluent reading. It also describes ways you can use interactive read-aloud, shared reading, guided reading, and independent reading mini-lessons to teach for phrasing and fluency in reading.

Contexts That Support the Development of Fluency

The four instructional contexts listed in Figure 8-2 offer varying degrees of teacher support in teaching children to build a reading process. Research on storybook reading with preschool children (Ninio & Bruner 1978; Snow & Ninio 1986) documents the value not only of reading aloud to children but of embedding the storybook reading in talk. According to these researchers, as parents read and talk about books with children, the children learn about story structure and character development, become familiar with the decontextualized nature of written language, and expand their vocabularies. They also begin to notice print. When children enter school, they continue to learn as they hear stories read aloud and interact with the teacher and peers (McCarrier 1992).

INTERACTIVE READ-ALOUD

Interactive read-aloud, as an instructional context, provides opportunities for students to:

- enjoy stories.
- become familiar with the sounds of written language, particularly literary language.
- become familiar with a variety of genres.
- discuss stories in terms of the text itself, in relationship to other texts, and in relationship to their own lives or the lives of others.
- experience powerful demonstrations of fluent, phrased, expressive reading.

Reading aloud provides the highest degree of support because you model what good readers do when they read. The focus of this chapter is on reading expressively, with phrasing and fluency. Good readers also read for a purpose—to enjoy a story or gather information. When you read aloud to your children, you demonstrate that reading is a meaning-making process that is facilitated when the reading makes the author's message clear. Most often, you will read to the entire class as a way to build a community of readers who share common knowledge about particular stories and topics. Often, because you read favorite stories over and over, children will join in on repeated phrases such as, "I'll huff, and I'll puff, and I'll blow your house down." Here, the children are participating in reading from their memory of the text.

SHARED READING

Shared reading is an instructional context that also offers a high degree of support to students because you and the children share the task. The size of the group depends on the instructional needs of students. Sometimes you might work with the entire class; at other times you might meet with a small group.

An essential feature of shared reading is an enlarged text. The text can be:

- a big book, which is an enlarged version of a text.
- a piece of interactive or shared writing in which the print is large and legible.
- a teacher-made chart.
- a text on transparencies for use on an overhead projector.

Shared reading is different from the joining in during interactive read-aloud that is described above. In shared reading, children are attending to the enlarged print.

Shared reading lessons begin with you reading the text to the children. Their focus is on meaning and enjoyment. After the children have heard and talked about the text, you might revisit it in order to help them develop specific skills or strategies.

GUIDED READING

Guided reading differs from the first two contexts in three ways:

- First, unlike interactive read-aloud and shared reading, children are grouped according to their instructional needs. Most teachers will have four or five groups of four to six children each.
- Second, you select books for each group that match their instructional level and needs.
- Third, you support students by orienting them to the book but do not read the story with them. Rather, you observe how children in a group are processing the text.

In guided reading, you use your observations to make a few teaching points after the lesson and to select the new book for tomorrow's guided reading lesson. Because you understand that reading is a meaning-making process, you always begin and end the lesson by talking about the story.

INDEPENDENT READING MINI-LESSONS

Independent reading provides children with opportunities to practice reading. You are not there to support children as they read, although you have provided support in terms of guiding their selection of texts. Texts used during independent reading vary from texts children have read in shared reading lessons or written during interactive writing lessons to books that they have read in their guided reading lessons. Because children are choosing books that are easy for them to read, independent reading provides time for them to practice phrased, fluent reading.

Supporting Fluency in Four Instructional Contexts

This section explores and provides examples of how you can teach for fluency and phrasing in the four instructional contexts described above.

INTERACTIVE READ-ALOUD

Through interactive read-alouds, you teach children that reading is a message-getting process (Clay 1991). Simultaneously, you foster the conditions for meaning-making through your phrased, fluent, and expressive reading. You model the kinds of reading behaviors you want children to exhibit when they are reading their own books by demonstrating that reading is meaningful. Because of how you use your voice, the narrative sounds like storytelling, and the dialogue sounds like talk.

Some books are better than others for demonstrating phrased, fluent reading. Books that contain dialogue offer excellent opportunities for expressive reading. Think of how you would use your voice to portray the characters in *Little Red Riding Hood* (Hyman 1983), showing the innocence of Little Red Riding Hood, the sneakiness of the wolf, and the frailty of the aged and sickly grandmother.

Most children's books lend themselves to modeling phrased, fluent, and expressive reading as well as modeling how readers construct meaning. The following example is from a second-grade classroom in which many students are English learners. Sharon, the teacher, prefaced the reading of the book she selected, *The Korean Cinderella* by Shirley Climo (1993), with an explicit demonstration of how to construct meaning about the story from illustrations and prior knowledge. The class had previously read several versions of Cinderella.

Sharon:	This is *The Korean Cinderella* by Shirley Climo. (*She opens the book to show both the front and back cover as a double-page spread.*) As I look at the illustrations, they remind me of Korea. The colors are very rich and deep, and I love that. (*She closes the book to show just the front cover.*) If you look at the character on the front, she looks like she is dressed for... something special.
Jorge:	A wedding.
Sharon:	A wedding. It could be.
Tana:	A princess.
Sharon:	A princess? Yes, that's possible.
Sujata:	Is Korea in China? (*Many of the children in the class are from Southeast Asia.*)
Sharon:	No. It is in Asia. Let's look at a globe. China is in Asia, also. They are both in that part of the world—on the continent of Asia.
Sujata:	Oh!
Sharon:	(*She points to the fan on the cover.*) She's using something to hide a part of her face. We'll find out what's going on.
Jorge:	She's ugly.
Sharon:	You think she looks ugly and that's why she's hiding her face? Hmmm. Is Cinderella usually ugly?
Sujata:	No!
Jorge:	Yes!
Sharon:	Well, maybe at the beginning. She's not really ugly, but she's not dressed well.
Elizabeth:	She's shy.
Sharon:	She's shy?
Sujata:	She's dirty. But why is she dirty?
Elizabeth:	Because she has to clean the house so much.
Sharon:	Yeah!
Chamrong:	She doesn't take a bath.
Sharon:	Could it be she doesn't have much of a chance to take a bath?
Chamrong:	(*His voice sounds as if he is reconsidering his comment about baths.*) Yeah.

Sharon: (*She points to the flower in the illustration.*) Notice this flower. This is sort of a little clue here.

Bunthean: Lotus blossom.

Sharon: It is a blossom. Not a lotus blossom. What kind of blossom do you think it is?

Sujata: Pear blossom.

Sharon: Pear blossom. You're right. (*Sharon turns to the endpapers.*) Even the endpapers are a deep, rich color. Look at this symbol. It's the same one that is on the fan. Another student told me that people have this symbol hanging in their cars. Have any of you seen that?

Children: Yes!

Sharon: Do any of you have something like that?

Children: No.

Sharon: There's that symbol again. See it on the fan? (*She indicates the illustration on the page opposite the title page. She turns to the first page of story.*)
Look at the illustrations now. Look at how important the illustration must be because the writing is only in this little white box. Almost the entire page is taken up with illustrations, so the illustrations must be very important.
(*She points to animals.*) And you see animals. So animals must play a very

Sharon Tate shows the cover of The Korean Cinderella.

important role in this story. This story begins, "Long ago, in Korea."
So this story begins: "Long ago" instead of "Once upon a time."
(Sharon begins to read again.)
"Long ago   in Korea   when magical
creatures   were as common   as cabbages,
there lived   an old gentleman   and his wife."
[Spaces indicate pauses during reading.]

As Sharon continued to read the story, she drew the children's attention to key parts of the illustrations in order to help them understand how pictures can be used to predict or anticipate what will happen next. She also helped students follow the story through the way she read dialogue. Children could tell by her voice whether the frail father, the matchmaker, or the mean stepmother was speaking.

SHARED READING

Let's look at ways to teach for phrasing and fluency in shared reading lessons.

Teaching Children to Read With Their Eyes

Shared reading provides an excellent opportunity for modeling phrased, fluent reading. Long before they learn how to read, children enter the world of communication through oral language, at first expressing meaning with only one or two words. For example, my daughter's first word was "tractor." We lived on a farm and she loved to watch our neighbor plow his fields. Rebecca used the word tractor to communicate two things. When she pointed at the window and said "tractor," she meant, "Lift me up so I can see Edmund on his tractor." When she pointed to her favorite Richard Scarry book and said it, she meant, "Read the page with the picture of the tractor on it." Eventually she expanded her one-word utterances into two- or three-word phrases that communicated what she wanted. Her speech was very precise; she even separated the syllables in "tractor." Her two- and three-word utterances were choppy rather than smooth, but soon she was talking a blue streak. Her talk had shifted from choppy utterances to a stream of oral language. As children acquire oral language, they expand the length of their messages from a single word to phrases, and then to complete sentences.

When young children start to read, they must learn to think about language in a different way. Now they must learn that the flow of speech is actually made up of separate units, called words. Think about the phrase "peanut butter and jelly." When we talk, we say it as if it were one word: "peanutbutterandjelly." In order to learn how to read, the young child must learn how to map speech onto print. Clay (1991) writes:

> Young children are trying to discover how the flow of speech can be cut into word segments. It is false to assume that the child knows that his oral sentences are composed of word units. He has to discover what the word units of his speech are. He learns to break his speech into words separated by pauses and tries to match units of speech to patterns in print. (p. 162)

Our task as teachers is to help the young child break up the flow of speech into word units. We teach the child word-by-word matching, that is, to point to each word as they read it. The coordination among eye, hand, and voice helps the emergent reader break the stream of oral language into individual words. We teach children how to break up the oral language "peanutbutterandjelly" into the individual words "peanut butter and jelly" by demonstrating word-by-word matching and encouraging them to do it themselves.

When word-by-word matching is well under control, however, we want the eyes to take over the process. We want readers to begin to combine words into meaningful phrases as their eyes move quickly across them. This is the time to move away from external mediators such as the finger or pointer, which ultimately can interfere with fluency.

During shared reading lessons, you can help students make the transition away from using an external mediator to track print. Instead of crisply pointing to each word, sweep the pointing stick across the page. The sweeping motion guides the readers' eyes to move more quickly. Another way to encourage your children to use their eyes to track across a line of print is to point to only to the beginning of each line. When the children finish reading a line of text, move the pointing stick to the beginning of the next line to support their return sweep and to maintain momentum and unison in their reading. Initially, when

A teacher supports children who are learning to track print.

emergent readers do not have the support of a moving finger or pointing stick, they might have difficulty keeping their eyes on the line of text that they are reading. Their eyes may jump to another line of print or they skip a line of text altogether. If this happens, go back to pointing or sliding under each word of the text but keep working with children to help them read with their eyes.

Teaching Children to Recognize Phrase Units

Teaching children to put words together into meaningful phrases is key to developing their ability to do reading that sounds like talking. A big question we ask ourselves is how to teach for phrasing and fluency. We know that we can model it whenever we read to our students. We also know that, once children control word-by-word matching, it is time for them to work for increased fluency and reading with their eyes. We want to teach them to recreate the stream of language by teaching for phrasing. Phrases within the sentence are separated by the briefest of pauses. Sentences are indicated through slightly longer pauses and changes in pitch.

One teacher was pleased that children were reading with good momentum and also learning to read with their eyes, but she wanted to give them a stronger demonstration of phrasing. She wrote the text on sentence strips and then cut the strips apart into phrase units, placing them in a pocket chart. Notice in the photograph below how she left space between the phrase units in order to emphasize that each group of words must be read together.

The texts you select for this purpose should be easy for all children in the group to read so that they can process the text quickly, with a minimum of problem-solving. We want their full attention on phrasing.

Using exaggerated space to teach for phrasing in reading

The teacher began the lesson by showing the children the original format of the text, a poem. She made a transparency of the page and placed it on an overhead projector. She and the children read the poem together from the transparency. Then the teacher placed the sentence strips in the pocket chart and they all read the poem again. Next, the teacher read the poem, cutting the poem into phrase units as she read. Finally, she and the children read the poem again, working hard to smoothly read all the words on each phrase unit card. The teacher and the children revisited this poem several times, so that

the children would get a feel for reading in phrases. The poem was left in the pocket chart so that they could practice phrased reading during buddy reading or independent reading. Remember that an exercise like this one would be undertaken only at an appropriate time for a particular group of readers. The rearrangement of text serves as only a temporary prop on the way to phrased reading.

Teaching Children to Read Expressively

Expressive reading is another important indicator of comprehending. Children can read a passage by grouping the words in each sentence into meaningful clusters but still use a monotone voice. You can help them by reading aloud to them frequently, modeling phrased, fluent, and expressive reading. Children will also hear this type of reading whenever they listen to stories on audiotapes at a listening center. Note that expressive reading is not overly dramatic or artificial; listening to expressive reading is like listening to a storyteller.

You can use shared reading lessons to teach children to be expressive readers. Again, it is important to choose a text that is easy for children to read. Stories with dialogue work especially well in teaching expressive reading. For example, *The Little Red Hen* (Galdone 1973) is a familiar story for many children. When children read the dialogue they can be taught to change the pitch and inflection in their voices in order to make the personalities of characters come alive. Part of what we are teaching children is that we read dialogue differently from narrative.

Select a repeated phrase or piece of dialogue from a book for teaching expressive reading. Enlarge the text on a chart or place it on an overhead transparency. Have the children join you as you read the enlarged text. After children are familiar with the text, it can be placed somewhere in the room for children to practice expressive reading during managed independent learning.

In the following example, the teacher chose to teach for expressive reading by using a refrain from one of the class's favorite read-aloud books, *Kate and the Beanstalk* by Mary Pope Osborne (2000). Like other Jack tales, the giant repeats a refrain throughout the book. The author has varied the giant's traditional refrain. Her giant roars:

> Fe, Fi, Fo, Fum'in,
> I smell the blood of an Englishwoman.
> Be she alive or be she dead,
> I'll grind her bones to make my bread.

One of the twists in Osborne's variant of the *Jack and the Beanstalk* tale is that the giant's wife, the giantess, has a refrain of her own. When Kate first comes knocking at the castle door, the giantess opens the door, grabs Kate, and chants:

Help me!
I need a servant!
The last one stole
our hen
and ran away!

The next time Kate knocks, the giantess repeats the refrain except for the phrase "our hen." The giantess does not know that Kate, who is in a new disguise, is the thief, so she hires Kate to replace the servant who stole the bag of coins. The giantess laments her dilemma by repeating the refrain, replacing "our hen" with "our money bag" in the text.

The teacher wrote both refrains on enlarged charts. In order to follow the story line, she wrote "our money bag" and "our hen" on separate sentence strips so that it would be easy to match the story line with the correct text.

Before she read the story, the children and teacher talked about how the giant and giantess felt. The giantess was desperate. The giant was hungry and looking for something good to eat. Then the children practiced how each character might have sounded.

The first time the children read the parts of the giant and the giantess during the interactive read-aloud, they all read both parts. Later, the teacher divided them into two groups. One group read the part of the giantess and the other group read the part of the giant. The refrains provided a powerful opportunity for teaching for phrasing, fluency, and expression.

Teaching Children to Read Punctuation

Writers use punctuation to indicate meaningful breaks in the text. For example, writers use quotation marks to indicate that someone is talking. They use commas to indicate that the reader should pause briefly, and periods to indicate the end of sentences. When children ignore punctuation, meaning-making is often disrupted.

Dialogue can be just as powerful for teaching children to attend to punctuation as it is for teaching expressive reading. Poetry is another excellent choice for teaching children the importance of punctuation. The refrains from *Kate and the Beanstalk* mentioned earlier could be used to focus attention on the purpose of punctuation as well as for teaching children to read expressively. In fact, expressive reading requires the reader to respond to punctuation.

Learning to Use the Structure of a Text

A teacher uses an overhead of the table of contents from The Life and Times of the Honeybee

When children become more skilled in using organizational tools, such as tables of contents, they can spend more time attending to information rather than searching for information. Knowing how to use organizational tools aids comprehension.

Many commercially-produced science and social studies curricula include big books for teaching key concepts. These big books are excellent tools for teaching children how to read expository texts. Often these books have a table of contents, an index, section headings, and captions or sidebars. The primary purpose for using these big books is to teach content included in the course of study—but they are also excellent materials for teaching children how readers use text features to aid in comprehending the text. For example, the table of contents not only helps the reader locate information, but it also gives the reader an idea of what the author thinks are the important concepts in this topic.

If you do not have enlarged texts for teaching children how a table of contents works, you can make a transparency of the table of contents from standard-sized trade books. For example, the study of the life cycle is part of the course of study in many primary grades. In the following lesson, the teacher enlarged the table of contents from the book *The Life and Times of the Honeybee* (Micucci 1995).

The children and their teacher looked through the titles listed in the table of contents. The group decided that the section with the title "From Egg to Bee" was probably about the life cycle of the honeybee. When they turned to page eight, they found just what they were looking for. Throughout the year, the teacher took every opportunity to demonstrate that readers can use the table of contents to find out how the book is organized and what topics the author included or chose not to include.

Final Thoughts on Shared Reading as an Instructional Context

Shared reading is a powerful instructional context for teaching children how to become more skillful readers. Teachers demonstrate the ways of reading that they want children to use in their own reading. They use an enlarged text displayed so that all the children can see. After giving a clear demonstration, teachers support the readers as they practice what they were just taught. The next two sections discuss how teachers teach for phrasing, fluency, and expressive reading during guided reading and in mini-lessons prior to independent reading.

GUIDED READING

Up until this point, I have discussed teaching for phrasing and fluency with groups of children who may not be at the same instructional level in reading. Teachers usually group their children heterogeneously in interactive read-aloud and shared-reading lessons. In guided reading, however, the children are grouped homogeneously, according to their instructional reading levels.

During guided reading, you support the children's ability to comprehend the text and to read with phrasing and fluency in two ways:

Students learn about section headings in a guided reading group.

- You select a text that matches the children's instructional level.
- You orient the children to the book through an introduction that:
  —gives an overview of the text so that children have the background they need to predict meaning.
  —fills in the gaps that the reader may have that could unnecessarily increase the difficulty of the text.
  —leaves the kind of reading work that will help each child become a better reader on the next book.

Figure 8-3 summarizes key features of a book introduction that support children's successful fluent reading of a text that provides children with new challenges. Whenever you introduce a book to children, you need to think about the features of book introductions that are listed in Figure 8-3. Consider the book *Mr. Putter and Tabby Pour the Tea* by Cynthia Rylant (1994) [Level J]. Most children can read this book at the end of first grade or the beginning of second grade. The story is divided into three sections. The title of the first section is "Mr. Putter." In this section we find out that Mr. Putter is lonely and decides to find a cat to keep him company. The second section is called "Tabby." This section explains how Mr. Putter selected Tabby—a cat just like himself. The last section, "Mr. Putter and Tabby," describes the relationship between Mr. Putter and Tabby and why it is so satisfying for both of them.

Before I introduced this story to a group of children I worked with recently, I asked if they had read other Mr. Putter books because that knowledge would shape my introduction. I wanted them to understand the relationship between this story and other stories they may have read. In this case, the children had read several other Mr. Putter stories. Before reading the book, I asked them to talk about what they already knew about

Role of the Book Introduction in Supporting Fluent, Phrased Reading

- Gives readers a sense of the overall meaning of the story.
- Helps readers understand how text works (the organizational structure).
- Familiarizes readers with unusual language structures.
- Draws attention to new and important words.

FIGURE 8-3

the relationship between Mr. Putter and Tabby. I told them that this is the story about how the friendship between Mr. Putter and Tabby began.

Level J books tend to be longer stories containing episodes that relate to one another in some way. Tools such as a table of contents or chapter headings help readers get a sense of the organization and structure of the text. In the case of *Mr. Putter and Tabby Pour the Tea,* I knew that reading the section headings would help the children understand what each section was about. In order to highlight the book's organization, I placed each of the three headings on a piece of chart paper to provide an overall picture of the book, and I drew the children's attention to the way the story was divided and helped them to form expectations.

Then I talked about the first section, "Mr. Putter." I encouraged the children to think about why Mr. Putter might feel lonely. They could understand and empathize with his problem. Then I asked them to consider the next section heading, "Tabby," and predict what might happen in this section. Could a cat be the solution to Mr. Putter's problem of being lonely?

I knew that the children would be able to solve most of the words in the story, but that the meaning of "company," as applied to a cat, might be challenging. Most eight-year-olds would think of Tabby as a pet. They might not equate pets with companions or company, so this literary language might be unfamiliar. I also thought that most of the group would not be familiar with the concept of clipping roses, so I talked about gardens and what gardeners do, using the language of the text. This background knowledge and their familiarity with language would help the children maintain a stream of meaning as they read these stories.

Clay says that every child deserves a good book introduction (Clay 1991). By incorporating the four points in Figure 8-3, I increased the probability that the children would be able to read more fluently and comprehend more easily. I needed to think about the parts of a good book introduction in relation to this text and these readers. First, I gave the overall meaning of the story by placing the story, *Mr. Putter and Tabby Pour the Tea,* in the context of other Mr. Putter stories they had read. In this book the author reveals why and how Mr. Putter got a cat. If the children did not know from other stories that Mr. Putter had a cat, the title gave them the clue that he does find a cat, someone to keep him company.

I pointed out the three sections of the book for two reasons. First, I wanted the children to use the subheadings to think about what might happen in the story. Second, I wanted them to begin to generalize their knowledge of how Rylant uses section headings to organize this book to the use of headings by other authors as an organizational feature in their texts. By learning how to predict the story from headings in this book, the children will become more expert at using headings to predict meaning in the other books they read.

In our book introductions we also want to introduce unusual language and language structures. For my introduction, I chose two concepts that I thought children might be

unfamiliar with: clipping roses and pets as company. I decided not to point out that sentences stretch over several lines of text because the children had read other Rylant books with the same text layout. As indicated in Figure 8-3, we can support readers by introducing new and important words. I talked about the two concepts, clipping roses and pets as company, but did not feel it was necessary to have the children locate these words in the text. My hypothesis was that they already had enough word-solving strategies to engage in problem-solving, especially as we had discussed the meaning of both concepts.

Mr. Putter and Tabby Pour the Tea lends itself to teaching for phrased reading because of its text layout, which indicates phrase units. Notice how the text layout supports phrased reading in the following text:

> All day long as Mr. Putter
> clipped his roses
> and fed his tulips
> and watered his trees,
> Mr. Putter wished for
> some company.

After the children had read and enjoyed the story, I copied this text on a transparency, and taught for phrasing. I pointed out that the single sentence extended over several lines of text. We read the sentence together and talked about its meaning. Then we practiced reading it in phrased units until our reading sounded phrased and expressive. I asked the children to read several pages of the story aloud during their independent reading and to monitor themselves for phrased reading.

INDEPENDENT READING MINI-LESSONS

During independent reading, children have opportunities to reread familiar books or read new books that are easier than their instructional level. For younger students, mini-lessons are not an essential part of independent reading. Sometimes, however, you may want to use one in order to draw attention to a particular behavior that will help children to become more efficient and effective readers. For example, you could quickly demonstrate reading with your eyes or reading with expression. I recently taught a mini-lesson to help children attend to punctuation during reading. I chose this mini-lesson because I had noticed that, in some cases, they were reading right through the punctuation at the end of sentences. In other cases, they paused at the wrong places, disrupting the flow of their reading.

I selected a page from a trickster tale that the children had composed and written during interactive writing lessons. (See Chapter 2 for a description of interactive writing.) The first

page seemed especially well suited for a mini-lesson on attending to punctuation. Both sentences began with phrases set off from the rest of the sentence by commas. There was also a series of animal names, separated by commas.

Before the children began reading their own books, we reread this page together, pausing after each comma and dropping our voices at the end of the sentence. Then I asked the students to choose a book from their browsing boxes and read one page from the book, paying special attention to punctuation. After they were finished reading, I asked one child to share a page from her book with the group. After she read, we praised her for reading the punctuation.

After this brief mini-lesson, I asked the children to choose two or three easy books from their browsing baskets. Reading an easy text minimizes the need for word-solving, and allows children to focus on looking for and using punctuation marks as they read.

The mini-lesson lasted about seven minutes. I asked one child to model for the group to ensure that all of the children understood that their task was to pause at commas, stop at the end of sentences, etc. After she read, we talked about what she did to make the reading enjoyable for us as listeners. The children could certainly have read books from their browsing

Learning about punctuation through interactive writing

baskets without a mini-lesson. But there are several important benefits of including a mini-lesson on attending to and using punctuation during reading as part of independent reading, including:

- Children attend to what their teachers attend to. Explicitly teaching the importance of punctuation makes children aware of its importance in reading.
- Each child has an opportunity to practice what he or she has learned after seeing a clear demonstration.

The mini-lesson gave a focus to the children's reading, helping them to become more fluent readers of punctuation.

Summary

Children need opportunities to practice fluent reading every day. They can read books from previous guided reading lessons or other texts that they find easy. They can read interactive writing or poetry that is displayed on charts in the classroom. They can read with a more fluent reading buddy or listen to audiotapes or stories, especially those which lend themselves to expressive reading.

In addition, children need to have opportunities to read outside of school. Schools can provide home book programs, such as the KEEP BOOKS® series from the Ohio State University, which are designed to support emergent readers. (See Appendix.) Children should also be able to check out books from the school library and take their guided reading books home.

Research indicates that there is a relationship between fluent reading and comprehension. Reading fluently, with phrasing, reflects recognition of the writer's intended meaning in combination with the reader's interpretation of the text. Fluent, phrased reading also reflects the joy of reading for meaning. As teachers, we can support fluency, phrasing, and comprehending through careful selection of texts and through teaching for these components across the language and literacy framework.

Ideas to Try

MEETING #1

1. Meet with grade-level colleagues from grades one, two, and three to discuss fluency and phrasing in reading. Have each participant prepare for the meeting by bringing an audiotape that illustrates one minute of fluent, phrased oral reading from a student in her or his class. Be sure that the student was reading without pointing and has full control of word-by-word matching. Also, be sure that the recording was made on the second reading of the book, after the student had read it once either orally or silently. Bring the written text so that listeners can follow along and notice punctuation.

2. Share tapes and generate lists of words and phrases that describe the reading. If any student had difficulty recording a fluent reading, discuss why that might be the case. Listen to the readings first, without looking at the written text.

   - How do the readers sound?
   - What evidence is there that they are noticing phrase units?

   Listen again and notice readers' attention to punctuation. If you like, mark phrase units.

3. Discuss the ways of teaching for fluency and phrasing mentioned in this chapter.

4. Leave the meeting with the goal of strengthening your teaching of phrasing and fluency.

MEETING #2

1. Identify two or three students in your class who read at about the same level and who seldom demonstrate fluent, phrased reading.

2. Record one minute of these students' reading of a text, one that they can read with about 95 percent accuracy and one that they can understand with your support.

3. Work intensively with these students for a two-week period. Do not increase the difficulty level of the texts they read, but use different ways to encourage them to read with phrasing and fluency.

4. At the end of the period, again record one minute of their reading (on the second reading).

5. Bring these tapes to a discussion with colleagues to share and discuss what you learned.

Chapter 9

Teaching for Comprehension in Guided and Independent Reading

Justina Henry

Working with your students in guided reading, you probably have found that teaching for strategies has paid off with more students becoming successful, strategic readers. Many teachers starting guided reading for the first time are surprised to find out how important it is to identify what students need to know next and to select an appropriate book for each lesson. These teacher decisions are based on analysis of observations of students as they read and discuss books.

In this chapter, I will describe the instructional decision-making of Leslie Stokes, a second-grade teacher in a central Ohio suburban school district, as she taught comprehending strategies to her transitional readers during mini-lessons in independent reading and guided reading. Her students have developed a reading process and are expanding their strategies as they meet the challenges of more complex texts. To prepare for a lesson, Leslie matches the needs of her students to an appropriate text. She analyzes the text to determine its demands on readers and plans for explicit teaching for strategies when she thinks her students need more support to take on effective processing. Her goal is to teach for an integrated use of strategies.

A Network of Strategies

Readers have a network of strategies that result in processing text with ease and understanding. Fountas and Pinnell (2001) state, "These cognitive actions are what readers do in order to understand text, but they are abstract notions. They occur simultaneously and rapidly, in a coordinated way, whenever readers read" (p. 310). Teachers always have the full range of strategies in mind (making connections, inferring, summarizing, analyzing, critiquing), and they help students think about their reading strategies and apply them to more complex texts. One instructional approach to developing reading comprehension is to draw readers' attention to effective cognitive actions during real reading experiences.

Observing and Supporting Comprehending Strategies in Interactive Read-Aloud

Although we can never observe the "in-the-head" operations of readers, we can hypothesize about readers' inner control of strategies by observing their overt reading behaviors (Clay 1991). If we listen and respond carefully to our students' reading and conversations about the text during guided reading lessons, aspects of their thinking will be revealed to us. We use this information to make in-the-moment teaching decisions that help expand students' understanding of the processes necessary for reading. As Fountas and Pinnell (1996) state:

> ...[W]e are not talking about a specific teaching approach to each new strategy but about a repertoire of interpretations and responses you can apply at any time to help the child to learn from reading text. Your moves must be focused and supportive, designed to bring forward examples that will help children learn "how to learn" in reading. (p. 149)

When children hear picture books read aloud, they bring a wealth of associations to the texts (Stephen & Watson 1994). We can become more aware of the ways readers develop networks of strategies to construct the meaning of stories if we analyze our conversations with our students during interactive read-aloud lessons. In read-aloud lessons, we model, acknowledge students' control of, and call for students to apply a variety of strategies necessary to understand the story at literal and inferential levels. To expand meaning, readers make connections, infer, summarize, synthesize, analyze, and critique the information in texts (Fountas & Pinnell 2001). These strategies for expanding meaning are applied by readers in an integrated way depending on the demands of the text being read.

Leslie pauses for students to think and respond while reading The Biggest Bear.

In read-aloud sessions, you read the words of the text, thus freeing students to experience the thinking processes involved in making meaning. Students can observe as you think aloud and model the processes. Often, students will volunteer their ideas as they become involved in the story. Even in the same lesson, you can call for students to apply a strategy that is necessary for understanding the text. With varying levels of teacher support, students can begin to realize what it means to read for meaning.

Leslie read *The Biggest Bear* (Ward 1952) to her second graders. During read-aloud sessions, Leslie usually read a section or page before pausing to give the students time to think. This wait time indicated to the students that she expected them to participate in thinking about and discussing the meaning of the text. This implicit invitation to contribute created opportunities for the students to experience and develop comprehension strategies. (See Figure 9-1.)

Realizing that her students were taking on the strategies for making meaning during the read-aloud sessions, Leslie decided to take a closer look at their behavior during the guided reading lessons to assess their control of these strategies in reading on their own.

Getting Ready for Guided Reading Lessons: Designing an Explicit Plan

Leslie's goal is for her students to become independent readers. She has a plan for explicit instruction that is implemented when she observes that her students need more support to learn comprehending strategies. The design includes ways to scaffold learning from high to low teacher support within the context of reading books in guided reading lessons. Through short, focused conversations with students, Leslie demonstrates and explains strategies. As students begin to learn something new about reading, she relinquishes control to the students through guided practice and independent practice. The basic structure of guided reading, along with important teacher actions, is presented in Figure 9-2. This structure incorporates focused, instructional conversations within real reading experiences.

This basic plan assumes that instruction requires "some varying proportion of responsibility from the teacher and the student" (Pearson 1985, p. 731). Because reading comprehension is a complex process, Leslie needs to be ready to show students that strategies are related and that they may need to apply many strategies while reading a single selection.

Graphic organizers are visual diagrams that help students become aware of the structure and organization of ideas. (See Fountas and Pinnell [2001] for a discussion of graphic organ-

Teaching for Comprehension in Interactive Read-Aloud

Leslie modeled making connections...

Text: *On the hill behind the barn Johnny's grandfather had planted a few apple trees. These were the only apple trees in the valley, and they were known as Orchard's orchard.*

Leslie: An orchard is a group of fruit trees. I've seen apple orchards and pear orchards.

...which stimulated student thinking:

Student: I was at my grandma's house and she has a woods behind her house and it kind of looks like that, but it's not. It doesn't have apples.

Leslie: Right. So she has woods but those trees don't produce any kind of fruit. This reminded you of your grandmother's trees and that helped you to understand what an orchard is.

She called for students to analyze the events of the story and form an understanding of how the plot was developing. Readers synthesized this information to predict what would happen next:

Text: *In the fall Mr. McCarroll got pretty upset when the bear spent a night in his cornfield.* (Pause) *In the winter he had a wonderful time with the bacons and hams in the Pennell's smokehouse.* (Pause)

Leslie: What do you think Mr. McCarroll and Mr. Pennell thought about that?

Student: All their work was ruined.

Leslie: What do you think they will do about it?

Student: They want to get rid of the bear.

Student: They might tell Johnny to give the bear away because he is trouble.

FIGURE 9-1

izers.) During guided reading lessons, Leslie and her students often create graphic organizers together on large charts. She has to be prepared to teach for strategies as needed in the guided reading groups. Part of her preparation for the guided reading lessons is to get the materials ready; an easel with a tablet of chart paper, markers, and whiteboards are close at hand at the guided reading table.

SELECTING AND ANALYZING THE TEXT

Leslie selects books for each of her guided reading groups. She has a three-ring binder that holds the notes she makes as she carefully reads each book. Important observations of students' responses to the text are added after using the books with her students. This book analysis is particularly helpful as her students begin to move into more complex fiction, such as chapter books. She thinks about how the episodes of the stories unfold and notes

Teaching for Comprehension Strategies Across the Guided Reading Lesson

STRUCTURE OF GUIDED READING:	TEACHER'S ROLE:
Plan the Lesson: Text Selection and Introduction	Read and analyze the text. Consider the demands of the text. Select important behaviors to emphasize.
Introduce the Text	Introduce the strategies. Tell why they are important to readers. Model/demonstrate effective strategy use. Explain and discuss the strategies.
Read the Text	Support/guide reading. Prompt for strategies.
Revisit the Text Teach for Processing Strategies	Discuss the meaning of the text. Model/demonstrate. Summarize learning.
Prompt Independent Reading	Remind students to use the behavior discussed.

FIGURE 9-2

appropriate stopping places for discussion. (See Figure 9-3.) These book notes are also helpful in planning for whole group mini-lessons that precede independent reading.

As she reads the stories, Leslie also analyzes her own reading process. For instance, she discovers that she automatically rereads when her understanding breaks down. If this strategy does not work, she rereads more slowly, paying closer attention to the phrasing signaled by punctuation and sentence structures. She realizes that she asks herself questions that keep her on track:

The Babysitter

Page

2 Students might ignore periods. They may read, "...doctor Nana..." and miss the meaning.

4 Students need to attend to comma (...stick,...) and how it's used in addressing the listener.

4 Good place to stop and predict what Tom will do next.

5 Text verifies prediction (..."ladder slipped and Poppa fell").

7 Students need to attend to quotation marks so they know if Poppa or Tom is speaking.

8-11 Need to understand layout

12 Meaning of "woke up"

14 Take perspective of mom. What will she say?

16 Students can rethink meaning of title.

FIGURE 9-3 Teacher's Book Notes for *The Babysitter*

- Did that sound right?
- Do I understand what I am reading?
- Is there something here I already know?
- What do I need to know?
- What will come next?

Leslie thinks about how she can teach for monitoring and fixing-up strategies as the need arises. As she reads each book, she notes places where her students may need to fill in the gaps. Thompson (1987) describes these gaps as places in the story where the reader must get meanings that are not explicitly stated: "spaces between sentences, chapters, events, details, characters, narrative viewpoints, textual perspectives and so on" (p. 123). Noting these places where students may need to bridge the gap helps Leslie anticipate difficulties her students may have when they read the book.

These insights help Leslie prepare to respond to students' needs as they emerge during the lessons. Her own reading experiences inform her teaching and help her plan and even rehearse the clear explanations she may need to make, particularly during any think-aloud demonstration in the guided reading lessons.

Teaching for strategies requires that teachers:

- understand that readers make meaning while they are reading a selection.
- observe and analyze students' reading behaviors for evidence that they understand what they are reading.
- select appropriate books.
- carefully read the selections, thinking about possible teaching points based on student need.
- make teaching moves that reveal to students how to construct meaning from their reading.

Being ready to teach a lesson helps us respond more effectively to students' needs. Our observations in one lesson help us to plan for subsequent ones, with some guided reading lessons including brief, explicit conversations. However, instructional decision-making is ongoing, and we must be prepared to act on students' confusions in the midst of each lesson.

Teaching for Strategies in Large- and Small-Group Contexts

This section examines examples of teacher-student interactions from two different reading lessons. The first lesson was a whole-group mini-lesson that Leslie conducted before independent reading. Her observations indicated that some students needed more explicit teaching and guidance to monitor their reading. She decided that most students would benefit from a whole-group discussion of strategic reading. The purpose was for the students to learn to more closely monitor their reading for meaning. In the second lesson, Leslie brought one of her guided reading groups together and provided explicit instruction in learning to recognize what is implied but not stated in the text.

WHOLE-GROUP MINI-LESSON: HELPING STUDENTS SEARCH FOR AND USE MEANING TO MONITOR THEIR READING

The students in one group have been reading Level H books during guided reading lessons. The stories, accompanied by supportive illustrations, usually have been similar to students' life experiences and easy for them to understand. (See Fountas and Pinnell 1996 for a discussion of text characteristics at various levels.) At Level H, books begin to include more episodes with more challenging ideas and vocabulary. In recent lessons at this level, Leslie observed that the children had little to contribute to the discussion of the story after the first reading. She realized that readers were not always monitoring for meaning and making the connections and inferences necessary to follow the plot and get to the deeper meaning of the stories. She reminded the students to think about whether they understood what they were reading and to reread if necessary, but this teaching generally came at the end of the lessons. Students did not immediately apply their learning with her support and guidance, because their lesson was over. She decided that most students in the class would benefit from a mini-lesson that focused on using punctuation and sentence structure to support self-monitoring for meaning. She planned for independent reading time to immediately follow the mini-lesson so that she could observe and confer with readers to support their processing, especially their self-monitoring.

Deciding that she needed a stronger focus on helping students monitor their reading, Leslie designed the whole-group mini-lesson. She selected *The Babysitter* (Randell 1997) [Level H] to use during the lesson at the easel. So that the students could easily see the print during their discussion, she enlarged the pages of the story. (Sometimes she copied the text onto a transparency to use at the overhead projector.) Then she prepared for the lesson by carefully reading the book. She decided that its compound sentence structures and dialogue would pose challenges to readers, especially if they ignored punctuation. The students gathered at the easel for the lesson.

Introducing the Text

First, Leslie *introduced the strategy*. She started the lesson by making a statement about self-monitoring. She said, "Today we are going to really listen to ourselves as we read, so that we can make sure that the story is making sense to us. Doing this will help you understand what you read." This introduction helped the children focus on the strategy so that they could use it more consciously while they read.

Next, she *explained why the strategy is important to readers*. She said, "Reading is not just reading the words. We have to think about the story as we read. If we become confused by the words or sentences, we need to stop and figure out the tricky parts. This is how good readers get better each time they read."

Then Leslie *demonstrated the strategy*, telling the students how she self-monitors as she reads: "I am going to read the first few pages of this book, *The Babysitter*. I am going to tell you my thoughts as I read—that will show you what it means to think about how the story needs to make sense to us as we read." She began reading:

> One day Mom had to take
> Baby Emma to the doctor.
> Nana went too.

Leslie, ignoring the punctuation, read, "One day Mom had to take Baby Emma to the doctor Nana went too." She said to the students, "Now that doesn't sound right. I think that Nana is the grandmother and not the doctor. I'd better read that again." Leslie then read the text correctly and said, "I didn't see that period after 'doctor' the first time I read. By rereading, I learned that watching for the periods helps me understand the story better." Leslie continued this think-aloud demonstration on the next pages, providing two more examples.

Then she *explained the strategy*, clearly stating what she wanted readers to do. She said, "I really understand the story so far because, as I was reading, I was always thinking about whether it made sense to me. If it didn't, I stopped and reread so I could figure it out. Noticing the periods helped me do that. Let's write one or two sentences on this chart

that will tell us what the story is about." The students offered ideas and Leslie wrote their sentences on the chart paper. (See Figure 9-4.)

Leslie then said, "Now it is easy to make a prediction about what will come next in the story. What do you think will happen next? Why?" She wrote the students' predictions on the chart paper.

Reading the Text

Leslie *provided guided practice* as individual students came to the easel to read aloud the rest of the short story. Leslie and the other students observed the readers. Occasionally, she intervened to prompt students to self-monitor. For example, to one student she said, "Does that make sense to you? Go back and reread. Think what would make sense and look right." She reminded them to attend to the phrasing and punctuation as a way to monitor their comprehension of meaning.

At the end of the reading, the class discussed the story. Leslie said, "As we read the rest of the story, we stopped if it didn't make sense. We reread or just thought about what we

FIGURE 9-4 Predictions for *The Babysitter*

knew and what would make sense. This helped us think about how the story really ended and if our predictions were correct." Leslie helped the students understand what it means to be accountable for their reading. She also demonstrated, with the help of the chart, how monitoring for meaning is important for predicting later story episodes.

Leslie *summarized new learning* at the end of the lesson. She discussed the meaning of the story with the children and pointed out that they had been checking on their own reading. She used an example from the students' current reading to point out some specific ways students had used effective monitoring. She conveyed the expectation that students would apply these ideas in reading other books. She said, "When you read your books today at the centers and during independent reading time, remember to think as you read. If it doesn't make sense to you, go back and try to figure it out."

Moving to Independence

Leslie planned time for *independent practice*. She followed this mini-lesson by observing the students and responding to their reading during brief conferences as part of their daily independent reading block. She looked for evidence that these readers could reestablish continuity of meaning when they did not understand the gist of the passage. Her observations helped her plan the next reading lessons. There were many other opportunities during the day for the students to read independently, during managed independent learning time—at the browsing box, reading journal, and poetry centers. Students were reminded at the beginning of center time to make sure they understood what they read.

HELPING STUDENTS GO BEYOND THE TEXT—INFERRING AND MAKING CONNECTIONS

Another group in the class was reading *The Bears on Hemlock Mountain* (Dalgliesh 1952) [Level M]. Level M texts challenge readers to make interpretations and understand subtleties of plot over longer stretches of text. Leslie wanted to support their developing strategies and planned to draw their attention to places in the text where they needed to make inferences, especially about Jonathan, the main character. She wanted the students to come to know the character by recognizing not only what is directly stated but also what is implied in the story. The students needed to be able to go beyond the literal meaning—to read *between the lines*.

In planning for the lesson, Leslie read the book and realized that as a reader, this text required her to make inferences about the main character. She could visualize what he

might look and sound like by connecting his situation to her own life experiences. These connections helped her make plausible predictions about what might happen next in the story. She also noted that she was asking herself questions, such as: "What did the author mean by_____? Why did the character say that? Do that?" This preparation deepened Leslie's understanding of how readers use a network of strategies—connecting, inferring, and predicting.

Introducing the Text

As the group came together to read Chapter 3 of *The Bears on Hemlock Mountain*, Leslie *introduced the strategy*. She began the lesson by talking to the students about making inferences. She said, "When we read today, we are going to pay attention to how the author helps us to get to know Jonathan, the main character in the story. Sometimes we have to think deeply about what the author's words mean to us. Doing this will help you understand what you read." This statement helped the students focus their attention on the author's words about the character.

Children read The Bears on Hemlock Mountain.

Next, Leslie *explained why the strategy is important to readers*. She said, "Good readers know that they have to read the author's words to create pictures in their minds. To do this, we sometimes have to think beyond what is actually stated in the book."

Leslie *demonstrated the strategy* by reading the beginning of Chapter 3 and telling the students how she makes inferences as she reads. "I am going to read the first part of this chapter. I am going to tell you my thoughts as I read. That will show you what it means to think beyond the words so I can really understand the character and the story."

Leslie read the text:

> "I know!" she [the mother] said to Jonathan, as he brought in an armful of wood,
> "your aunt Emma, over across Hemlock Mountain, has the biggest iron pot you ever laid eyes on."
> "I never laid eyes on it," said Jonathan.

Leslie stopped reading and commented on the thoughts running through her mind. She said:

> As I am reading, I can see Jonathan and his mom in my mind. It reminds me of how I talk to my daughter at home. I think Jonathan's mom is telling him about the pot because she is going to send him over there to get it. But as soon as he hears her say "Hemlock Mountain," he says he's never seen the pot. I think he is making an excuse and is trying to keep her from telling him to go for the pot.

Leslie continued to read:

> "Then you are going to," said his mother.
> "But it's a long way and the pot is heavy," Jonathan said.

She stopped reading and said:

> The mother really doesn't tell Jonathan to go for the pot. I had to think about what her words meant: "Then you are going to." I think Jonathan is afraid of going up the mountain and he's making an excuse not to go. Jonathan doesn't really say this, but I know what he means because it reminds me of my daughter and how she tries to make excuses about doing some chore for me. I think he is trying to convince his mom that he shouldn't go. All that the author wrote was, "But it's a long way and the pot is heavy." I had to read between the lines to figure it out. I can picture Jonathan's face in my mind—he probably is not looking very happy.

Then Leslie *explained the strategy* she had demonstrated and said, "I really understand the story so far because as I was reading I was always thinking about how the author *showed* me with words what the characters are like. The author's words reminded me of my life, and I used this to help me figure out the story. Let's write on this chart one or two sentences from the book that show us that Jonathan is afraid of going up the mountain."

The students offered suggestions and Leslie wrote their sentences on the chart paper. (See Figure 9-5.) They reread the text in the chart and she said, "The author doesn't exactly tell us that Jonathan is afraid; we have to go beyond the words in the book to really understand this. As you read the rest of the chapter, think about how the author shows you what

FIGURE 9-5 Students learn to make inferences by discussing how the author shows rather than tells about the main character.

Jonathan is like and how he feels. A picture in your mind may help you understand what the story is about and what the characters will do next."

Leslie helped the students understand more about what it means to make inferences during reading. She demonstrated how she thinks about what she reads to get to a deeper meaning of the story. Using the chart helped the students reflect on the author's words, uncover some implicit meanings, and understand how these inferences aid in making predictions.

Reading the Text

The students participated in *guided practice* as they read the rest of the chapter. Leslie observed and sometimes asked a student, "What does that mean? Why do you think that?" Students' responses helped her decide whether they could make inferences based on implicit information drawn from the text, and also whether they could provide justification for these inferences.

Next, Leslie *summarized new learning*. After the students finished reading, they discussed the story and made additions to the chart. Leslie emphasized the thinking involved in reading between the lines. She provided a clear example from her observations of one reader's thinking process.

Moving to Independence

Concluding the lesson, she told the students they would have opportunities for *independent practice* during independent reading time and at the centers. She reminded them to think beyond the author's words to understand what the author is trying to show them. Leslie also put the chart in the independent reading center. She introduced the next chapter and explained, "As you read the next chapter in this book at your seats, think about some other ways the author describes Jonathan. When you come to the center, add your ideas to the chart. We'll talk about these ideas the next time we have our guided reading lesson."

Summary

Engaging students in conversations about their thinking processes within the context of real reading experiences supports their use and expansion of comprehending strategies. We can address the use of a particular strategy by momentarily stopping the reading to explicitly discuss the process that is being applied. We can adjust our teaching within and across lessons by:

- observing students' responses.
- preparing for guided reading lessons by increasing our knowledge of the books we have selected and the processes readers will need to use to make meaning.

Our teaching can help our students expand their network of strategies and develop the responsibility and know-how for their own learning.

Students have opportunities to apply reading strategies during independent reading time.

Ideas to Try

1. Explore students' development of their ability to think beyond the literal meaning of the texts. Focus on strategies related to inferring and making connections. Select the discussion after reading the text for your observation of students.

2. Prepare for a meeting with colleagues by observing your students as they discuss texts they read in guided reading. As you select texts over a week of teaching, think about the demands on the readers:
   - What inferences will they need to make?
   - What connections will be possible for them to make?

3. Make some notes on students' discussion of each text. You might use an observation form like the one below.

Observation of the Discussion After Reading	
What texts require:	**Observations of readers:**

4. Observe your students closely as they discuss stories *after* reading them. Take notes on their behaviors.

5. Afterward, reflect on the lesson. Ask:
   - What is the evidence that students were making inferences or making connections?
   - Did students make the inferences and connections that I predicted would be necessary to understand the text?
   - What were the surprises in my observations?
   - What important inferences and connections did students miss?
   - Were the texts too easy? Too hard?
   - How can I help students expand their ability to think beyond the text? In the introduction? In the discussion after reading?

6. Bring your notes and the texts that students read to a meeting with grade-level colleagues. Discuss your exploration and your reflections on helping students expand their ability to think beyond the text.

CHAPTER 10

Extending the Meaning of Texts: Beyond the Book in Guided Reading

Gay Su Pinnell

Reading means thinking—before, during, and after you process a text. From the moment you pick up a book or article, you have expectations. As an adult reader, you are not consciously aware of the process, but you will immediately activate background knowledge to bring to the reading. The integration of readers' background knowledge with information in the print, before and during processing, leads to the construction of understandings, or comprehension. As we read, we constantly employ comprehending strategies: making connections and inferences, summarizing and synthesizing information, and perhaps even critiquing or analyzing the text in some way.

After reading a text that we have understood, we have a useful summary in our minds that allows us to call up the important ideas, responses, or details. This summary implies a kind of selection process as to what is important to retain. For nonfiction texts, we probably remember the *new* information gained as well as any surprises we may have encountered. There may be a special connection with the topic if something in the informational texts can be connected with your personal experience. For example, you might give special attention to an article on China if you have visited there or if your family's roots are there. Occasionally, a text will prompt a deeper reflection after reading. Perhaps there is a character's dilemma or a tragic or funny turn of events that you keep returning to in your mind, without deliberately meaning to do so. Or the text may trigger memories that inadvertently come to mind for several days after reading it. You might discuss these memories or responses with friends.

If you are participating in an established discussion group, you might even make some notes or draw out some important contrasts in or events from the book. This *extended* reflection focuses on the meaning of the text; usually, we find that our own understanding is richer because of this reflection. You can almost always remember a book (even one you did not particularly like) that you discussed with your reading group; texts read without conversation may soon be forgotten.

For young readers, extending the meaning of a text through discussion, writing, or other means can help them not only to understand a specific text but also to expand their comprehending powers in general. This chapter explores the purposes and advantages of extending texts and provides several examples of doing so.

What Does It Mean to Extend the Meaning of the Text?

Extending the meaning of a text means going beyond the literal meaning to perform some kind of analytic thinking. Individuals are always thinking about what they read. Thinking about meaning is integral to the introduction and the reading of a text, and important when revisiting the text after reading as well. But extending the text generally means going deeper into the process, connecting analysis with some kind of representation. Intermediate-level students are frequently required to go *beyond* a text to extend the meaning, and writing is often required as evidence of their thinking. (The high-stakes proficiency examinations certainly require such cognitive action.)

Extending meaning provides explicit demonstrations of how readers think about texts after reading, and how they can put their ideas into writing or some other kind of representation to communicate them to others. Extension is *not* about proving to someone that you read a text. It does not involve retelling so much as it involves reflecting. The goal of extension is to help readers make their own ideas clear; extension also communicates the idea that good readers think *while* reading but also think *after* reading. The kind of analytic work that you do in extending the meaning of text will influence students as they read because they will notice more details and build meaning around the important comparisons or other organizational structures in the text. Through extension, they can learn more about how texts *work*, so that they are better able to derive the information they need for deeper understanding. Extension can also help them begin to make judgments about a text in terms of its accuracy or quality.

Remember that in guided reading, students are processing texts that have been especially selected to be "just right" for them in terms of reading instruction. With the support of the teacher's introduction and skilled teaching, children in a group can successfully process these texts, meaning that they can read with high accuracy and understanding. Most words in the text fall into one of the following categories:

- Known words that are quickly and automatically recognized.
- Accessible words that can be quickly solved with the strategies that children currently control.
- Challenging words that offer opportunities to expand word-solving strategies (with the support of your introduction, interactions during reading, and teaching after the reading).

Values of Extending the Meaning of Texts

- Give children support to engage in deeper analysis and reflection.
- Explicitly demonstrate how to think about a text after reading.
- Prompt children to be more analytic and make better connections while reading.
- Show them how to communicate their thinking in speaking (or speech) or writing.
- Help them see the inner workings of texts.
- Help them see how to make connections between what they read and what they already know and have experienced.
- Show them how to place ideas (in writing or other representation) in relation to each other.
- Show them how to make judgments about a text.

FIGURE 10-1

The problem-solving that readers do takes place against a backdrop of accurate reading. Comprehension has been supported by your introduction, which helps readers understand a text's main ideas and organization. So a book read in guided reading is ideal for teaching students how to extend meaning.

VALUES OF EXTENDING THE MEANING OF FICTIONAL AND FACTUAL TEXTS

Extending the meaning of texts that they read has high instructional value for children, especially as they become more competent at writing and able to read more complex texts. (See Figure 10-1.)

Extending meaning can prompt children to become more analytic in thinking about a particular text and should carry over to their reading of other texts. Through extension, you can demonstrate to children how to make the kinds of connections that enhance understanding. You can show them how ideas are organized in a text and guide them to grasp an important concept: that readers are required to *think* about their reading and to make judgments.

SOME CAUTIONS ABOUT EXTENSION

The major caution about extending the meaning of a text is this: Don't overdo it! In addition, be sure to:

- Have a real reason for extending the text.
- Engage children in extension only when the particular text warrants it.
- Use extension only when the text has potential for helping children learn something they really need.
- Remember that not every text is worth extending.

If extension is overdone, you can eat up a lot of time working on it, and that can have two consequences:

- You can take up so much time over the course of a week that children read only a few pages during that period.
- You can take up so much time on a given day that you miss reading with another group.

No matter how valuable the extension activity might be, it should not take the place of reading continuous text.

In guided reading, some texts serve the purpose of adding to readers' ability to sustain meaning while processing massive amounts of text. Children need to read and read and read. In the process, they pick up a great deal of new vocabulary, increase fluency, and build a more extensive knowledge of texts and how they are organized. But, as I have pointed out, some texts do not warrant extension. It is not that these texts provide nothing to think about—any text worth reading presents an opportunity to comprehend. But it may not be necessary to extend such texts. If you extend a text that does not really warrant extension, little learning occurs, and you run the risk of beating it to death and thus boring students and making them reluctant to read. Sometimes the best next action after talking about a book is simply to read another book. If students think they have to do an activity after every text they read—especially if this activity is writing—they will not look forward to reading. Be especially cautious with kindergarten and first-grade students, for whom writing takes longer and is more difficult.

Given these cautions, though, well-selected extensions clearly can be helpful to students. They also form a foundation of reflecting about and responding to texts that supports students' test-taking skills—skills that they will need in the third, fourth, and fifth grades.

Extended texts require short pieces of writing that provide evidence that the reader can think beyond the text; they also require analysis and comparison of texts. While primary students' reading should not be directed toward test taking, the kinds of extensions you use can naturally guide students to more analytic ways of looking at texts.

COMPARISON—EXTENDING THE MEANING OF FICTIONAL AND FACTUAL TEXTS

There are important differences in extending the meaning of fictional and factual texts. (See Figure 10-2.) I use the term "factual texts" because I like the idea of saying what a text *is* rather than what it is not (Freedman 1992). Factual or nonfiction texts have become much more important in elementary school—even primary grades—in recent years. We need to be cautious in asking students to read factual texts with extremely difficult concepts when they are just beginning to put together a reading process. We can, however, begin to introduce factual texts on familiar topics into guided reading lessons when students have built a basic reading process and are becoming more flexible in the kinds of structures they can use. Extending the meaning of the factual texts students read will help them to make this step.

It is easy to see that extending the meaning of both fiction and factual texts requires using all kinds of structures for thinking, including:

- Comparing and contrasting events, people, or natural phenomena.
- Following organizational patterns, such as sequence in time.
- Seeing relationships across time, among events, and for natural phenomena and processes.
- Thinking about characters' properties, motivations, attitudes, and actions.
- Predicting what may happen.
- Thinking about underlying causes.
- Finding evidence for hypotheses and conclusions.
- Reflecting on and reporting your own responses to a text.

In extending the meaning of fiction texts, the reader is working with what happens among people, between people, and within people. These occurrences may be created in the imagination of the writer, and may even be fantasy, but they have roots in the reality of basic human issues and problems. Characters may feel friendship or love for each other;

Extending the Meaning of Fictional and Factual Texts

Extending the meaning of a text means going beyond the literal meaning of a text to perform some kind of analytic thinking and to represent that thinking in a way that others understand.

FICTIONAL

Examples:

- Making hypotheses as to characters' motivations and thoughts.
- Predicting actions and events based on past events.
- Identifying the organizing structure of a text.
- Identifying evidence that points to conclusions about the meaning of the text.
- Describing relationships among elements of the text, e.g., setting (time, place) and the attitudes and motivations of characters or the events of the plot.
- Identifying the overarching theme of a story, e.g., friendship or love, triumphing over fear, loneliness, family and pets.
- Identifying how events in a narrative happen in a sequence and how one is connected with another.
- Identifying the problem of a narrative and generating alternative possibilities for solving it.
- Drawing conclusions about a character and evaluating his or her actions.

FACTUAL

Examples:

- Identifying and using the organizing structure or structures of the text.
- Using information in the text to interpret subsequent information as it is given.
- Understanding how ideas, events, or steps in a process are organized in a sequence and how one leads logically to another.
- Identifying comparisons that reveal the properties or characteristics of matter or human events.
- Identifying causes for phenomena—why physical or social events happen.
- Identifying and interpreting language that describes important characteristics of natural or social phenomena.
- Identifying main and subordinate categories of information (and linking to headings, subheadings, and sub-subheadings when necessary).
- Identifying and interpreting natural or social problems and their solutions.

FIGURE 10-2

they may feel fear of something in the environment or of other people. Characters are motivated by their underlying experiences, and they change in relation to events. Events may be understood in sequence, with one thing leading to another as the plot unfolds. Most texts for primary children are organized in temporal sequence rather than using literary devices such as *flashbacks*, but some present stories within stories that readers have to understand structurally.

Factual texts present ideas in juxtaposition to each other. Usually, ideas are organized into categories. To describe a species of animal, for example, the writer may present information in categories—what they eat, where they live, how their skin/fur feels, what their young look like and are called. The writer may use comparison and contrast to help readers understand natural or social phenomena (e.g., birds that fly and birds that do not fly). Writers of nonfiction may also use a sequence in time to explain natural or social phenomena (e.g., showing how tadpoles become frogs or how a dam is built) or show readers the causes of phenomena with step-by-step explanations (e.g., how water becomes polluted or what makes a volcano erupt).

Ways of Extending the Meaning of Texts

When you involve children in extending the meaning of texts, be sure to vary the texts and lessons because children will get tired of doing the same thing time after time. The activities also should also be suited to your purpose. Some ways of extending the meaning of texts are listed in Figure 10-3 and discussed briefly below.

EXTENDED DISCUSSION

A simple way of extending the meaning of a text is through discussion. Of course, you will always be discussing a text after reading it; but you may want to increase the time for and depth of discussion, depending upon the text. There are many different ways to organize discussion, including:

- Writing or drawing, then talking with a partner.
- Talking with a partner and then sharing in the group.
- Writing or drawing, then talking to the whole group.

Teach young children how to turn to a partner and talk for a few minutes, taking turns; then show them how to think of one important thing they said to share with the whole group. To help them refine their listening skills, ask them to repeat one thing their partners said.

As shown in Figure 10-4, one teacher who was working with early readers selected a text that was simple to read but actually contained some abstract concepts. The text was *Making a Memory* by Balinger (1997).

The idea of *making a memory* can be understood by young children but requires inference. These children read the text at very high accuracy, but the teacher wanted them to think about the meaning. She asked them to think about an object that they owned and that helped them *remember* something. She suggested examples, such as a teddy bear or a rock that they had collected. Children thought of objects such as a doll or a piece of jewelry. It was not important that children understood the idea of *memory* in an abstract sense, but that they thought about simple keepsakes and connected them to the story. Each child drew a picture of his or her object and talked about the object with the group the next day, which helped everyone reflect on the meaning of the story.

SHARED OR INTERACTIVE WRITING

Group writing is a highly effective way to quickly extend the meaning of texts. You might choose to do the writing yourself, involving children in the composition; this is *shared writing*. Alternatively, you might decide to have the children share the pen by coming to the easel and writing some of the letters and words; this is *interactive writing*. (See McCarrier, Pinnell, & Fountas 2000.) Interactive writing has the added value of focusing children's attention on the details of print; however, it takes longer and can produce less text in the time allotted. The decision about which method to use should be related to the children's needs.

As shown in Figure 10-4, the teacher used shared writing as a follow-up to extended oral

Some Variations in Extending Texts

- Extended partner discussion with guiding questions.
- Shared writing to demonstrate writing about text.
- Interactive writing to demonstrate and engage children in the process of writing about a text.
- Charts or diagrams (on easel with the whole group).
- "Quick writes" shared in partners or with the whole group.
- "Quick sketches" shared with partners or the whole group.
- Interpretive oral reading in partners or with the whole group.

FIGURE 10-3

Extending the Meaning of *Making a Memory*

TEXT: *Making a Memory* (Balinger 1997) LEVEL: D

GENRE: Fiction

PURPOSE—TO HELP STUDENTS TO:

- extend concepts (memory as an abstract idea).
- make connections to personal experience.

DESCRIPTION/SUMMARY OF TEXT:

This text is about a little girl who looks at a number of items that remind her of her memories. The text is framed by a picture of the girl looking at a number of items on a shelf. She is thinking about five items that remind her of each age between one and five. A thinking bubble appears on each page, showing the girl at each age. The text ends as she is making a memory for her dad by drawing something. The text is easy—one line of print and almost all of the words are high-frequency words except for *memory*. But the concept is abstract.

EXTENSION: The teacher asked children each to think about something they had that helped them remember something. She suggested some examples, including pictures, a toy, or something they might sleep with. Each child was asked to draw a picture of the memory and to bring it back to the group the next day. Then, the teacher asked each child to show the picture and talk about it. She put together a book, sized 11 by 17 inches, with print big enough that everyone in the group could see it. On each page, she printed a repetitive phrase, such as "This is Michael's memory," and "This is Javon's memory." Children were then asked to write a sentence or word about the object presented. They could label the object or write something. Two children simply labeled the picture:

Cassie wrote: "I love my teddy bear."

Karin wrote: "This is my book bag from my grandma."

FIGURE 10-4

discussion. After each student showed his or her picture and talked briefly about it, the teacher quickly put together a four-page book. This book measured 11 by 17 inches (small enough to conveniently hold in your hand) and contained print large enough to be seen by a small group. She glued each child's picture on a page and wrote, "This is ________'s memory" below it. She was careful to put the four words on one line and to place the print consistently on each page. Right beside the picture, she put one or two words as a label. Then, the group quickly read through the book. On the front she wrote, *Our Memories*, but she did not staple the book together. For writing that day, each child wrote another sentence about his or her picture. The result was a book that the students could place in their browsing box or the class library.

Another example of shared writing is shown in Figure 10-5 on the next page. The teacher was working with a small group of emergent readers who were reading a caption book called *Lunch* (Pinnell 2000) [Level A]. A caption book is a very easy book with repetitive language, extremely simple text, many high-frequency words, high picture support, consistent layout, and familiar content.

After reading *Lunch* and discussing it, the teacher made a *fold book* for each child. She took one piece of paper and folded it, as shown in Figure 10-6.

3	2 fold 1 (down)
4	**Title** 1

fold 2 (across)

Diagram of the four-page fold book from the KEEP BOOKS® Guide. **FIGURE 10-6**

Extending the Meaning of *Lunch*

TEXT: *Lunch* (Pinnell 2000) LEVEL: A

GENRE: Caption Book

PURPOSE—TO HELP STUDENTS TO:

- recognize patterns of language and understand how they help in reading.
- connect pictures with words and use them to understand the meaning.

DESCRIPTION/SUMMARY OF TEXT:
Lunch is a simple "caption book"—it contains one simple sentence in one line of print per page, and the print is directly related to the illustrations. On each page, a little girl goes through a cafeteria line and picks up one kind of food. The text on every page reads, "I like [kind of food]." On the last page, the text reads, "I like lunch."

EXTENSION: After an introduction, a group of emergent readers read through the book. The teacher's primary objective was to help them match word by word, and they did this successfully, with only a few errors. The teacher noticed that on a few content words (notably "sandwiches" and "bananas") several children hesitated and asked to be told the words. The goal here was not to learn these words; they are too hard for emergent readers and not useful. All members of the group successfully read "I," and "like," high-frequency words.

They could not have read words such as "apples," "bananas," "pizza," "sandwiches," "cookies," "milk," and "lunch" successfully in isolation (without picture support), but that is not a problem. These children were having their first experiences in reading and needed to move through a meaningful text on their own. The teacher wanted them to know that the pictures, as well as the first letter of a word, will help them figure out words they don't know. She decided to give them more practice in both reading and writing so that they could notice the details.

The teacher quickly made a *fold book* for each child by folding in half a piece of 8.5 by 11 paper and then folding it once more. The result was a four-page book. (See Figure 10-6.) On the front of each book, she wrote *"I like"* and asked each child to write his or her name. On the left inside page, she wrote *"I like* _______" and had each child write in the name of some kind of food (just like in the book) and draw a picture. To write the food's name, she helped them to "say the word slowly and think what to write." She filled in letters the children didn't know. She then asked each child to write about another food on the other page and to put their name on the front of the book. She ended the lesson by saying, "Bring your books to reading tomorrow and we will read them to each other."

FIGURE 10-5

She wrote *Lunch* on the cover of each book and had the children write their names below it. Then she asked the children to create two pictures of something they liked for lunch, one picture on each of the two inner pages. Thus, the book would have only two pages of print. Going around to each child, she wrote *I like* and helped each student think of and write the third word of the sentence (something for lunch). On the back of each book, she wrote *The End*. (The fronts and backs of these little books can be prepared in advance.) Each child read his or her book and brought it to the group the next day. Then the children each took home a book connected to the meaning of this story. This extension helped children learn a great deal about how print works, and to recognize patterns of language and the usefulness of pictures to check meaning.

QUICK WRITES AND QUICK SKETCHES, FOLLOWED BY DISCUSSION

As children grow more sophisticated in their use of written language, they can do a quick bit of writing, often preparatory to sharing and discussion. You might ask them to do the following, for example:

- Write some of the words that *Amelia Bedelia* (Parrish 1992) gets mixed up and be prepared to read your list.
- Write a sentence or two about the character you find most interesting.
- Write something that this story made you think about.
- Write something new that you learned or that surprised you.
- Write an important question you have about what might happen next in the story.
- Write a prediction.
- Write what you think might be the answer to the problem.
- Write about something you either like or don't like.
- Write a summary of what you've read so far (one or two sentences with *only* important details).
- Write the main idea of the story.
- Write some words that describe how a character feels (or that describe a character).

These "quick writes" form a foundation for discussion. In addition, they closely resemble some of the kinds of writing that students will be expected to do on proficiency tests. Frequently engaging in quick writes, perhaps in a Think Book (as described in Chapter 13 of this book) allows students to create a written record of some of their best thinking and also to self-evaluate their writing.

An alternative to quick writing, and one that students like, is quick sketching. This option is probably most effective as students become able to truly understand the difference between making a picture and quick sketching—probably in second grade. Quick sketches are not detailed drawings that take a long time to complete. Teach students how to sketch the bare basics of what they are thinking, demonstrating this process yourself. In three to four minutes, they can sketch something important from the setting or an important object that has significance in the story—a character, important traits, or a prediction of what they hope will happen next. Sketches, too, are a good foundation for talking. In explaining their drawings, students use language to talk about the text and, thus, deepen their understanding.

INTERPRETIVE ORAL READING

Another way to extend the meaning of texts is to think about how they should sound when read aloud. Select texts carefully for this option—not every text lends itself to being read aloud several times. Children should first read the text for meaning and discuss it. Then select a piece of the text for them to practice reading several times and then to read aloud. They can discuss how one's voice can make the story meaningful and enjoyable for others to hear. Students can even tape-record their readings so that others in the class or younger children can listen to them.

For example, a repetitive text such as *Henny Penny* (Zimmerman 1989) can be divided into parts for the characters and a narrator. This enjoyable tale has enormous potential for interpretive reading. Groups of children can join in on refrains; characters can assume different voices. When you read aloud with fluency and phrasing, you provide your own interpretation of the author's intended meaning; that is, you plumb the deep meaning of the text (see Chapter 8 for an exploration of the relationships between fluency and phrasing and comprehension). Other ideas for engaging children in interpretive reading are:

- Have children read a segment of the text as shared reading; discuss the way voices should sound.
- Have children share parts as partners, reading aloud to each other several times.
- Read the text yourself to demonstrate interpretive reading and then have the children read it as a group.

- Ask individuals to practice reading a small part of the text and have them read one after another.
- Ask children to work as partners to think of two ways to read a sentence or group of sentences. Talk about how the meaning is a little bit different depending upon which way the text is read.
- Divide the children into two groups and have each group read alternate lines of a text, or have one group repeat the reading of the same lines of a poetic text.
- Have the children practice interpretive reading in preparation for a performance for the rest of the class or another group.

Once children have learned to practice interpretive reading for themselves, they can do it as an independent activity. The problem, of course, is that the noise level may be disturbing to the group during reading workshop. Find another time in the day to schedule a practice and/or teach them to work softly, with a final practice at performance level.

CHARTS AND DIAGRAMS

Charts and diagrams can help students create a deeper understanding of a text. Graphic organizers have been used for years to provide a structure for directing students' attention to certain aspects of texts. I recommend using charts, diagrams, and graphic organizers, but with a great deal of caution. Be careful not to make a diagram into a worksheet that students simply struggle to fill out without thinking. Using diagrams effectively with students requires conversation, negotiation, and mutual decision making. For primary students, use the easel and work together to show them how to think in different ways about a text. Talk about what to put on the chart. This will be a powerful demonstration, one which helps students to see the inner workings of text. The demonstration might be anything from a simple listing of comments about the text or what students learned about a topic to a more complex diagram that illustrates the relationship between ideas. Below are a few examples.

Extending the Meaning of a Nonfiction Book

Nonfiction texts are quite difficult for young readers, and, in general, we do not use ones with complex content knowledge for children who are just beginning to put together a reading process. Young children do not have the necessary background knowledge to process complex nonfiction text, and they also still are struggling to match word-by-word, use visual information, and integrate sources of information. At this point, we cannot expect them to learn a lot of content from their reading.

A teacher selected a text called *Who Lives in a Tree?* (Canizares & Moreton 1998) [Level E] for a group of early readers who had established word-by-word matching. As shown in Figure 10-7, the text is easy but contains some difficult content words.

The sentence structure is quite simple: "[Animals] live in trees." But some of the animals were familiar to children and others were not. The teacher's goal was not to have the children learn to read all of the animal names, or even to learn about animals. She was relying on what the children knew; her strategy was to help children bring what they knew to their reading of an informational text. Working with the children, she asked them to generate the names of animals they knew, and they created their own chart, even adding to it some other animals that they knew lived in trees. The result was a chart that they could read and comprehend, using content knowledge as well as high-frequency words and general reading strategies.

Extending the Meaning of *Who Lives in a Tree?*

TEXT: *Who Lives in a Tree?* (Canizares & Moreton 1998) LEVEL: E

GENRE: Nonfiction

PURPOSE—TO HELP STUDENTS TO:

- understand concepts [many animals live in trees].
- understand concepts [names of familiar animals].
- figure out the first word of a sentence using the picture and first letter.

DESCRIPTION/SUMMARY OF TEXT:
This book's text is very simply patterned; however, its difficulty is greatly increased by the fact that each sentence begins with the name of a different animal who lives in a tree: raccoons, butterflies, foxes, ladybugs, chipmunks, hedgehogs, porcupines, owls, and bats, which live upside down. This text will require quite a bit of discussion in the introduction. Each page includes high-quality photographs of animals.

EXTENSION: Children needed to know the names of the animals to understand the text, so the teacher provided a rich introduction. The children processed the text fairly well, remembering most of the names of the familiar animals.

After the reading, the teacher decided to make a quick chart with some of the names of the animals. She wrote the question: "Who lives in a tree?" at the top of the chart.

She did not include all of the animals, because the point of the lesson was not to try to memorize unfamiliar animal names. She invited the children to remember animals from the text and to retell it. As they came up with the names of animals, she made a quick drawing of each on the chart. Then, she asked them to remember the text and wrote the sentence about the animal beside each one. They read it together. Next, she invited children to add to the chart. They added "Birds live in trees" and "Caterpillars live in trees." (See below.)

The final text had five lines, which the children read several times. There was a brief discussion of how to figure out the first word if it was really hard (check with the first letter, look at the picture, think what it could be, and say the word). The piece of writing went up in the room and was read by this group several more times.

Who lives in a tree?

- Raccoons live in trees.
- Squirrels live in trees.
- Owls live in trees.
- Birds live in trees.
- Caterpillars live in trees.

FIGURE 10-7

Extending the Meaning of *Stories Julian Tells*

Ann Cameron's books about the stories that Julian and his younger brother Huey tell are a wonderful resource for teachers. Each story involves a young boy telling something about his family life. In this example, I worked with a group of second graders who had previously read *The Stories Huey Tells* (Cameron 1995) and were now reading *The Stories Julian Tells* (Cameron 1981) [Level N.] (See Figure 10-8; also see Chapter 4.)

The children in the group were reading with high accuracy, so they had no trouble processing the text. But I wanted them to understand it at another level. One of my goals in the introduction was to help them understand and appreciate the author's use of figurative language, such as:

> "A wonderful pudding," my father said. "It will taste like a whole raft of lemons. It will taste like a night on the sea." (p. 2)

The children enthusiastically talked about the idea of using interesting language to describe just how good the pudding really was.

Another goal was to help these beginning readers to think about characters. This story, which was interesting and easy to read, was a good place to start. I made a chart—one for Julian and one for Huey—and began to generate ideas about how the boys were alike and different. The children were able to look through the two books and several stories to draw out some statements about the characters. The chart was kept in the classroom as a resource; as individuals or groups read more about Julian and Huey, they added to the chart.

Extending the Meaning of *The Stories Julian Tells*

TEXT: "Catalog Cats" (Cameron 1981) LEVEL: N

GENRE: Realistic Fiction–Short Stories

PURPOSE—TO HELP STUDENTS TO: understand characters.

DESCRIPTION/SUMMARY OF TEXT:
This text is a collection of short stories told by a young boy, about seven years old. Each chapter is a different story; the central characters are Julian, his little brother Huey, and his dad.

In this story, Julian's dad asks the boys if they liked to plant gardens, and they said "yes." Dad announced then that he would order a *catalog*. Afterward, when the boys were alone, Huey asked Julian, What's a catalog? Julian is very imaginative, and spun a tale about a catalog being full of "catalog cats" that jump out and run around when you open it. Huey believed Julian and asked his father every day if the catalog had come; he even dreamed about these wonderful cats.

When the catalog came and Dad opened it, Huey began to cry. Julian was forced to confess that Huey thought the catalog had cats in it. Dad looked stern and Julian thought he was in trouble, but Dad solved the problem by telling Huey that catalog cats were invisible and moved so fast you couldn't see them. Also, cats didn't come in the catalog; they had to be requested. He added that catalog cats were around the garden, and if you worked hard, they helped you by making the work go faster, even if you couldn't see them. The story ends with Huey's written request for catalog cats.

EXTENSION: A group of second graders had read *The Stories Huey Tells* and the first story in *The Stories Julian Tells*. Their discussion after reading focused on Julian and his imagination. The teacher asked them to talk with their partners about something they imagined when they were little. They could also share something a younger brother or sister or cousin imagined. They talked for a few minutes and then the teacher asked for one or two examples from the group.

The teacher then turned the discussion to what Julian and Huey were like. In some ways the two boys are alike and in some ways they are different. She generated ideas from the group and got comments such as:

> "They both got imaginations."
> "Julian is big and Huey is littler."
> "Huey gets Julian in trouble."
> "Julian is bossy."

She then guided the children to record their ideas on a comparison chart. This chart could be added to as the group read more stories in *The Stories Julian Tells*. If children read more books in this series, they could return to the chart and add more comments.

Julian

* Likes lemon pudding
* Has imagination
* Tells stories about Huey
* Bosses Huey around
* Gets in trouble
* Likes Gloria
* Likes the dark

Huey

* Likes lemon pudding
* Has imagination
* Tells stories about Julian
* Believes what Julian says
* Gets Julian in trouble
* Likes Gloria
* Doesn't like the dark

FIGURE 10-8

Extending the Meaning of *The Little Red Hen*

A folktale is organized in a very traditional way. The bare bones of the story are easy to see. There are a series of events, predictable language, a predictable conclusion, and, often, a lesson to be learned. Working with a group of first graders who were reading *The Little Red Hen* (Galdone 1973) [Level J], I helped them reflect on the structural elements of this text. (See Figure 10-9.)

First, I asked students to think of the characters in two categories: the ones who worked and the ones that were lazy. They had no problem making this distinction. The characters in folktales are flat, meaning that they are not complex. What they seem to be on the surface is what they are, and they seldom change except when they are learning a very obvious lesson.

During the first day of reading this 37-page story, the children generated the first two tasks that the Little Red Hen accomplished—she planted the wheat and tended the wheat. At each point in the plot, the lazy animals simply said, "Not I." On the second day of reading, the children finished the story and listed several more events. The lazy animals said, "Not I," until the last event, when, of course, they said, "I will." This simple chart helped readers to look closer at the structure of the story and provided them with an explicit example of temporal sequence—an important way of organizing both fiction and nonfiction texts.

Extending the Meaning of *The Little Red Hen*

TEXT: *The Little Red Hen* (Galdone 1973) LEVEL: J

GENRE: Folktale

PURPOSE—TO HELP STUDENTS TO:

- understand the structure of the folktale.

DESCRIPTION/SUMMARY OF TEXT: In this familiar tale, the Little Red Hen does all the work to bake a cake, from planting the wheat to baking it. The lazy cat, dog, and mouse refuse to help. At the end, the Little Red Hen ate every last crumb of the cake herself. After that, the cat, dog, and mouse became willing helpers.

EXTENSION: After the introduction, children read this 37-page story over two days in a guided reading lesson. After they discussed the whole story (and how the characters changed) on the second day, the teacher guided them to make a story map to show sequence of events.

She drew two rows, one to show what the Little Red Hen did, and one to show what the cat, dog, and mouse did. Children generated the following:

Characters	What they did							
Little Red Hen	Plant the wheat	Tend the wheat	Cut the wheat	Take the wheat to the mill	Gather the sticks	Build the fire	Mix the cake	Eat the cake!
Cat **Dog** **Mouse**	Not I Not I Not I	Not I Not I Not I	Not I Not I Not I	Not I Not I Not I	Not I Not I Not I	Not I Not I Not I	Not I Not I Not I	I will! I will! I will!

And then they were all eager helpers!

FIGURE 10-9

Extending the Meaning of *Henry and Mudge Get the Cold Shivers*

The *Henry and Mudge* series by Cynthia Rylant provides many stories about a young boy and his huge dog Mudge. These stories are full of emotions that surround everyday life experiences. In *Henry and Mudge Get the Cold Shivers* (Rylant 1989) [Level J], children first read about Henry's sick days, when he stays in bed and gets lots of presents. (Mudge gets crackers.) But then Mudge gets sick, and Henry is very worried. Rylant describes the visit to the vet and the way Henry takes care of Mudge.

This extension (see Figure 10-10) illustrates the use of the compare/contrast structure to analyze an aspect of text. One characteristic of Rylant's craft is the way she juxtaposes Henry's experiences, emotions, and attitudes with Mudge's experiences, emotions, and attitudes. The text is engaging, partly because of this parallel structure. While these second graders were not ready to examine craft in a formal way, the teacher wanted them to recognize what the writer was doing. She asked them to compare Henry's sick days with Mudge's and to make a chart of items for each character. (See Figure 10-10.) The children added some of their own inferences, ideas that were not explicitly mentioned in the text. They underlined the items that were actually mentioned in the text, as opposed to what probably happened but was not mentioned. They also starred the things about Henry and Mudge's sick days that were exactly alike and checked those that were similar. An interesting discussion took place around the idea that Henry got Popsicles and Mudge got ice cubes. One student brought up the two ideas, and the children agreed that the articles were alike because they were frozen and melted when you eat them. Finally, they drew lines between items that were connected. These second graders had analyzed a text and clearly extended the meaning.

Extending the Meaning of *Henry and Mudge Get the Cold Shivers*

TEXT: *Henry and Mudge Get the Cold Shivers* (Rylant 1989) **LEVEL:** J

GENRE: Realistic Fiction

PURPOSE—TO HELP STUDENTS TO:

- notice and remember details that make the story interesting.
- understand the structure of the text, i.e., the way information is organized to make the story interesting.

DESCRIPTION/SUMMARY OF TEXT:
This story in the *Henry and Mudge* series focuses on Mudge's trip to the vet. The story begins with a description of what happens when Henry gets sick—he stays in bed and gets Popsicles, comic books, and crackers. (Mudge eats the crackers.) Then, Mudge gets sick and has to go to the vet, who diagnoses him with a cold. Mudge didn't like going to the vet, as shown in a memory "bubble" from his "puppyhood." Henry fixes a "sickbed" for Mudge and gives him ice cubes, a rubber hamburger, a rubber hot dog, and crackers. (Henry eats the crackers.) This book is full of emotions from childhood: Henry worries about Mudge and takes care of him. The story's parallel structure makes the text coherent.

After reading the story, the children discussed how Henry must have felt when Mudge was sick; he'd never been sick before. They also found evidence in the text that Henry cared about Mudge:

> "He put his old blanket and baseball mitt and pillow in Mudge's bed."
>
> "He was worried in the doctor's office."
>
> "He brought him things just like Henry's mom and dad brought him things."

They discussed the word "vet" and compared it to "doctor."

EXTENSION: The teacher asked the children to compare Henry's sick days and Mudge's sick days by listing what happened in each. They made a chart:

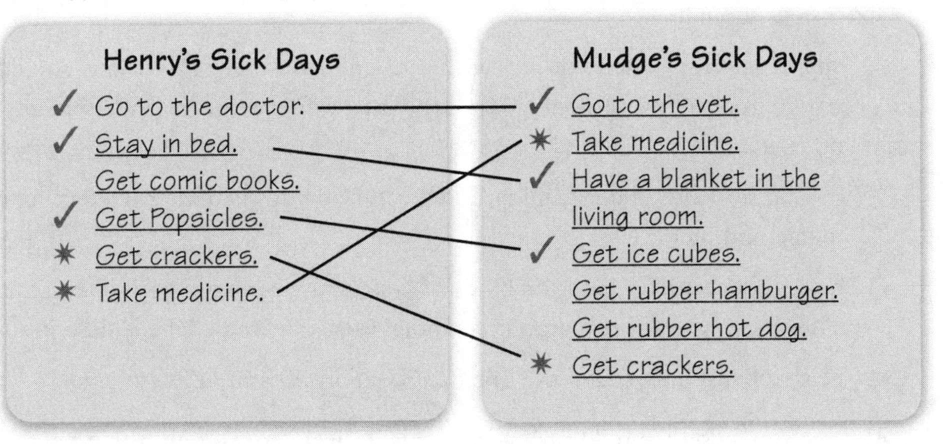

They underlined the events that were actually mentioned in the story after adding ones they had guessed had occurred. They put a star by the things that were exactly alike and a check by the things that were almost alike, connecting those items with a line.

FIGURE 10-10

Extending the Meaning of *Nate the Great and the Lost List*

The *Nate the Great* mysteries are a wonderful resource to help young children begin to understand this genre.

As shown in Figure 10-11, I worked with a group of second graders who were learning more about the organizational structure of a mystery. In *Nate the Great and the Lost List* (Sharmat 1981) [Level K], Nate (a young, self-styled detective) and his dog Sludge set out to find his friend Claude's grocery list. The children read the story over two days. Each day, at the end of the designated reading, I asked them to list the clues that they had uncovered. One of the understandings here is that when you read a mystery, you notice details that are important to the plot. At the end of the reading, we had listed all the clues. We then went back and reflected on the reading.

We asked: "Why was that detail a clue?" We also discussed whether the clue was informative or not. After all, a detective finds many clues and rejects some. Using a very simple story, this list helped children uncover the structure of a mystery tale.

Summary

Extending the meaning of a text is not an add-on activity or an exercise that you do after reading every text. Keep in mind the cautions I explained when planning extension activities. As you work with texts, you will be able to sense when a natural extension will help to deepen students' understanding of a particular text and expand their comprehending abilities. The extensions should:

- engage students' interest at a deeper level and help them understand the inner workings of texts so that they can apply that information to understanding other texts.
- expand students' understanding of textual elements, such as characters, setting, theme, and plot.
- help students understand the kinds of structures frequently used in informational texts, such as compare/contrast, temporal sequence, cause/effect, description, etc.
- help students understand the organizational patterns in different genres.

Above all, extension should involve students in lively conversation that enhances their enjoyment of texts. Comprehension is in fact *about* enjoyment, not a tedious exercise undertaken to obtain a grade or prepare for a test. As adults, we enjoy reading because we comprehend it. Extending the meaning of a text should contribute to students' insights and enjoyment.

Extending the Meaning of *Nate the Great and the Lost List*

TEXT: *Nate the Great and the Lost List* (Sharmat 1981) LEVEL: K

GENRE: Mystery

PURPOSE—TO HELP STUDENTS TO:

- learn more about the organizational structure of a mystery.

DESCRIPTION/SUMMARY OF TEXT: Nate the Great and his dog Sludge set out to find his friend Claude's grocery list, which is essential if they are to have lunch.

EXTENSION: As children read the story over two days, they were asked to identify and report clues that helped Nate solve the mystery of the missing list. After their reading on day one and day two (at the end of the story), the teacher wrote the clues on a chart, along with why those clues were important.

Nate the Great and the Lost List		
Clues	**Why Is It a Clue?**	**Is It a Good Clue?**
The paper blew to Rosamund's house.	Maybe Claude's list blew the same way.	Yes
Rosamund was all white.	She was making pancakes that tasted fishy.	Yes
Fang had a paper.	It might be the list that he dropped.	No
Eggs and baking powder were on the list.	Nate made pancakes and used eggs and baking powder.	No
Rosamund mixed everything together to make cat pancakes.	The list looked like a recipe to her for fishy pancakes.	Yes

FIGURE 10-11

Ideas to Try

1. Meet with grade-level colleagues to discuss the role of extension in guided reading and to plan for using this technique.

2. Prior to the meeting, choose at least three books to use for the next week's guided reading lessons for each group. Bring these books to the meeting.

3. During the meeting, talk about what you want students to learn to do as readers. Then, through discussion, select two books that offer appropriate opportunities for extension. Using this chapter as a resource, plan two extensions. Plan to use a chart to demonstrate the process to children.

   - List materials you will need and organize them so that you can move quickly into the extension activity.
   - Write a succinct statement of what you will say to the children so that they understand what you want them to do as well as why they are doing it.
   - Draw the chart with a few examples on it. (You will be asking children to generate examples, but you will want to have a few in mind to show them what you mean.)

4. After the meeting, gather materials and implement the extensions with your students.

5. Have a follow-up meeting to share written products and talk about what children learned.

CHAPTER 11

Interactive Read-Aloud: Supporting and Expanding Strategies for Comprehension

Diane E. DeFord

Young children can be quite insistent when they want to hear one of their favorite stories—so much so that I know some parents groan at the thought of reading *that* story one more time. I can remember my own joy as a child while listening to a story about Poppy, a tiny fairy. My mother never seemed to tire, though, of my frequent requests to read Poppy, or of hauling me up onto her lap and opening the worn Child Craft book that held my favorite story. What is it that drew me to request that story and others, to relish in hearing them time and again? It was emotional satisfaction and the joy of learning. These books were associated with being in a warm, safe place, and there was excitement in hearing their familiar language, experiencing an anticipated event, or savoring a character's dilemma. I still read some books again and again, as if they are friends to become reacquainted with after an unwanted separation.

I have observed children in many classrooms who have this same experience when listening to stories read aloud. I was in a New Zealand classroom with my camera a few years ago and snapped the picture below. The faces of these children show how engaged they are in the story being read to them by their kindergarten teacher.

Kindergarten students listen to their teacher read aloud.

I recently watched this same magical response appear in a group of sixth- through eighth-grade teachers. I was reading a short story to them—"Licked" by Paul Jennings (1995). These teachers laughed, choked, and cried out in amazement at points during the reading. One teacher was so caught up in this bizarre tale that she ran out of the room during the story. When she heard that Andrew, the young main character, licked some "chewy brown goo" and "crunched a bit of crispy black stuff" off a yellow flyswatter, she put her hand over her mouth and ran. When she returned, she was quite pale.

Books offer new information, new worlds to visit, powerful language, characters that make us cry or laugh, and experiences that we make our own, even if we have not actually encountered them in our own lives. There is a certain power in what Cullinan calls "fundamental lessons"—those lessons instilled in each one of us as books are shared. She says:

> Children who do not hear stories will have few reasons for wanting to learn to read. Those who have stories read to them will become readers and inevitably will become parents who read to their own children. It is a family legacy to be passed on to the next generation. Family storybook reading could break the cycle of the crippling inheritance of illiteracy that plagues many families (Taylor & Strickland 1986).

When we feel we have something to learn, our engagement is high. No matter where we are, or how old we are, a good book captures us and transports us into a different place. This is magical. Beyond pleasure, books help us learn, even teaching us lessons we are not aware we have learned. But we learn, nonetheless.

In one classic research study conducted in England in 1986, Gordon Wells showed the powerful lessons that children learned from reading experiences prior to school. Wells studied children from two years of age until they finished sixth grade. He found that children's literacy knowledge at age five was the single, strongest predictor of student achievement at age 10. Children who attained higher scores on a knowledge-of-literacy test before school began were more likely to have parents who read more and owned more books; these parents were also likely to

Children's independent reading further develops their knowledge of reading and writing.

read more often to their children. In subsequent research, Wells found that these children showed more interest in reading and writing, asked more about the meanings of words, noticed more about letters, and were likely to spend more time on activities associated with reading and writing.

Children's progress in reading and writing is the product of adult-child (or sibling-child) interactions that involve literacy, the child's independent explorations of written language, and observations of others using written language (Teale 1986). These interactions continue to have an impact throughout the elementary school years. The literacy experiences children engage in with parents and teachers, and their daily, independent reading makes a difference in their literacy achievement. The time parents spend in dinner conversation, for example, and in support of students' schoolwork, reading, and discussion of their personal interests, has an impact on students' literacy achievement (Anderson, Wilson, & Fielding 1988).

Wells' research (1986) found that the amount of help parents gave with schoolwork and the model they provided of the value of literacy in their own lives (the frequency with which they engaged in reading and writing themselves) contributed to student achievement in literacy. In the study by Anderson and his colleagues (1988), among all the different ways children spend their time in second through fifth grade, reading books was the best predictor of reading achievement. Unfortunately, on most days, most children did little or no book reading outside of school.

If we are to have an impact on children's literacy levels, we must make sure that we demonstrate the importance of books to children every day, during the school day. Sharing books through interactive read-alouds within the literacy framework of the school day can make a big difference in how children use books and what they understand about books as they read and write. This chapter describes interactive read-alouds, sets forth some guidelines for selecting and using books during interactive read-alouds, and discusses how interactive read-alouds support and extend children's strategies and comprehension.

What Is Interactive Read-Aloud?

Reading aloud to children has long been a central part of the reading curriculum in schools (Holdaway 1979; Teale 1984; Wan 2000). The use of the term "interactive" is purposeful, intended to suggest that during read-aloud there should be an intentional, ongoing invitation to students to actively respond and interact *within* the oral reading of a story. Jeane Copenhaver (2001) tells of a story-reading time one night with her six-year-old daughter, Alison. Alison kept interrupting her and Jeane kept saying, "Alison, let me finish this page, and *then* you can tell me what the page makes you think about or remember," or

"It's not polite to interrupt the person who is reading to you." As she thought about the interactions she and Alison had had that evening, she realized that she was *discouraging* her daughter from connecting this book to her own life. Realizing this, she was chagrined.

Of course, this pattern of interaction—adult reads, child listens—is all too often the way that read-aloud is enacted in a classroom setting. If there is interaction during read-aloud time, it is either explicitly invited by the teacher or children raise their hands for permission to speak. Recent research suggests that when a different pattern of interaction is encouraged—a more authentic conversational pattern—children are encouraged to use their own experience, their peers, and the teacher to engage in *meaning-making* (Beach 1993; McGee 1995; Wells 1995). This type of interaction is far more supportive of students' developing strategies and comprehension, as well as more empowering for the learner (Huck, Hepler, & Hickman 1993). Hickman (1992) refers to this type of response pattern as *free response* to literature. She explains that "if children are given a chance to make their own comments about stories before their attention is directed one way or another by focused questions, they will reveal perceptions and preoccupations that they bring on their own to literature" (p. 187). In the give-and-take of an interactive read-aloud, readers share experiences, bond with one another, and become active participants in the unfolding of the story or text. Active learning is the goal as you and your students discuss high-quality literature, nonfiction, and poetry.

Selecting and Using Books for Interactive Read-Aloud

The first and most important criterion for selecting books for interactive read-aloud is to find texts that will interest and engage students. A book's illustrations could be particularly interesting, or its topic could be one that draws upon students' interests and experiences, but the text ought to connect with their own lives. It is critical to select books that have themes, topics, and characters that lend themselves to meaningful discussions; that have artistic qualities that students can appreciate; and that will introduce children to new genres, authors and illustrators, and styles of writing (Fountas & Pinnell 2001). Because children bring their own cultural and racial histories to the story setting, interactive read-aloud offers an excellent opportunity to introduce them to different cultural and racial experiences. How they relate to these different experiences depends upon the choices you make for interactive read-aloud (Diller 1999; hooks 1995; Tatum 1997).

Selecting books that you love will demonstrate your own excitement about reading. Your excitement will be contagious, and your students will clamor for the opportunity to be the first to get their hands on each read-aloud book. If you think about interactive read-aloud as a public forum for discussing books (both short and long) that serve a variety of purposes (to inform, to enjoy, to encourage connections, to introduce interesting characters, etc.), you will be able to plan a balanced curriculum. So it is helpful to keep an ongoing record of the books you read, and to sample students' responses to gauge the success of the texts you choose. When they request to hear books again, you will know that you have struck a chord and found a book that helps them continue to learn with repeated readings.

As children experience a repertoire of books by the same author, or books that have noticeable similarities or differences, they will naturally begin to make comparisons and relate one book or illustration to another. As you help children interpret events and characters' actions from different perspectives, they will begin to make their own observations. Careful attention to their responses (both verbal and nonverbal) will help you gather information about their awareness of text features, characterization, themes, or cultural practices. Then, as children become more sophisticated, you can build upon their responses and introduce more complex texts. Louise Rosenblatt (1969) was one of the early proponents of encouraging a more open response to literature. She suggests that if we "wish young people to participate in literature, we have to be concerned about the world they live in, the experiences they bring to the text. We must offer them works to which something in their own lives, their own preoccupations, and their own linguistic habits can serve as a bridge" (p. 1,012). Rosenblatt challenges us to provide a "more fertile kind of inductive process…in which the students themselves raise the questions" (p. 1,011). When we select books that engage children in discussion and response, they can join with us in creating links between their own world and the world of books.

Planning an Interactive Read-Aloud

Figure 11-1 offers suggestions for planning an interactive read-aloud. First, read the book you selected and think about its best characteristics. Decide where you might want to stop reading and encourage children to think about the language, story, and/or illustrations. If the book has some natural sections or breakpoints where children can offer comments, predict, or respond, you may want to mark them in some way. (Many teachers find sticky notes helpful for this purpose.) Be prepared to respond as a reader yourself, and also be able

to guide the discussion when necessary. Some easy-to-spot points to invite children into the conversation are:

- when you arrive at informational sections, such as the endpapers;
- when the children are thinking about what they know or guess about the story; and
- when they want to talk about a particular character based on information gained from the cover, illustrations, or back of the book.

Before you start, make sure the children are seated comfortably, preferably where they can see the book's illustrations. Talk with them about why you chose this book, and give them some information about the book, the genre, the author, and/or the illustrations. There are some wonderful books available about authors, from which you can get bibliographic information designed for use with children. In addition, numerous Web sites offer such information (see the resource list of Internet sites for authors at the end of this chapter).

As you read, watch the children for their verbal and nonverbal responses. Draw them into conversation as it seems appropriate, or pause so that they have a chance to respond. Remember that the observations, questions, and connections triggered by the reading are important to this experience.

Planning an Interactive Read-Aloud

- Read the book to decide on places to stop or pause.
- Consider natural break points.
- Respond as a reader yourself.
- See that children are seated comfortably.
- Make sure they can see the illustrations.
- Set a purpose and provide necessary information.
- Draw children into the conversation.
- Observe students' responses.
- Make notes as necessary.

FIGURE 11-1

Supporting and Expanding Strategies for Sustaining Reading

Interactive read-aloud is a perfect setting in which to demonstrate and discuss strategies that sustain the reading process. Read-aloud allows you to provide a model of phrased, fluent reading. It helps children to notice and savor the beauty of written language, to expand their vocabulary and experiential base, and to extend their thinking. You can show the children how to focus on the sound and meaning of new or unfamiliar words and on subtleties of meaning. Fountas and Pinnell (2001) point out systems of strategies that help sustain the reading process, and discuss a range of problem-solving strategies for recognizing or decoding words and deriving meaning in connected text. (See Figure 11-2.)

For example, it is necessary that readers monitor their reading for how they keep their processing on track. While processing a text, readers check that what they say looks right (a visual check), whether it makes sense (checking for meaning), and whether it sounds right (a check for grammatical or syntactic appropriateness). If their reading does not fit with all three of these cueing systems, then they need to reread to correct possible errors, phrasing, or the use of punctuation. This type of monitoring keeps the reading process moving forward with meaning as the goal. As readers progress through the text, they gather information that is important to their continued understanding. They may identify literary concepts such as the plot, theme, symbolism, or hints to different characters' intentions.

For readers to keep their attention on meaning, their word-solving strategies need to be quick enough to read unfamiliar words and to maintain fluency, or to adjust their reading to a variety of circumstances (when the reading is hard, or when it is easy). As you plan for and conduct interactive read-aloud sessions, you can guide, model, and talk about the reader's craft in ways that will support children's processing when they read independently.

Strategies for Sustaining Reading

- Monitoring for meaning, syntax, and visual information
- Predicting
- Word-solving
- Gathering information
- Maintaining fluency
- Adjusting reading in relation to the text and purpose for reading

(Fountas & Pinnell 2001, pp. 312-313)

FIGURE 11-2

Supporting and Expanding Strategies for Comprehension

As children talk about books, they naturally use the kinds of strategies that support and expand comprehension. When they make connections and form analogies that connect books to their own experiences and to the world around them, they are deepening their understanding. In conversation with others, language users are required to synthesize information, make inferences, analyze information, summarize information, and make judgments. Interactive read-aloud is intended to be a *structured routine* where the conversation is about books, authors, experiences, and the construction of meaning that is propelled forward with each new book. These routines serve as structuring situations (Wertsch 1985; Wood, Bruner, & Ross 1976) in which you purposefully transfer responsibility (for thinking and acting like a reader and writer, for making judgments, etc.) from you to the group and then to individual children. The guidance provided during interactive read-aloud helps children develop systems of strategies for comprehending text (Fountas & Pinnell 2001). You model these strategies, guide children to use them within the discussion, and praise children when they initiate using these strategies for themselves.

The key strategies that are supported within interactive read-aloud are connecting, inferring, summarizing, synthesizing, analyzing, and critiquing. (See Figure 11-3.) These strategies support and extend comprehension. The goal is to observe children's use of these strategies and the opportunities texts provide for highlighting these strategies within text, so that children can increase their ability to use them during independent reading, guided reading, and writing workshop.

The connections that children make can be quite varied—connections between books by the same author, as well as between the read-aloud text and other books that deal with the same topic, illustration techniques, social issues, characters, and historical events.

Strategies for Expanding Meaning

- Connecting
- Inferring
- Summarizing
- Synthesizing
- Analyzing
- Critiquing

(Fountas & Pinnell 2001, pp. 314-315)

FIGURE 11-3

These connections lead readers to use their skills of comparison and contrast to explore similarities and differences. During an interactive read-aloud you may encourage the children to relate their personal experiences, world experiences, and other text experiences to extend meaning. Making such connections leads readers to go beyond the literal meaning of a given text and to talk about what is implied by characters' actions, events, and motives. These inferences in turn lead children to form hypotheses; respond emotionally to feel empathy toward characters and other people; and create sensory images about characters, plot, setting, and themes. They learn to understand what is implied, but not stated.

Relating one thing to another, inferring, and summarizing are the building blocks of thinking. As readers compare and contrast, then summarize or distill information from a variety of sources, they must synthesize information and integrate new knowledge into their existing knowledge base. Learning how to analyze texts and offer critiques of the books they read provides children with the most complex strategies they need to learn. Unfortunately, these strategies are often taught through worksheets rather than in ways that most benefit children. In interactive read-aloud, however, books are shared in a more natural context to help children understand how the different genre are organized and how they serve different purposes. Children learn to recognize the different features of texts—the unique forms of language used in poetry, the factual base of informational materials, and the characteristics of different forms of fiction (tales, realistic fiction, etc.).

As children analyze illustrations, look at maps and charts, and learn to use literary features of text, they grow in their ability to comprehend and respond to texts. This process is the essence of expanding comprehension. Interactive read-aloud is the support system children need to learn these complex strategies and apply them independently.

Summary

Our goal is to support readers. We want them to grow in confidence, become articulate, and be able to engage in rich conversations about books. If we are reflective in our interactions with children, they will learn to be reflective themselves. If we support them in thinking critically, they will become more sensitive to the writer's craft. But most of all, we want to instill in them the love of the craft of books—illustration, rich language, and symbolism. We are building the resources that readers will draw on throughout their lives, and creating lifelong readers.

The journey is exciting. When books are shared aloud, different perspectives, richer analyses, and broader learning opportunities result because of the diversity inherent in today's classrooms. The love of books, new experiences, and the beauty of language are discovered through the pages of wonderful books.

Ideas to Try

1. Share several of your favorite picture books with a group of colleagues and look carefully at both the text and illustrations to identify unique characteristics of the author's or illustrator's craft that you might discuss with students during an interactive read-aloud. Such sharing usually leads to new insights about the book.

2. Review one or two of the professional books, journals, or Web sites listed at the end of this chapter to select new books for your school or classroom library. Visit a bookstore to look at other new titles before making your decision.

3. Videotape your class while sharing a book during an interactive read-aloud. Look for ways you invited children to respond. What worked? What did not? What new insights do you have about your students as readers because of their participation in the reading of the book?

4. Ask your local librarian for assistance in finding books related to some favorite read-alouds your students have enjoyed. Find books by the same author or illustrator. Look for books with similar themes or characters. Read the new books with your class and invite them to make connections between the familiar favorites and the new stories.

Professional Resources for Teachers

PROFESSIONAL BOOKS

Kaleidoscope: A Multicultural Booklist for Grades K-8 by Barrera, R. B., V. D. Thompson, & M. Dressman, Eds. NCTE Bibliography Series. National Council of Teachers of English.

Beyond Words: Picture Books for Older Readers and Writers by Benedict, S. & L. Carlisle, Eds. Heinemann.

Picture Books: An Annotated Bibliography with Activities for Teaching Writing by Culham, R. Northwest Regional Educational Laboratory.

Multicultural Literature for Children and Young Adults by Kruse, G. M., K. T. Horning, & M. Schliesman. Wisconsin Department of Public Instruction. University of Wisconsin-Madison.

Beyond Heroes and Holidays: A Practical Guide to K-12 Anti-racist, Multicultural Education and Staff Development by Lee, E., D. Menkart, & M. Okazawa-Rey, Eds. Network of Educators on the Americas.

Adventuring with Books: A Booklist for Pre-K-Grade 6 by Pierce, K. M., Ed. NCTE Bibliography Series. National Council of Teachers of English.

Children's Books from Other Countries by Tomlinson, C. M., Ed. Scarecrow Press.

PROFESSIONAL JOURNALS OFFERING BOOK REVIEWS

Journal of Children's Literature. Children's Literature Assembly.

Language Arts. National Council of Teachers of English.

The Horn Book Magazine. Horn Book, Inc.

The New Advocate. Christopher-Gordon Publishers.

The Reading Teacher. International Reading Association.

INTERNET SITES

Web Search Engines

www.google.com

www.bess.net

www.yahooligans.com

www.ajkids.com

www.kidsclick.org

Additional Author Sites

www.ipl.org/div/natam/
This site, the Internet Public Library site for Native American authors, was developed by graduate students at the University of Michigan. It contains information on more than 450 authors and 1,400 books, and includes links to more than 1,400 additional sites.

www.lang.nagoya-u.ac.jp/~matsuoka/AmeLit.html
This site provides links to sites to research classic authors (Edgar Allen Poe, Nathaniel Hawthorne, etc.) for older students and adults.

www.ucalgary.ca/~dkbrown/authors.html
The Children's Literature Web Guide (CLWG) includes Internet resources related to books for, and authors who are writing for, children and young adults. The site has quick references for the different children's book awards, discussion boards for children, and information about conferences. There are also resources for parents and teachers, journals, book reviews, research guides, and indexes to aid users in doing Internet research. This site is maintained by the University of Calgary.

www.people.virginia.edu/~jbh/author.html
Authors On the Web includes biographical sketches of authors. It is organized in alphabetical order for ease of locating featured authors (for both adults and children).

falcon.jmu.edu/~ramseyil/biochildhome.htm
This Internet index to children's and young adult authors and illustrators is maintained by the Internet School Library's Media Center. There are bibliographies of authors, conference and presentation dates, chat rooms, and personal information about authors.

www.scils.rutgers.edu/~kvander/Authorsite/index.html
Rutgers University maintains this site featuring biographies and autobiographies of children's and young adult authors and illustrators. The site links lead to information about resources for teachers.

www.ipl.org/div/kidspace/askauthor/authorinfo.html
The Internet Public Library offers answers to Frequently Asked Questions and biographical information on favorite authors.

www.carolhurst.com/authors/authors.html
Carol Hurst's Children's Literature Site reviews authors (Avi, Betsy Byars, Eric Carle, Barbara Cooney, Dr. Seuss, Jean Fritz, Kevin Henkes, Pat Hutchins, Kathryn Lasky, Lois Lowry, James Marshall, Phyllis Naylor, Katherine Paterson, Seymour Simon) and provides links to professional sites.

www.cynthialeitichsmith.com/authors-illustrators.htm
This is Cynthia L. Smith's Web page about authors and illustrators of children's books. The site includes multicultural and ethnic categories as special features.

www.edupaperback.org/top100.html
The Educational Paperback Association's top 100 authors page includes biographies of each author and grade-level designations. This site often includes special features (African American History Month, book awards, etc.).

www.childrenslit.com/f_mai.htm
This site allows you to "meet children's authors" through detailed biographies and reviews of books by favorite writers.

PART III

Facilitating Effective Teaching Through Organized Productive Independent Work

The chapters in Part III present information on the support system for effective teaching and learning. Without good organization and management, teaching for comprehending strategies is impossible. The first chapter in this section explores what makes managed independent learning work, while Chapter 13 explores shifts in management and teaching that will meet learners' needs as they grow more sophisticated in their ability to read and write. The final chapter presents some frequently asked questions about classroom management.

CHAPTER 12

Problem-Solving Managed Independent Learning: What Makes It Work?*

Barbara Joan Wiley & Justina Henry

*This chapter is based on a presentation entitled, "What Makes Managed Independent Learning Work?" which was given by Barbara Joan Wiley, Kecia Hicks, Sheila Blue, and Sue Oxenrider at the June 2000 Literacy Collaborative Institute, Columbus, Ohio.

We get our best information about teaching and learning by looking closely at what happens in classrooms. As researchers and teachers, we are faced with a decision. Should we look at a phenomenon when something is going wrong to figure out what is causing the problem and what will fix it? After all, much of our information on reading has come from studying learning difficulties. Or should we find situations where something is working well and search for what is making it work, as Clay (1966) did in her landmark study of good readers? Her findings provide much insight into early literacy learning, as well as how to help young struggling readers.

We wanted to investigate a topic that is of constant concern to teachers: how students can learn to work productively and independently on literacy tasks. Teaching students to be independent is an important educational goal. Independent students learn more every time they read and write because they have a system in place that supports them as message-makers and problem-solvers.

We wanted to know what independent students understand about routines, self-selection of just-right tasks (neither too easy nor too hard), and self-regulated behavior that keeps them focused and on task. We also wondered how teachers supported students as they learned about the students' routines, their work choices, and their self-managed behavior. Following Clay's lead, we set out to study a classroom where managed independent learning, as well as reading instruction, was working. We looked for a classroom with students who were highly engaged in reading and writing tasks while working independently. Moreover, it was important to us that the students in this classroom typically made average or above-average literacy progress during a school year as shown by end-of-the-year text leveling (Clay 1993) and writing rubric assessments (Fountas & Pinnell 2001).

We wanted to find out what happens in such a classroom—that is, what does the teacher do that works and what do the students do that works? We also felt it was important to learn about the thinking processes of a teacher whose students were achieving success. Because of our concerns about independent work, we were especially interested in analyzing what the other children were doing while their teacher taught reading to a small group. We expected that this close look at independent learning and how it is achieved in a classroom would offer valuable insights that could help other teachers.

A Close Look at Managed Independent Learning

Managed Independent Learning (MIL) is the time, usually during the morning, in which children work independently while you work with small groups of students teaching reading. If you are going to successfully teach students to build an effective reading process, you must match books to children and teach intensively. Because of the wide range of students' abilities, no one book will fit every child's skills. By working with small groups, you can provide books with just the right amount of challenge to help students learn more. But what are the rest of the children doing? Whatever it is, they must be working independently, learning something about reading and writing, and fully engaged in the task at hand.

Throughout our experiences helping teachers with their instruction, we have noticed that MIL was highly successful in some classrooms; but in others, teachers struggled to correct activities that were at best unproductive and at worst chaotic. The question that drove our research was, What makes Managed Independent Learning work? The answer to this question is important, because students typically spend two or three hours of the literacy block working independently in centers and only 30 minutes with their teachers in a guided reading lesson. For them to make steady progress, their independent time needs to be as valuable and productive as the time they spend with the teacher.

THE CLASSROOM

We conducted our study in Leslie Evans's second-grade classroom in a central Ohio suburban school district. The 23 students in her classroom came to her with varying abilities in reading, ranging from early (Level D) to self-extending (Level R) readers and writers (Fountas & Pinnell 1999).

Data were collected for one school year, 2000-2001. The entire literacy block was videotaped every fourth week and the teacher was interviewed monthly. Field notes were taken to capture the structure of the day, researchers' insights, and tentative emerging patterns and themes. We analyzed these data to determine both how and why MIL worked in Leslie's classroom.

WHAT WE DISCOVERED

Our analyses revealed a reflective teacher who problem-solved issues related to independent learning on a daily basis. As MIL was introduced and eventually became established in her room, Leslie asked herself a series of questions. For example, early in the year, she wanted to know how effectively she was teaching the routines so that her students could work alone without her assistance. Once they were independent workers, she wanted to be certain that they were learning something powerful as they worked independently. She then questioned how she could teach them to manage their own learning. (See Figure 12-1.) Often the solving of one problem would lead to asking another question requiring yet another solution. She moved cyclically from problem-posing to problem-solving and back again.

EXPLORING LESLIE'S QUESTIONS

In informal interviews, Leslie shared her reflections regarding the routines, content, and self-regulating behaviors needed to make independent learning work. We also analyzed our videotapes and field notes and discovered even more valuable insights regarding the series of questions Leslie was asking herself.

Leslie's Issues and Questions

ISSUE:	DEFINITION:	QUESTIONS:
Routines	A series of activities performed according to standard procedures.	How can I teach the students to work independently during reading time?
Content	Work that offers just the right amount of challenge—not too easy and not too hard.	How can I make the independent work activities more powerful?
Self-Regulating Behavior	The child's ability to organize and monitor his or her own behavior.	How can I teach the students to manage their own learning?

FIGURE 12-1

How Can I Teach the Students to Work Independently During Reading Time?

Although Leslie's goal was to eventually release control of centers to her students, in the first few weeks of school independent work time in her classroom was highly structured and carefully monitored. Centers were introduced gradually, one or two a day, until children could care for supplies, successfully complete tasks, and maintain a comfortable noise level.

At the beginning of each day, during whole-group meeting time, Leslie explicitly taught the children what they were to do in centers. Some centers had an assigned task, and Leslie held the children accountable for a product. Each center also had several activities from which the children could choose after they had finished the assigned task. They stayed in the center until they were told that it was time to move on. Each child was assigned a partner with whom to work.

After the children had spent about 20 minutes in centers, Leslie asked the children to clean up and come to a community meeting. At this meeting, Leslie reviewed expectations, helped the children evaluate their own behavior, and asked them to share what they had accomplished. The children then moved on to the second center of the day.

As the students worked, Leslie walked around the room and monitored what was happening. She praised the students when appropriate. One day, early in the year, Leslie told the children, "Wow, what organized students you are! You got right to work on your job. When you were done with your job, you found something else to do at the center. Really nice job." Leslie would also offer reminders and suggestions as needed. Her goal was to eventually work herself out of the job of closely monitoring the students.

During the first month of the school year, Leslie was faithful to the adage "Less is best." She began by using a simple workboard that was easy for the children to follow but which gradually became more complex. Quality was valued over quantity. For every student, the last icon each day was independent reading. So, when Leslie glanced around the room and noticed that the majority of the

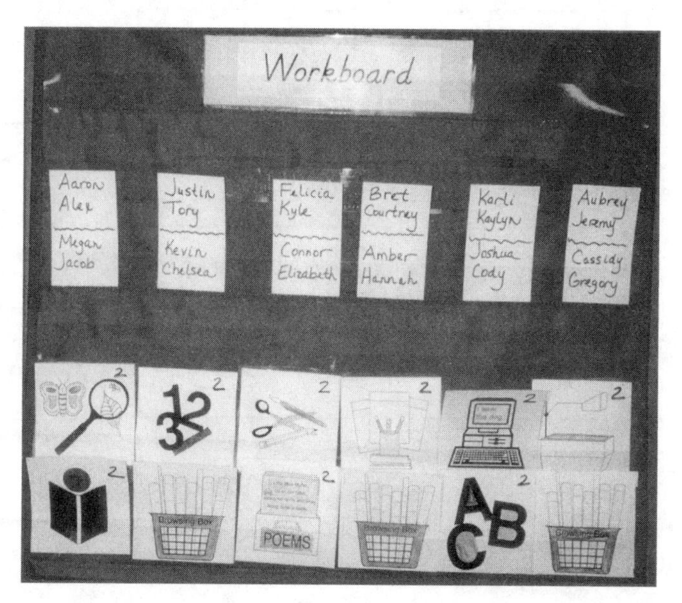

A simple workboard

students were reading at their desks, she stopped what she was doing and called an end to center work, thus providing time for independent reading.

In this classroom, many of the literacy centers were ongoing activities rather than short-term ones that would last only a day or two. The children went to these centers every day and knew exactly what to do, making time-consuming, daily explanations unnecessary. This also freed Leslie from having to create new centers each week. For example, when working in the browsing box center, the children read four books from the box, alone or with a partner. At the writing center, they wrote letters, poems, notes, or journal entries. The children quickly internalized the expectations for these ongoing centers. They learned the meaning of the center icons: what to do, what was expected, and what the rules were. (See Figure 12-2.)

Leslie felt that the time she had spent organizing and managing centers, and making the process easy for herself and her students, was time well spent. As the children learned to monitor their own behavior and learning, Leslie began to assess their individual abilities. By the third week of school, baseline assessments were completed and analyzed, and she began conducting guided reading lessons.

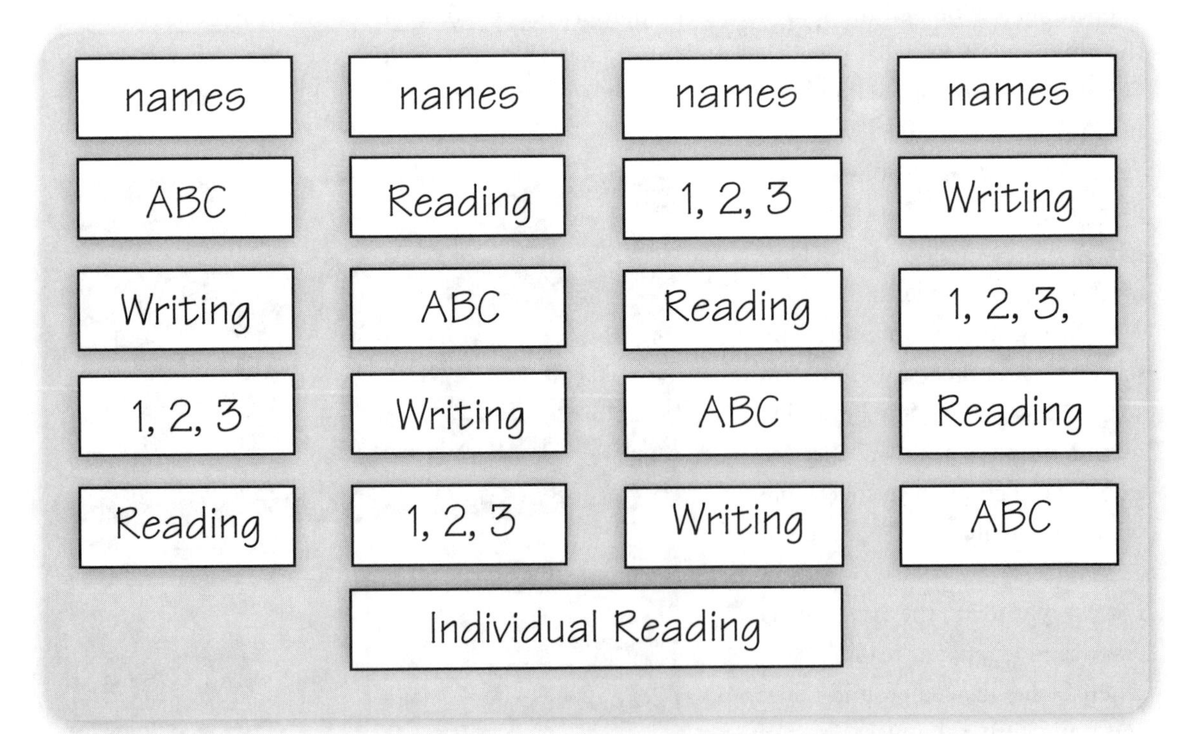

FIGURE 12-2 A more complex workboard

How Can I Make the Independent Work Activities More Powerful?

Once the students understood the routines for independent time and knew where to go, what to do, when to move, and why supplies need to be organized, it was time to up the ante. Leslie began to focus a greater portion of her attention on challenging each child appropriately every day in every work area. Early on, at the beginning of the year, she had asked herself, "What can these children do alone?" She observed each child closely, every day, and analyzed the information she was collecting to assess what each student could do independently.

Then she used her district's goals to determine what her students needed to learn next. For example, Leslie knew that a curriculum goal was that her students to be able to write a poem. So, early in the year, she asked herself, "What is an initial step that these children can take right now that will eventually lead them to this goal?" She decided to have the children memorize a different poem each week for a month, hoping that they would learn more about poetic devices such as rhyme, meter, images, and sound. This knowledge would take them one step closer to actually authoring a poem themselves.

Leslie kept striving for just the right amount of challenge. She knew that if the work was too easy, the children would spin their wheels. If it was too difficult, it would be a waste of their time and they would stop trying. Her driving maxim was, "Give them challenges they can successfully meet, because that's when the lightbulb of learning goes on." Independent work time in second grade is quite different from the centers that students were used to in kindergarten. Kindergarten children move from center to center, exploring magnetic letters in the ABC center and looking at their favorite books in the library center. In second grade, there is more sustained reading and writing time. For example, during work time, Connor would be investigating the rainforest by reading books and writing interesting facts on index cards. He later categorized these cards and used them to prepare a project that summarized his learning, which he shared with the class.

Next, Leslie began working to make sure that the learning that was taking place in centers and other independent work was generic knowledge that could be transferred from one context to another. She did not want her students merely to memorize items of knowledge. Instead, she wanted them to become strategic problem solvers. By engaging in meaning-making, problem-solving behaviors, her students would develop self-extending systems to help them to get better at something the more they practiced it. For example, when the class was studying about states in the research center, Kevin brought from home a huge book filled with information. While reading the book, he gleaned many interesting facts. He noticed that many states had the same state bird. He wanted to categorize the states by their state birds and create a bar graph to display his knowledge. He also wanted to learn the year that every state joined the union. He was not just learning isolated facts; he was learning the investigation strategies of focused attention, logical thinking, and deliberate memory.

Leslie also began to provide more and more opportunities for the children to have a choice in what they studied. She felt that the eagerness that resulted from having choices would support learning at a higher level. One center that she wanted to implement was a Challenge Me Center. She had heard about how successfully this was working in Sue Oxenrider's classroom. At a workshop, Sue had picked up a flier about this center written by a second-grade teacher, Jeffery L. Williams. In this center children were asked to investigate something that they really cared about, such as a favorite animal or flags of different countries. Their work could go on for several days or several weeks, depending upon the students' goals and their plans for sharing their learning with the rest of the class. First, students selected their personal challenge and wrote a few sentences about what they would learn and why they wanted to take on this challenge. When their challenge was completed, the students shared their project with the rest of the class, which usually inspired even more students to take on challenges. Aubrey, for example, became deeply engaged in learning how to count and spell in Spanish and in so doing was learning about a different culture.

Offering students choices empowered them to learn. Leslie found that her centers were more powerful when she ensured that the children had successful challenges, when she taught for strategies, and when she offered choices.

How Can I Teach the Students to Manage Their Own Learning?

After Leslie realized that the students were working smoothly and learning, she saw a need to refine their attitudes about how to work more diligently in centers. In order for their learning to accelerate, they needed to understand more fully their roles as students. This teaching shift—from routine procedures to work habits—was particularly evident in the interactions that took place during the community meeting at the end of the reading period. Early in the year, Leslie talked about routines and the expectation of productive work. Later in the year, the focus was on valuing learning. Leslie encouraged her students to learn the strategies of focused attention and self-regulation. These interactions between teacher and students supported independent learning. By talking about such words as "focus," "self-control," and "concentrate," Leslie was demonstrating the type of language her students needed to guide their behaviors (Bodrova & Leong 1996).

In September, during the group discussion, Leslie taught her students to value the routines of putting their names and the date on their papers. She encouraged them to use good handwriting. At this time she also praised them for working well together and keeping busy.

Leslie's language was explicit and offered rationales, which supported her students in following and internalizing the organizational patterns and rules of the classroom. Early in the year, a typical community meeting after reading period included interactions that focused on expectations and routines. (See Figure 12-3.)

Using Explicit Language to Clarify Expectations and Solidify Routines

Leslie: Everybody was working very nicely with their partners. I cannot say enough about how well you worked together. People were following the directions on the cards. I saw Jacob going to the card at the reading center. He found the card, read it, and did his job there. One of the things I want to talk about again is this: when you are done with your job at the center, turn in your paper and do something else productive at that center. I was talking to Cody about that. Cody, can you tell everyone some of the things they can do at the Word Study Center when they are finished there?

Cody: Link letters, magnetic letters, pictures.

Leslie: Good. You can see what Cody did. (Holds up Cody's paper from the Word Study Center.) He remembered to put his name and the date on his work so I can see it. You can see how nicely he worked. And again, his handwriting is really nice. His spelling is not perfect, but it is really close. I am able to read it. I can tell that he said the words slowly and put down the sounds that he heard, and most of his words are spelled right. What productive work! Really nice job. Who would like to share something that they did today? Hannah?

Hannah: I wrote a letter.

Leslie: Hannah was at the Writing Center and the job was to write a letter to a friend. Hannah wants to share her letter. If you notice Hannah's work, she has her name and a date on it. Very nice handwriting. You can tell she took pride in her work. Now she is going to read us her letter.

FIGURE 12-3

Using Explicit Language to Emphasize the Role of a Student

Leslie: I am going to start out by asking what you learned today, Hannah.

Hannah: I found a golden retriever that was named a different name.

Leslie: What state were you researching?

Hannah: Maryland.

Leslie: Right, this book says that Maryland's state dog is the Chesapeake Bay Retriever. Some retriever dogs are similar but have different names, just like the rocks we are looking at in the Science Center. One is sandstone, and the other is limestone. Now, let's look at what Hannah does because I always like how Hannah takes her time when she works. She concentrates and finishes whatever she does, and always, always tries her best without being told. Did you find a book over there that was useful to you to find this information? Was it the green one?

(Hannah nods.)

Leslie: So she found that the green dictionary that I showed you this morning was very useful in finding information she needed.

(Hannah shows and reads her research booklet.)

Leslie: I like how well you worked on it. You are such a hard worker. Who else learned something today? Brett.

Brett: I learned at the Research Center that North Carolina is not just smooth; it is also bumpy.

Leslie: Yes, Brett, let's share your book. I think you are another good example of someone who always focuses on his work and reads very carefully to see what he is supposed to write.

FIGURE 12-4

In October the group discussion after center time sounded quite different. Leslie prefaced each exchange with a child by asking, "What did you learn today?" Essentially, this discussion highlighted what the children were learning, how they were learning, and why they were learning. When children fine-tune their work habits, they learn more and they learn faster. A community meeting after reading period in October included interactions that focused on defining the role of a student. (See Figure 12-4.)

Leslie started the year by teaching her students the routines and expectations of centers. As the children internalized the procedures for independent work time, her focus shifted to providing her students with successful challenges. Next, she helped her students value their learning and take on the role of a serious student.

Summary

Leslie is a reflective teacher. She began the year by asking herself, "What do I think second graders can do independently?" Once this question was answered, she moved on to ask, "How can I up the ante so they can learn new things?" When she was certain the children were working with just the right amount of challenge, she began to ask herself, "How can I support them in taking on the role of a serious student who is a self-regulated and self-motivated learner?" The shift was from other-managed to self-managed behaviors, from actual to potential abilities, and from reactive to deliberate learning.

Leslie's thinking does not stop here. The process is both an ongoing and a recursive one. Her observations of the students in her room will continue to drive her practice from day to day, month to month, and year to year. Effective teacher decision-making is directly related to what the students know and what they need to know next. It was important for Leslie first to teach for knowledge of routines, then to ensure just-right challenges, and next to define what it means to be a student. New teaching points emerged as needs dictated.

Each time Leslie addressed a problem and solved a problem with her students, she led them one step closer to her goal of making Managed Independent Learning work in her classroom. She saw value in her students becoming independent learners who get better at what they do every time they do it because they know how to learn. Leslie, like Clay, strategically defined teaching and learning as "meaning-getting, problem-solving activities which increase in power and flexibility the more they are practiced" (Clay 1991, p. 6), and in so doing she made MIL work for her and her students.

Ideas to Try

1. Think of a new center or routine activity that you want your students to be able to use or do independently while you work with a small group in guided reading. (Alternatively, think of a center that is not working well in your classroom and start over to make it more effective.) Select an activity that will be productive in terms of reading or writing—one that all students can do simultaneously the first few times you work on it.

2. Ask a colleague to observe your classroom or join you at lunch or after school to look at the physical arrangements and materials in the center.

3. Together, analyze in detail exactly what the children will have to do to use the center effectively. Walk through the sequence of expected actions while your colleague takes notes. Use this list of details as a guide to the explicit teaching needed to establish routines.

4. Now plan the introduction of the center or activity. Questions that will help include:

   - What materials will students need? Organize the materials in the place where students are expected to complete the activity or in a highly accessible place if all students are working at their desks or tables. Eliminate clutter by making sure that all materials are separated into containers. Label the containers and the place on the shelf where they are supposed to go.
   - What is the sequence of actions students will be expected to undertake from beginning to end? Plan to demonstrate the actions and have students demonstrate for the group.
   - Is the activity simple enough that the students in your class can learn it? If not, simplify the sequence of actions.
   - How long will it take for students to learn the routines? Plan to establish the routine over several days.
   - How can students be involved in their own learning? Plan to have students self-evaluate their performance of the routines each day. Also, ask them to talk about what they have learned. This follow-up discussion is very important in helping students become self-managed and take ownership for their learning.

5. Implement your plan over a period of two weeks. Gradually withdraw your supervision and support as students become more independent, but keep a watchful eye. Reteach routines as needed.

6. Meet with your colleague to share what you learned from the experience. Remember, as students learn more of these routines, they *learn how to learn* them, and it will take less time to teach them. Every new activity, though, will require teaching.

CHAPTER 13

Shifting Teaching and Management to Meet Learners' Changing Needs: Transitions from Primary to Intermediate

Gay Su Pinnell & Irene C. Fountas

Given the remarkable changes in learners described in Chapter 4, it is evident that the curriculum must be adjusted to support student growth. Figure 13-1 outlines the language/literacy framework for primary and intermediate grades, with a transition framework for grades two to three. Each version of the language and literacy framework is conceptualized as three blocks of instructional time.

Adjusting the Language/Literacy Framework

The primary framework provides for three blocks of instructional time, for a total of about two-and-a-half to three hours, usually in the morning (see Chapter 2). The intermediate framework provides for an hour of reading workshop, an hour of writing workshop, and a combined time of 30 minutes to an hour for the language/word study block. Obviously,

A Transitional Language and Literacy Framework for Grade Two	
Language/Word Study Block (30 to 60 minutes)	Interactive Read-Aloud/Literature Discussion Word Study Mini-Lesson/Buddy Study System *Select from:* • Interactive Edit • Modeled/Shared/Interactive Writing • Modeled/Shared Reading • Handwriting
Reading Workshop Block	Independent Reading Guided Reading Independent Literacy Center Work
Writing Workshop Block	Independent Writing and Conferring (after mini-lesson) Guided Writing Interactive Writing (small group)

FIGURE 13-1

approaches in the language/word study block are not used every day. Also, in intermediate grades, these activities may be scattered at different times in the day. For example, you might end the day reading aloud a chapter or two of a favorite novel. Or you might do five minutes of interactive edit just before lunch by placing a sentence or paragraph on a chart and asking students to copy and edit it using standard editing marks. Have the whole class work together and discuss each edit on the chart focusing on any aspect of convention or craft that you want to teach.

When students enter second grade, they will be working in a way that looks very much like the primary framework; when they end second grade, they should be working in a way that looks more like the intermediate framework. These shifts will not be sudden, but they should be carefully explained and demonstrated to children when they take place. Each change in the schedule, the workboard, or the ways you expect children to work should be signaled by a brief, explicit lesson.

For example, the workboard might change to show that all children should begin the reading workshop with independent silent reading. Teach them how the room should be during the first 15 minutes when everyone is reading and no one is talking. Explain that you will be talking individually with some children in whispers and will call the first group soon. Make this change a mini-lesson that extends over several days. At the end of the morning, ask children to talk about how the quiet in the room helped them do their best reading and thinking.

In the next section, we will describe several adjustments within each block of the framework that might be appropriate at some time during second grade. Your decision-making will depend on the children you teach—on their experiences and on the strategies and skills they demonstrate.

Language/Word Study Block

The language/word study block includes interactive read-aloud and discussion, interactive writing, modeled/sharing reading, modeled/shared writing, handwriting, and letter/word study. This block usually involves whole-class instruction. The word study mini-lesson sets the scene for some active exploration of phonics and spelling principles, usually in the word study or ABC center.

In second grade, continue to use interactive read-aloud to present books to children that they cannot yet read for themselves. The texts you are reading to second-graders help to expand their comprehending strategies. (See Chapter 11.) You can also begin teaching them how to talk with each other about literature. With your guidance, they can begin deeper discussions of texts.

Most teachers we know like to introduce the Buddy Study System, which is described in Chapter 2, in the last part of grade one or at the start of grade two for the following reasons:

- Children are ready for a more deliberate and systematic approach to studying words and how they work.
- The routines are easy to understand and implement.
- The variety of routines teaches children four different ways to learn spelling patterns.
- The system makes it possible for children to learn basic principles that they can apply to all of their spelling.
- There is a good balance among direct teaching, demonstration, and student application.
- There is a good balance between partner and individual work.
- Children choose some words and are guided to others that illustrate the principles being explored.
- The Buddy Study System provides for about 10 minutes of independent work each day during reading workshop.

You will continue doing word study mini-lessons with active application; however, Buddy Study moves students toward conscious attention to conventional spelling. The Buddy Study System provides for five days of learning activities surrounding six to eight words.

DAY ONE: CHOOSE, WRITE, BUILD

Provide a mini-lesson on some spelling principle (e.g., dropping the silent e before adding "ing"). The mini-lesson usually results in a chart of the words that illustrate the spelling principle. Make the chart together with the children, explaining the examples and getting them to generate more. At the end of the mini-lesson, place a few examples on the word wall.

Have children choose three words from the chart that illustrate the spelling principle and three words from their words to learn lists, which are kept in their writing folders. As you have writing conferences with children, help them select words to place on the list of words to learn.

Students can also choose words from high-frequency word lists. For second graders, use the 100 most common high-frequency words. Each child has one of these lists in his or her

writing folder. Over several days, give practice tests and have children highlight the words they know; the words they do not yet control can be selected for Buddy Study. For children who know all of the words, you can find more on the list of 500 high-frequency words. These lists of words are provided in Appendixes 4 and 5 of Pinnell and Fountas (1999).

After choosing words for the week, ask each child to write them on a small card that is kept in a library pocket mounted on the wall. Check the cards for accuracy, because the children will use them all week to check their work. It is important to have these cards (with children's names on the outside of the library pocket) in a visible place. If you want the children to take their words home, have them make a second copy of the card. Then have the children make their words three times with magnetic letters, each time checking with the accurate spelling letter by letter.

DAY TWO: LOOK, SAY, COVER, WRITE, CHECK

The children will use a study technique called *Look, Say, Cover, Write, Check*, which helps them learn how to look at words, recognize patterns, and remember them. Take manila folders and cut the front cover to make either three or four flaps (depending on how many times you want children to study and write each word). Have each child insert a sheet with columns in the folder. In the first column, the child writes one of the words chosen for the week, checking letter by letter with the accurate word on the card. Then, the child looks at it carefully, says it, covers it with the first flap, lifts the second flap and writes it, finally checking letter by letter with the accurate word in the first column. For the same word, the child performs *Look, Say, Cover, Write*, and *Check* one or two more times. The process can be repeated for each of the week's words.

DAY THREE: BUDDY CHECK

Have children work with a partner who has similar spelling skills to give each other practice tests on the week's words. The buddies check each other's tests. If a word is misspelled, the child looks at it carefully and then tries again one or two times. Have children highlight parts of words that they want to remember.

DAY FOUR: MAKING CONNECTIONS

For each of their words, ask children to search for and make connections with other words that they *look like* or *sound like*. They can also search for words that mean the same or the opposite of each word. Use mini-lessons to teach how to make connections in several different ways. Start with simple connections and show explicitly how to write them.

DAY FIVE: BUDDY TEST

Have partners give each other a test by dictating the word and using it in a sentence. Usually, children take this test in a special booklet so that you can look at progess over time, but you may choose to use loose paper. Grading these tests provides feedback on what children have learned. If a child misses a word, you may want to place it on the "Words to Learn" list. You can also use the information to identify a few children who may need small-group work on a principle.

The Reading Workshop

In the reading workshop block, which is described in Chapter 2, you create a context that allows for two things to happen:

- You work with children in small, homogenous, guided reading groups so that you can match books to readers and teach for effective strategies.
- While they are not in the small group, children work independently in a productive activity related to reading, writing, or word study.

Expect significant shifts in guided reading and independent work in second grade.

INDEPENDENT WORK

Independent work in the reading workshop block focuses on reading, writing, and word study so that children gradually learn the function of a sustained period of time for literacy-related activities. For kindergartners and beginning first graders, the independent work activities are of short duration (10 to 20 minutes); some active movement and talking in low voices is expected. Some of the work might be done at the children's desks or tables; other work would be done in centers. You would usually avoid centers such as building, blocks, or games, moving them instead to another part of the school day.

Some important transitions will be taking place in the independent work the students are expected to do; some of these are described in Figure 13-2.

For kindergarten and first-grade students, there is quite a bit of variety in the independent work activities, although you would not usually have every one of the choices going on at once. The centers described in Figure 13-2 are ongoing; for each, the children have learned a particular routine that does not vary. For example, when they work on their personal poetry books, the routine might be:

Changes in Independent Work During the Reading Workshop Block

KINDERGARTEN → GRADE 1 → GRADE 2 → GRADE 3

Independent Work:	Transitions:	Independent Work:
Reading around the room using a pointer to reread charts and poems on the walls. Putting together stories or poems in the pocket chart and reading them. Reading (usually rereading) several short books from browsing box books that are familiar and easy. Writing and illustrating short pieces in a writing center. Listening to stories read aloud in the listening center. Using the overhead projector (placed on the floor) to display poems or stories on the wall to be read. Reading from the poetry box (poems on large cards that have been previously read in shared reading). Gluing a familiar poem (from shared reading) into a personal poetry book, reading it, and illustrating it. Completing an assigned task in the word study center (directly related to a mini-lesson). Reading with a buddy.	*From several shorter independent work activities to longer periods of reading and writing.* *From working in centers most of the time to working individually at desks or tables most of the time.* *From a variety of active centers that involve talk with others to longer sustained individual time in reading and writing.* *From a hum of soft voices reading and talking to longer periods of silence.*	Silent reading of a self-selected book for independent reading. Writing about reading in a Think Book. Engaging in the daily activities of the Buddy Study System (spelling). Completing assigned word study tasks (directly related to mini-lesson). Using computers to produce written products. Writing longer pieces sustained over several days or longer. Reading poetry books. Reading picture books in the classroom library. Selecting and copying poems for a personal poetry book.

FIGURE 13-2

1. Glue the poem (i.e., a duplicated version of a poem that they have read in shared reading that day) onto one page of the notebook.
2. Illustrate the poem.
3. Read the poem to yourself.
4. Read the poem to a buddy.

What does vary in these centers is the material the children read and write, and the aspects of words they study. You are always changing the content, but the process remains the same.

Over the first-grade year, children learn to modulate their voices so that they are reading very softly, and they make the transition to silent reading. Much of their reading is automatic, and they are reading much longer texts. There should be an expectation for longer periods of reading; and, because they are reading silently, there will be silence in the room. You will gradually increase the time the students spend reading independently, and

Sample Plan for Managing Independent Work in the Reading Workshop Block

T'alor Michelle Javon Maya	Daisha Dominique Tiara Melvin	Jeremy Jazmyne Grace Brittony	Jahlil George Nora Amber	Patrick David Madeleine Kara
Independent Reading	Independent Reading	Independent Reading	Independent Reading	Independent Reading
Buddy Study System	Buddy Study System	Buddy Study System	Buddy Study System	Buddy Study System
Reading Journal	Think Book	Word Study Center	Computer or Reading Journal	Listening Center

FIGURE 13-3

they will spend more time on self-selected books, so there will be less work in browsing boxes, which contain previously read texts. There is a big difference between rereading three or four short books from a browsing box and sustaining the reading of a 30- or 40-page text over a couple of days. There will be less work in centers and you will be choosing the quieter centers.

A sample management plan for a group of second graders is illustrated in Figure 13-3. This plan can be changed each day simply by rotating the names of the children. Notice that all of the children begin with silent, independent reading and then move to the Buddy Study System. What they do after that will depend on whether it is Day 1, 2, 3, 4, or 5, but each day's lesson provides a structured routine that the children understand. The third activity is more open-ended, often takes place in a center, and may involve writing.

BEGINNING TO USE A READING JOURNAL

Children who are more fluent in writing can begin to write about their reading using a reading journal. As they move up the elementary grades, they will be regularly using a reading response journal. To get them started in second grade, introduce the journal as a special book that they will use only to write about their reading. In the reading response journal, they may list the titles of books they read; once or twice a week, you can guide them to write about their reading. The activity is guided by suggestions and/or questions, such as, "Write what your favorite character is like," or "Write what you think is going to happen at the end of the story." You do not want to institute daily writing of a routine nature, because the writing will be become superficial and will detract from reading time, as children will want to get their writing done instead of spending time on reading. Be sure that the children understand that the reading journal is a special book that they will use when you work with them in reading.

If you like, divide the reading journal into sections. In one section, children can list the titles of books that they read and/or write or sketch in response to their independent reading. Be cautious with this, however—you do not want children to think that they will be required to write every time they read. Careful planning and instruction will help children realize how writing can be a tool for communicating about and reflecting on their reading.

INTRODUCING A THINK BOOK

As children move into second grade, they can make greater use of writing for a variety of purposes: taking notes; using writing to organize thinking; writing down simple, helpful rules and principles; making lists; and so on.

A new item for second graders is a "Think Book," which helps children become accustomed to using notebooks and journals. (See Figure 13-4.) The Think Book may be used at any time during the day. Students can use the Think Book to:

- write notes or vocabulary for social studies, science, or the content areas.
- record observations of experiments.
- make charts to record observations of phenomena over time.
- make lists of details or experiences to talk about later.
- make quick sketches, sometimes labeled, for later discussion.
- write notes that can form the beginning of a piece of writing in writing workshop.
- respond to the interactive read-aloud.
- extend the meaning of or follow up on a book you have read aloud to them.
- complete a focused writing assignment in the content areas.

FIGURE 13-4 A sample of a Think Book

Teach children how to keep the Think Book in a special place and to use it *only* when you directly ask them to write something. Depending on what you want to use the Think Book for, it can have several sections.

DOCUMENTATION OF INDEPENDENT WORK

One of the challenging questions for teachers is, "How do I know that children are doing their independent work?" Some adjustments in the amount of documentation are outlined in Figure 13-5.

Documentation is difficult with young children. For example, you do not want to have kindergartners and most first graders record the titles of all the books they read; in a good classroom, they read hundreds of short books. And it takes them just about as long to write down a title and page numbers as it does to read the book. Such documentation is simply a waste of time. For young children, it is enough to say, "I read all the books in the yellow tub." As they become more fluent writers and are reading fewer (but longer) books, children can easily keep a list of the books they have read. As mentioned above, the reading journal can be used for this purpose. Simply glue a sample form for the list in the first few pages of the reading journal. Students can also keep a reading workshop pocket folder with gussets for their lists and other work.

Younger students can engage in active learning work without formal documentation. You will be constantly monitoring their activity by scanning the room and interacting with them between groups. At the end of the time period (or at the end of the language/literacy block), have the students evaluate how their time was spent. They can self-evaluate their work, reporting orally, or the group can make comments on how the work went in general. This self-evaluation is a good procedure to use throughout the elementary years.

Older students can do more documentation of their independent work, although, again, you do not want to overdo it. What if you had to write about everything you did in your workday? Chances are, you would not get much done. Children will be doing one activity every day for the Buddy Study System, and the work from these activities will be placed in their folders for you to examine.

Changes in Documentation of Independent Work: Primary to Intermediate

KINDERGARTEN → GRADE 1 → GRADE 2 → GRADE 3

Documentation of Independent Work:	Transitions:	Documentation of Independent Work:
A workboard provides guidance to help them remember their schedules for the work period. There is minimal documentation of the books read because these books are familiar; also, it would take children too long to copy titles. Children have a system for turning in written products from their work in the writing center. Many activities have no documentation, although some centers may have a check-off system. Teachers monitor engagement by scanning and walking around between groups. At the end of the block, teachers have the group report and self-evaluate independent work.	*From mostly oral reporting to a combination of oral reporting and written documentation.* *From little writing in response to reading to regular writing in response to reading.*	Children keep a list of the books they have read in a folder or a Think Book. Children work on pieces of writing over several days or longer periods, which they keep in a writing workshop folder. Children keep a list of words to learn, from which they can select for the Buddy Study System. Children turn in the forms completed each day as part of the Buddy Study System (spelling). Children document their word study activities in writing (possibly in a Think Book). Children write or sketch in response to books they have heard read aloud or read for themselves. At the end of the block, teachers have the group self-report and self-evaluate.

FIGURE 13-5

GUIDED READING

In guided reading, children move from oral reading of short texts to silent reading of a combination of short texts and longer chapter books. You will use the same basic structure for guided reading, but with a few variations, as noted below:

- **Introduction of the text.** Children are growing more sophisticated as readers, but they still need you to introduce texts. Remember that you are asking them to read a text that provides for new learning. They will be applying the strategies they have already learned to a longer, more difficult text, and, in the process, expanding their reading systems. The introduction is key to the successful processing that builds good reading strategies. There are several ways to introduce a text. If you are introducing a chapter book such as *Henry and Mudge* (Rylant 1987), you may introduce the whole book and focus only on what you want students to read (for example, the first two stories). Or, you may introduce only the part of the text you want them to read today, and continue introducing sections as the children are ready to read them. You will find that your introductions take a little more time on the first day of reading a chapter book.
- **Reading the text.** Children read the text silently to themselves. You can go around and sample oral reading and sometimes interact briefly with individual students. Just ask them to lift their voices to an audible level when you come to them. Remember that there will be no other voices in the room, so students can read very softly. At this time, you can take notes. After sampling their reading, you may want to confer with individuals elsewhere in the room or even get another group started. For second graders, it is best to let them stay at the table to read rather than going to their desks, so the transition from introduction to reading will not be interrupted and the children will be more focused. It might be helpful to have two guided reading tables in a second- or third-grade classroom.
- **Discussing and revisiting the text.** After reading, revisit the text to discuss any aspect of meaning and encourage the children to support their thinking with evidence from the text.
- **Teaching for processing strategies.** After a brief discussion that helps you judge readers' responses to the text, you can work on any aspect of the reading process to which you want to draw students' attention. Your teaching will be directed to what your students need to know next. (See Chapter 1.)

- **Extending the meaning.** (Optional) As students become more at ease with reading and writing, you may want to work more on extending the meaning of the text—that is, using writing, interpretive reading, or charts to look deeper into texts. (See Chapter 10.) They may also write in their reading response journals or Think Books (as guided by the teacher).
- **Word work.** (Optional) For students who are having some difficulty in decoding words and/or understanding how they work, take a minute or two and do some lively, game-like word work.

Writing Workshop in Primary Grades

The basic structure of a writing workshop remains the same for second graders, except that they will be writing longer pieces and will be expected to write for a longer time without talking to others. Gradually increase their writing time and begin to involve them more in the revision aspects of the writing process.

INDEPENDENT WRITING

Independent writing includes a mini-lesson, individual writing, conferring with the teacher, and sharing. Most teachers find it helpful for each child to have a writing folder with side pockets and resource materials in the gussets. These resource materials could include a list of topics the child wants to write about as well as his/her words to learn lists. Children keep the writing that they are currently working on inside the pockets, while finished pieces are stored in a file.

Second graders can participate in all phases of the writing process, but you would not want to make it laborious by including too much editing and revising. Children are still writing expressively, drawing on their own experiences. They can learn to do simple proofreading—crossing out rather than erasing, and using techniques such as "spider legs" to add material. Have strips of paper available so that children can add sentences or phrases, glue them on, and fold them over. They should also be responsible for accurately spelling all words that they know. It is not necessary to copy every piece of writing. Second graders simply need to write and write, becoming fluent and expressive in the process.

GUIDED WRITING

Second-grade students can work more independently in writing than younger children because they can spell so many words. They also will have learned how to use resources such as the word wall, personal dictionaries, and high-frequency word lists. When students have learned the routine of working independently and silently, you can begin to bring together small, needs-based groups to work on a specific aspect of writing. These small groups allow you to teach efficiently because you are working on just what that particular group needs to know. Other children can proceed with their writing rather than working on concepts that are too easy or too hard for them to understand. Group work may focus on any aspect of writing—conventions, strategies and skills, or craft.

INTERACTIVE WRITING

Some second-grade students look much more like first graders in their development of a writing process. These students need more modeling and support. Interactive writing is an excellent tool to help these students understand the conventions, strategies, and craft of writing. Bringing them together in a small group makes it possible to explicitly teach the concepts they need to know; the group support helps them to go beyond the writing that they could do alone. The essential elements of interactive writing are outlined below; a detailed description is provided in McCarrier, Pinnell, & Fountas (2000).

- **Composing the text.** In this exercise, you build the writing on some kind of experience that the children have shared. Many teachers use children's literature (e.g., books you have read aloud during the language/word study block). The students could be working on the same assignment that other students are doing individually, but they will be making an enlarged version on chart paper. Involve the students in planning and composing the text. They can discuss and negotiate every aspect of this text, but it should be a group decision. You will be guiding the composition, so that it is one that the group will be able to write with your assistance, as well as providing opportunities to learn. You will have an overall sense of where the text is going; compose one workable chunk at a time (a sentence or two).

- **Constructing the text.** Once the text or a workable piece of it is composed, students usually say it out loud one or two times together so that they can remember it. (With second graders, it may not be necessary to say it more than once.) Guide the process of writing the text word by word and letter by letter, sometimes sharing the pen with the

students. Your decision-making focuses on what to write yourself and what to invite an individual student to contribute. A good rule of thumb is for you to write the words and parts of words that the students know well, as well as those that are well beyond their knowledge. For words and concepts that they nearly know or are within their grasp, invite a student to write. Provide such opportunities only a few times during the construction of a text, because you want the process to move along quickly and you do not want to teach too many things at once. Select those items that have high instructional value. You can also attend to punctuation and text layout during the construction.

- **Reading and extending the text.** A text is reread several times during construction and remains a source of reading afterwards. Hang it in the classroom so that students can use it as a resource. When part of a text has been written interactively by a small group, you may want to have students do a little more writing on their own to add to the group text because:

  - they will have just seen a clear demonstration of writing on the topic and have worked together as a group to generate a lot of ideas.
  - some of the words related to the topic may be more available to them.
  - writing a short piece individually will not be as daunting as composing an entire piece alone.
  - they will have the satisfaction of finishing a good piece of writing.

We find that interactive writing is quite helpful to children who have had less experience in writing. It is also effective for working with English learners who are facing the challenge of learning to write in a language that they are also learning to speak.

Summary

Understanding the learning shifts that take place during second grade requires looking across the language and literacy framework from kindergarten through fifth or sixth grade. There are changes throughout this period because students are sustaining reading and writing for longer and longer blocks of time. The children will be producing more complicated writing and increasing their use of writing across the framework. The major changes I have discussed in this chapter are summarized in Figure 13-6.

It makes good sense to look across the elementary years and make some decisions about the optimal times to introduce new demands and responsibilities to students. It is rewarding for children to know that they are graduating, so to speak, to new challenges, so each year should offer new tools and new ways of working. When you introduce something new, make a big deal out of it! Each year's work builds on the previous years, and there is great continuity when the language and literacy framework is implemented throughout the grades—though each year is special. If your students realize that they are changing, they will feel a sense of accomplishment in making those changes, and the process of learning will make each year exciting.

What's New in Second Grade?

- Less center work in general and quieter centers
- Longer periods of silent independent reading
- Longer periods of silent independent writing
- Use of interactive writing with children who need more support rather than with the entire class
- Introduction of a reading journal for written response to books
- Introduction of a Think Book
- Introduction of the Buddy Study System for spelling

FIGURE 13-6

Ideas to Try

1. Meet with colleagues in grades one, two, and three to explore changing your management plans to meet their needs.

2. First, have a general discussion of your students, perhaps sharing in grade-level teams and then with the whole group. Discuss:
   - What are your students able to do independently as readers and writers?
   - How long can they sustain independent reading and writing work?
   - How do you predict they will change over the next two months?

3. Share the schedules you currently use, as well as your management plan for the reading workshop time.

4. Now look at the transitional framework presented in this chapter. Use it as an example of shifting the instruction as students become more proficient. Discuss with colleagues:
   - What changes should I make in my schedule and management plan for reading workshop now?
   - What changes should I make during the next two months?

5. Make a plan for the gradual shifting of work in the reading workshop block. You will need to explain and demonstrate each change to the students; and you will also want to monitor behavior to be sure the change was appropriate.

6. Schedule a follow-up meeting to discuss the changes in your reading workshop time and what you learned from it.

CHAPTER 14

Questions and Answers About Classroom Management

Gay Su Pinnell

Over the last 10 years, I have had constant interaction with teachers about guided reading and other components of the language and literacy framework. Teachers have posed many insightful, practical, and important questions, and together we have sought answers. In this last chapter of this book, I share many of these recurring questions. The answers to them are not mine alone. Indeed, they have come from discussions among teachers from many parts of the United States and Canada. We are all experts, and we are all learners. Here, I have summarized some answers from our ongoing dialogue.

I have selected seven frequently occurring questions for discussion in this chapter. Some teachers have asked about keeping children's interest during large-group instruction. Others have questions about guided reading and independent work time. Teachers want to know how to work with small groups and simultaneously manage the children who are working independently. That is quite a challenge, but I have received many excellent suggestions from teachers. I hope that the following questions and answers are helpful to you.

Question 1: How can I keep children from fidgeting around and disengaging during whole-group instruction?

Have the whole group together for many activities designed to create a community of learners, including reading aloud, word study mini-lessons, interactive writing, and discussion. Here are some ideas for promoting self-control:

- It is essential to have a large-group area that will accommodate the entire class comfortably. It is preferable to have a rug in the area so that children can be more comfortable; some teachers use small carpet squares that children take out and put away. To test your whole-class area, have everyone sit there. Can all of the students sit comfortably, without touching anyone else? Be sure that no one is sitting under (or almost under) a desk or table when you check your space.
- You should sit in a low chair right in front of the children. You should be able to see every one of them, and they should be able to see you.

- Be sure that all the children can see and hear you as you read aloud or work at the easel. If the children in back feel the need to get up on their knees, you might have a row of small chairs back there. Children will be disruptive if they cannot see and hear, and we cannot blame them. To test this, sit yourself in every part of the rug area. Can you see the easel well? This is also a good way to see whether glare (from overhead lights or windows) interrupts children's vision.

- Be sure that there is an empty area right in front of you so that children can quickly come up to the easel and stand comfortably when you are doing interactive writing. Do not let children creep right up to where you are sitting.

- Teach children precisely how to sit as they work together in a large group. Some teachers ask children to check whether they are sitting on their bottoms with legs crossed, their elbows are in, and their hands are in their laps, perhaps clasped. No one should be touching anyone else. Demonstrate (or have a child do it) and ask them to look at each other and really think about how they are sitting.

- During the first weeks of school, be very firm about having children check themselves. If you are inconsistent, they will always be waiting for you to remind them. Do not allow children to lie down even if they are quiet or you feel like putting up with it. It will be difficult for you—and confusing for them—to correct this behavior later.

- Try seating your children with their backs toward a wall or bookshelf. It is natural to place yourself with your back to a wall. Think about finding a seat in a restaurant; do you gravitate toward the booth against a wall? There may be something human about wanting your back covered. Children may feel more secure if they have a place to sit within a defined area.

- Seat your children so that they are not looking at the doorway—a source of obvious distraction. This suggestion may conflict with the previous one, but it is also worth a try.

- Think about the amount of time you feel comfortable sitting on the floor. How long is it before you feel the need to stretch or change position? Keep your lessons fast-paced and within reasonable limits.

- Finally, be sure that you are doing something that engages children's interest—reading good books, having interesting discussions that involve everyone, and engaging in authentic interactive writing are key. Avoid long, tedious whole-group sessions.

Question 2: How do I get everything done in the allotted time?

Time management is a real problem for all teachers. There is simply not enough time in the school day, so skilled management is necessary throughout the day. Here are some suggestions for making the most of the time you have:

- Analyze your schedule and set priorities. Categorize activities as high priority—children's reading, writing, and oral language learning—and low priority. Be ruthless in cutting down the time for low-priority items.
- Think in weekly terms rather than in daily terms. Look at the amount of reading and writing instruction over the course of a week. On some days you will have many interruptions (e.g., assemblies or time for music, art, or other activities), but other days may offer opportunities for concentrated time. I do not mean to imply here that music and art, as special areas of the curriculum, are not valuable. But every time children leave the classroom, instruction is interrupted. It is advantageous to cluster these activities in order to give yourself a longer planning time and also to cause fewer interruptions in reading and writing time.
- Have something for children to do as soon as they come into the room. In many schools, children arrive at staggered times. Children who take the bus arrive at different times than walkers; having children sit at desks to wait for late arrivals wastes time. Many teachers have children immediately begin to read from book boxes or write in their journals.
- Find an efficient routine for children to hang up coats, turn in materials, and begin to work. Practice this routine.
- Create efficient ways to accomplish housekeeping tasks, such as taking the roll and determining lunch status. Some teachers have a sign-in board. As children come into the room they move their names to present. Some boards even have a space for lunch (buying, packing, etc.).
- One glance at the sign-in board can give you the information you need. Use mini-lessons to teach your children to use the system. Reduce opening business whenever possible; you may be using rituals that are unnecessary. Do those that are necessary quickly. For example, the calendar can be considered within two or three minutes. It may not be necessary to count the number of days of school every day,

especially if all the children can already count to high numbers. Instead, spend the time reading aloud to children and discussing literature.

- Make materials quickly accessible to children. For example, one teacher we know has children's folders (color-coded by subject) in different crates. The children are divided into committees of five, and each committee has its folders in one crate. The crates are in different parts of the room. When children need to retrieve their writing workshop folders, they scatter to different points of the room. Only five children are getting into a given crate to retrieve materials. This simple system eliminates the lines and inevitable delays that occur when all the children are getting materials from one place.

- Having sharp pencils available in a can reduces the amount of time you or the children spend at the sharpener during classtime.

- Mini-lessons are just that—quick, focused, powerful lessons. They are not intended to be long and drawn out. For a week or two, estimate the appropriate time for each mini-lesson you do. It might be three, five, or eight minutes, depending on the lesson's complexity and the number of examples you think you will need to elicit from the children. Set a cooking timer for the estimated time. When it goes off, are you still introducing the lesson? Are you halfway through? Are you writing the last examples on the chart? This exercise will help you be more aware of pacing in the lesson. You want children to actively participate; I am not suggesting that you shut them down when they are offering their ideas. But you want to keep your own language precise and to the point, which will make the mini-lesson more effective and more efficient.

- Work with colleagues and the principal to establish efficient school routines. For example, the staff member who picks up your lunch schedule and attendance does not need to interrupt instruction if you have an established system. The intercom takes up entirely too much time in most schools. A word of the day or thought for the day will not be meaningful for primary children.

- Monitor the time you spend talking to the children. It is important for you to have conversations with the children. You will find that the less talking you do, the more children will learn and the faster lessons will go.

- Develop routine systems for yourself so that you can efficiently accomplish tasks. For example, color code folders for various subjects so that you can find them quickly. Establish a system of checking reading journals over the week. Some teachers have the Monday Kids, Tuesday Kids, etc. Students' journals are examined in turn, depending upon which day a child is assigned to, and the teacher responds to students on the appropriate day. This way, you have five to seven journals to look at each day rather than a whole pile at the end of the week.

- Use the interstices (in-between times) in the day to do incidental teaching. If you have five minutes before lunch, you can review a mini-lesson or read aloud a bit of a familiar, well-loved story. If children are lining up, they can sing a song or enjoy shared chanting of a favorite poem (thus promoting phonemic awareness). If children are lined up in the corridor, be sure there is something on the wall they can read.

- Have materials well organized and ready to use, so that children can get to work immediately. The better your classroom is organized, the more time you will save.

Question 3: How can I keep children from interrupting me when I am working with small groups in guided reading?

The less children know about the routines of the classroom, the more they will interrupt you as you try to confer with individuals and work with small groups. The reverse is also true. Teaching routines explicitly will help. If you are being interrupted frequently, that means the children have not practiced the routines enough. Other factors also play a role in reducing interruptions. Some suggestions are listed below.

- Be sure that only one kind of material is in a container and clearly label each kind of material with words and an icon (a small, clear picture or symbol). Then label both the container and the space on the shelf or table where it is located. Store together materials that share a common function. For example, pencils, markers, different sizes of paper, rulers, and scissors would go in the writing center or a writing supplies area. Within each center or area, have all the tools that are needed for it. You would not, for example, want children who are working in a science exploration center going across the room for paper, pencils, or rulers.

- Explicitly teach children where the materials are and have them practice getting and returning them. You will want to do this for one center at a time, starting with the materials needed most. If the children need more support for this process, make a game out of it by asking them to point (or say) as quickly as possible where to get items such as markers, paper, browsing boxes, and so on.

- Another reason children may interrupt you is that they have problems doing tasks that they do not know how to solve. In this case, the children are actually trying to solve the problem by asking you for help. That is certainly better than simply sitting passively, acting out, or disrupting the work of other children; however, interruptions still make it impossible for you to be effective in teaching small groups. Make a list of common problems, then teach children how to solve these problems. For example, spelling words are a common source of interruption. Teach students that if they do not know how to spell a word, they should: (1) look at their personal dictionary; (2) look at the word wall; or (3) say it slowly and get down as many letters as they can.

- Be sure to analyze the work that you give students to do. If it is too hard or complex, they will interrupt you because they cannot remember details. The tasks you are asking students to do may be all right for some students but too hard for others. For example, trying to read books from a browsing box that contains books that are too hard will frustrate students. Simplify the tasks as needed so that every student can be successful. This does not mean that the tasks must be at the level of the least-knowledgeable students. Tasks that are too easy will cause other disruptions because the more advanced students will complete tasks too quickly or become bored.

- Make some work multilevel in nature, with opportunities for the advanced students to go further and a simple version of the task for less advanced students. For example, you might present a mini-lesson on words that have the pattern, i-consonant-e. Discuss the sound of i when the pattern is in a word and generate examples such as kite, write, white, bite, and ice. Most of the children will generate examples to match the chart, and an application activity might be to make three chart examples in magnetic letters, then say the words, and then record them in a word study notebook. Encourage students to find more examples from the word wall or other references. Less advanced students could concentrate on making an easy exemplar

several times with magnetic letters and then writing it. More advanced students might be given the same words with -ing endings and asked to write what changes when they add the ending.

- Finally, analyze the interruptions you do receive. For one or two days, record what students are asking of you during independent work time. Chances are, you will come up with four or five categories of interruptions, such as:

  "How do you spell this word?"
  "I need to go to the bathroom."
  "I can't find..."
  "My pencil needs sharpening."
  "_____ is bothering me."

- Plan a mini-lesson for each category that you encounter. You can avoid pencil-sharpening noise and disruption by keeping a can of sharp pencils and another can labeled pencils to be sharpened. A student whose pencil needs to be sharpened simply puts it in the pencils to be sharpened can and takes another from a can of sharp pencils. Each afternoon, have one student sharpen all the pencils (or do it yourself). You might also want to wipe these pencils each day with a sanitizing paper, which you can buy at any drugstore.

Question 4: How can I keep children from interrupting each other during independent work/guided reading time?

It is very important that children learn to sustain themselves in independent tasks. Indeed, this is an important life skill, not one that is relevant only for literacy or school. Children can help each other by trying not to create distractions, but you will need to teach them how to do that. You will also need to teach them that it is the responsibility of workers not to allow others to distract them.

- First, be sure the environment is very well organized so that students can be independent. Then, be sure that every student can perform the tasks that are asked of him or her. Strategically place centers so that the traffic patterns work for you rather than against you. If students have to go through other work areas frequently (for example, from their desks to the word wall), that traffic will disturb the independent work of others.

- In mini-lessons and whole-group discussions, talk about your class as a community. Always say "our work" and "we" rather than "my." Even young children can begin to learn that they have a responsibility to contribute to the learning of others in the community. As you begin the year and are teaching routines, end the morning and afternoon session with self-evaluation. Ask children what they did that helped others learn (e.g., talked quietly, did not interrupt, got their own materials and put them away, and so on).

- Be sure to locate your guided reading table so that you can see the entire room from it. That way you can frequently and quickly scan the room, noting potential problems or disruptions. Do not allow children to lie under tables to read or write, but ask them to use the comfortable spaces you have provided for them. They should be in your full sight. This does not mean that you need to stop and interrupt the group every time you see a problem; often, children will resolve problems for themselves, and they need to learn to do so. But you will be able to quietly intervene if needed.

- Between guided reading groups, you can do a quick turn around the room to remind individuals of what their goals are and gently move them back on task. A quick checkup helps children keep on track.

Question 5: How can I keep the noise level in my classroom within reasonable limits during independent work/guided reading time?

It is natural for young children to talk, laugh, and sometimes shout. Children may come into school with the habit of speaking in loud voices; after all, some families just have exuberant voices. It is not a problem at home because there are fewer people and everyone accepts a certain level of volume.

This is not the case in your classroom, however, where a high noise volume will disrupt teaching and learning. It is important to remember that people learn how to talk in a place while they are in that place. If children have learned to talk loudly in one place, they can learn to talk softly *in* another place, especially when they are given a very good reason for it: "We talk softly so that all of us can do our best thinking." Here are some suggestions:

- Teach voice modulation just as you would teach anything else—with a mini-lesson that involves explicit demonstration, with practice, and with self-evaluation. Some teachers have used a chart such as the one in Figure 14-1.
- Through demonstration and practice, you can teach each of your students what voices 0 through 4 mean. Then you can remind them (and refer to the chart on the wall) when an activity is to be conducted in a 0 or 1 voice. This technique is much more effective than just telling children to be quiet; some of them actually might not know what you mean by quiet.
- Plan the quieter centers for your literacy time; avoid blocks or drama, which naturally lend themselves to louder voices. You can also put noisier centers across the room from quieter centers. If some students are talking loudly, then everyone gets a little louder in order to be heard. The noise level escalates without anyone being conscious of it.

Voices in Our Room

0	1	2	3	4
Work Time	Conference	Group Time Reading Writing	Meeting Time	Outside Recess
No Talking or Other Noise	Whispers	Quiet Voice	Medium Voice	Loud Voice

FIGURE 14-1

- Above all, do not escalate the noise level by talking loudly yourself. Find some way (a soft bell tone will work) to get the attention of the whole class when necessary. Talk very quietly when you confer with individuals and just loud enough for the small group to hear when you are conducting guided reading lessons. If your voice is booming out during guided reading, students will be tempted to talk louder simply to be heard. You actually will evoke better listening by talking softly. In other words, follow the rule of 0–4 voice levels yourself.

Question 6: How do I do independent work and small-group instruction if I have a very small classroom? How can I make the best use of space?

It seems that classrooms are never quite big enough, but if you have an unusually small space, here are some suggestions:

- First, discard every single item that you do not absolutely need. You will be surprised how many materials are used seldom or not at all. The beginning of summer is a good time to accomplish this task. Examine all of your equipment, materials, and other items. If you did not use an item during the school year (or used it only a few times), give or throw it away. A classroom is like a laboratory or operating room; it should contain only the items you really need and each should have a specified place.

- Once you have reduced the amount of your materials, be ruthless in finding a specific place for each item. Place each kind of material in one container. Label shelves and containers with words and an icon, so that it is easy to find where to put containers. You may have to make some tough choices if you do not have space for everything.

- Be sure that your storage cabinets, shelves, and other pieces of furniture are not large. Big filing cabinets or storage units can take unnecessary space. A large teacher's desk may not be necessary. Remember that large tables have useless space in the middle. By using smaller furniture, you can generate more space for people, yet store materials just as efficiently.

- Use your walls and other display spaces efficiently. You can create display space (which can double as a reading activity—e.g., with a pocket chart) by placing a low shelf perpendicular to the wall. Children can use browsing boxes (in tubs on the shelves) on one side of the shelving; on the other side, they can work with a poem in a pocket chart.

- Have some centers that are permanent and others that change so that you have only a few to set up. That way, space can do double duty. The art center, for example, which you might use in the afternoon, can be the poetry center in the morning, where children post copies of the poems they read in shared reading.

- Teach routines very carefully, especially the routine for how to speak quietly (see Question 5). When working in a small space, teach children how to work without touching or bumping each other. It is especially important for them to work within their own space.

Question 7: How can I be more efficient in my management of small-group reading instruction?

All of the suggestions listed above will certainly help you be more efficient in general. If you are interrupted less often, you will be able to accomplish your goals with guided reading groups in less time. But, in addition to broader classroom management, you will need to attend specifically to the management of small-group work. Here are some suggestions:

- First, be sure that your materials are well organized and available. Think of how much time can be wasted in searching for your white dry-erase board or a marker. Before you know it, four or five minutes have gone by; meanwhile, your small group is sitting idly and growing restless. One of the best systems we know is to keep a small cart on rollers with plastic tubs or shelves right next to the table where you do guided reading. You can buy one of these small carts at any office supply store. This cart can be rolled back in a corner when you are not using it. Or, you can have a small set of shelves near your chair. On the cart or shelves, place: (1) books to be used for each group; (2) your clipboard with student records and prompts taped to the back; (3) markers and dry-erase board; (4) magnetic letters arranged in muffin pans or tackle boxes; (5) sticky notes, paper, markers, pencils, and other supplies.

- Prepare for your lessons a week or a few days at a time by checking your running records and observational notes and thinking forward to the books that will be appropriate for reading lessons. Choose several books and have them available in multiple copies (held together by elastic bands or in baggies). Each day, think about the reading and confirm or change your book selection for the next day. On a sticky note, write key words or phrases for your introduction so that you can present it as efficiently as possible.

- Carefully monitor your own talk during the introduction. It is easy to eat up time by repeating something over and over or talking a book to death. An introduction is meant to be a brief and lively discussion. Give yourself guidelines for how much time you want to spend on a book introduction and set a timer if necessary. This action will help you become much more conscious of time.

- Carefully monitor children's talk. You certainly want children to initiate conversation and to offer ideas from their own experience and their previous reading. But you do not want the conversation to go so far off track that it will not help the children when reading the new book you are introducing. You walk a fine line here, because you also do not want to cut children off when they are offering ideas. If you sense that the discussion is becoming rambling, gently guide students back to the text they are considering. Usually, however, it is our teacher talk that wastes time rather than students' offerings.

- Monitor the use of time throughout the lesson. Gradually, you will learn how much of the text to have students read each day, and you will get better at selecting texts. For example, if the text is too hard, students will struggle with it and too much time will be required to read it. A well-selected text will mean that students can read most of the new book accurately, with a few problems to solve; consequently, the lesson can move along. Also, select your teaching points so that you are not trying to do too much. If you do some word work, make it quick and like a game; one or two minutes is enough. Again, if you are new to guided reading, you may want to use a timer to remind yourself that a fast-paced lesson with focused attention is more effective than one that is tedious and drawn out.

- If students are reading a longer section of text (and especially if they are reading silently), consider leaving them at the table to read while you do something else. For many children, staying at the table helps to sustain engagement. You can listen to each one read for a few moments, prompting or interacting as appropriate, and then move away to begin working with another group or conferring with individuals. We are even beginning to think that in second-grade classrooms, two guided reading tables might be desirable. You can introduce a text and listen briefly to students read in the first group, then move away to another table or area and introduce a text to the second group, again listening to a few children read before moving away. You can go back to the first group for discussion and word work, followed by a discussion with the second group. Many teachers even find time to confer with a few individuals and/or take a walk around the room between groups to support students' independent work.

Summary

Chances are, these questions and answers will raise many more in your mind. As teachers, we are always asking questions because we approach our work in the spirit of inquiry. The more we learn, the more questions we reveal. When you have questions, the best thing you can do is turn to colleague support. Such ongoing sharing will be helpful to everyone.

Ideas to Try

Meet with grade-level colleagues to discuss classroom management.

1. Generate a list of questions about classroom management.
2. Categorize the questions.
3. Prioritize the questions, putting the most important or critical ones at the top of the list.
4. Select the two most important questions. Brainstorm for answers to each question. The rules of brainstorming are:
   - Anyone may and should suggest anything that comes to mind.
   - No one may criticize another's idea during the course of brainstorming. In other words, do not choke off discussion by saying, "I tried that and it did not work."
   - People may piggyback on others' ideas by suggesting extensions and alternatives.
   - You can come back to the ideas later and select those that you really want to try.
5. From the list of brainstormed ideas, select those that you think will be productive and agree to try them.
6. If you do not have enough suggestions, agree to search for information—from other teachers, from the literature, from professional readings, and from experts.
7. Regroup in a month to share your experiences and information. Select new questions to consider.

Appendix

KEEP BOOKS® BOOK LIST AND ORDER FORM

EMERGENT READER

pre-kindergarten, kindergarten, beginning first grade

Big-CB Big Caption Books

CB Caption Books — *levels A,B—1,2*

Dinosaurs
Trucks
What Do I See?
Traffic!
Look at Me!
Balloons
The Farm
Watch Me!

sCB Spanish Caption Books (LIBRITOS MÍOS)

Dinosaurios
Camiones
¿Qué es lo que veo?
El Tráfico
¡Mírame a mí!
Globos
La Granja
¡Mírame!

ER1 Emergent Readers 1 — *levels A,B—1,2*

Playing
Boo-boos!
Zoo Animals
Building a House
The Swimming Pool
Scrub-a-dub-dub!
Getting Dressed
My Cat

Big-RS1 Big Rhymes and Songs 1

RS1 Rhymes and Songs 1

To Market, To Market
Hey! Diddle, Diddle
Fuzzy Wuzzy
Hickory, Dickory, Dock!
Teddy Bear, Teddy Bear
Five Little Ducks
Five Little Monkeys
This Little Pig

NR Nursery Rhymes

Itsy Bitsy Spider
Mary Had a Little Lamb
Jack and Jill
Old Mother Hubbard
Humpty Dumpty
One, Two, Buckle My Shoe
Little Boy Blue
Little Miss Muffet

sNR Spanish Nursery Rhymes (LIBRITOS MÍOS)

Al Juego Chirimbolo
Cinco Pollitos
Los Animalitos
Los Maderos de San Juan
Los Pollitos
Naranja Dulce
Tengo, Tengo, Tengo
Un Elefante Se Balanceaba

EARLY READER

kindergarten, first grade

1 Set 1 *levels C—3,4*

Gingerbread Girl
Making a Peanut Butter and Jelly Sandwich
Keeping Warm
Our Van
The New Baby
My Map
My Mom Likes Blue
My Backpack

2 Set 2 *levels C,D—3,4,5*

Lunch Box
Max's Birthday
My Snowman
Together
Good Morning
Going Places
Let's Pretend
Party Time!

mA CB Letters, Words, and Numbers Caption Books *levels A,B,C,D—2,3,4,5*

Making a Mask
How old are you?
School Times
What do I see in the tree?
The Garage Sale
Vegetable Soup
Sandwich Shapes
Pigs at the Pool

LETTERS, WORDS, & PHONICS

LSW1 Letters, Sounds, and Words *levels A,B,C,D,E—2,3,4,5,6,7,8*

Caption Book Format

Baby Animals
Patty
Up in the Sky
What Will I Eat?
The Zoo
My Room
I Like To Go
Will You Play With Me?

Extended Stories in Beginning Reading Format

The Tree, a Bee and Me
Patty's Cat
Billy Loves Baseball
Betsy and Her Bug
Always Listen to Mother
Jake's Day
Don't Break the Eggs!
Mole's Nice Hole

LSW2	**Letters, Sounds, and Words**	
	Caption Book Format	**Extended Stories in Beginning Reading Format**
	Up, Up, Up	*My Dump Truck*
	Field Day	*A Good Place To Hide*
	Growing Up	*Brad's Tooth*
	Going to the Farm	*Mother Bird*
	Eating Breakfast	*Watching TV*
	BIG and little	*My Little Brother*
	My New Bike	*James Goes to the Hospital*
	Can I?	*My Seed*

TRANSITIONAL READER

first grade

3	**Set 3**	*levels D,E—6,7,8*
	Come Over	*Feeding the Birds*
	The Zoo Trip	*Our Favorite Snowman*
	The Three Little Pigs	*Growing a Pumpkin*
	Lunch Time	*The Soccer Game*
4	**Set 4**	*levels F,G—9,10,11*
	Notes to Me	*Max and Mutt*
	Burnt Cookies!	*Reading At Home*
	Almost Ready	*My Messy Sister*
	My Brother's Motorcycle	*Goldilocks and Baby Bear*

SELF-EXTENDING READER

first grade, beginning second grade

5	**Set 5**	*levels G,H—12,13,14*
	The Mystery of the Chocolate Chips	*The Smoke Detector*
	The Birthday Present	*Mugs*
	Mutt Goes to School	*Hold On!*
	Monkey Tricks	*The Gingerbread Man*
mA	**Letters, Words, and Numbers**	*levels G,H,I—10,11,12,13,14,15*
	"That's Not Fair!"	*Is It Lunch Time?*
	Wait for the Change	*Too Many Pets*
	The Contest	*What a Night*
	The Treasure Hunt	*Clickety-Clack*

KEEP BOOKS® ORDER FORM

KEEP BOOKS are little paperback books specially designed to support children's beginning reading strategies. These books have black-and-white illustrations and cost as little as 25¢ per copy. Many school business partners sponsor these books so that children can collect them—that is, take them home to keep.

BILL TO: Name_______________

School_______________

Address_______________

____

City, State, Zip_______________

Phone_______________

P.O./Check No._______________

SHIP TO: Name_______________

Address_______________

____

City, State, Zip_______________

Phone_______________

PAYMENT

All orders must be accompanied by a check, purchase order or a credit card number.

❑ Payment enclosed
(Check or P.O. payable to The Ohio State University)

❑ Charge to: ❑ VISA ❑ MasterCard

Name on credit card:_______________

Card #_______________

Exp. date_______________

Signature_______________

International customers and inquiries regarding our Limited Rush Service, please contact the Shipping Department. Please keep a copy of your order for future reference.

Mail this form to:
OSU KEEP BOOKS
807 Kinnear Road
Columbus, OH 43212

For information about shipping or status of your order, call: 1-800-678-6484; Columbus area, call (614) 292-2869

For information about KEEP BOOKS, call:
1-800-678-6484

If ordering by credit card or P.O., fax the form to:
OSU KEEP BOOKS, (614) 688-3452

Please visit our Web site at www.keepbooks.org

PLEASE INDICATE THE QUANTITY ORDERED FOR EACH ITEM.

KEEP BOOKS 400 books, 50 copies of 8 different titles

Item/Set	Quantity	Price	Total
Set CB Caption Books		$100	
Set NR Nursery Rhymes		$100	
Set RS Rhymes and Songs		$100	
Set ER Emergent Readers		$100	
Set 1		$100	
Set 2		$100	
Set mA CB Letters, Words, & Numbers		$100	
Set 3		$100	
Set 4		$100	
Set 5		$100	
Set mA Letters, Words, & Numbers		$100	
Set sCB Spanish Caption Books		$100	
Set sNR Spanish Nursery Rhymes		$100	
Letters, Sounds, & Words 400 books, 25 copies of 16 different titles			
Set LSW1		$120	
Set LSW2		$120	

Mini Sets for Tutors or Volunteers 80 books, 5 copies of 16 titles. Please indicate quantity ordered for each Mini Set (no substitutions).

Item/Set	Quantity	Price	Total
Sets CB and NR		$30	
Sets CB and mA CB		$30	
Sets 1 and 2		$30	
Sets 3 and 4		$30	
Sets 5 and mA		$30	
Sets sCB and sNR		$30	
Sets LSW1		$30	
Sets LSW2		$30	
BIG KEEP BOOKS (8) Big CB		$20	
BIG KEEP BOOKS (8) Big RS1		$20	
		Subtotal	
		*Add Shipping 10%, minimum $4.95	
		GRAND TOTAL DUE	

*For residents of Alaska and Hawaii, please add 25% per set for shipping and handling.

Bibliography of Professional Books and Articles

Anderson, R. C., P. T. Wilson, and L. G. Fielding. 1988. "Growth in Reading and How Children Spend Their Time Outside of School." *Reading Research Quarterly* 23: 285-303.

Askew, B. J., and I. C. Fountas. 1998. "Building an Early Reading Process: Active from the Start!" *The Reading Teacher* 52 (2): 126-134.

Bagley, S. 1997. "How to Build a Baby's Brain." *Newsweek*, Special Edition, spring/summer: 28-32.

Beach, R. 1993. *A Teacher's Introduction to Reader-response Theories*. Urbana, IL: National Council of Teachers of English.

Beaver, J. *Developmental Reading Assessment*. 1997. Glenview, IL: Celebration.

Blevins, B. 2000. Unpublished study of the relationship between phrased, fluent reading and comprehension scores on the DRA. Thurgood Marshall School. Manassas, VA.

Bodrova, E., and D. Leong. 1996. *Tools of the Mind: The Vygotskian Approach to Early Childhood Education*. Englewood Cliffs, NJ: Merrill.

Bruner, J. S. 1983. *Child's Talk: Learning to Use Language*. London: W.W. Norton & Co.

Clay, M. M. 1966. *Emergent Reading Behavior*. Unpublished doctoral dissertation. University of Auckland Library. Auckland, New Zealand.

Clay, M. M. 1991. *Becoming Literate: The Construction of Inner Control*. Portsmouth, NH: Heinemann.

Clay, M. M. 1991. "Introducing a New Storybook to Young Readers." *The Reading Teacher* 45 (4): 264-273.

Clay, M. M. 1993. *An Observation Survey of Early Literacy Achievement*. Portsmouth, NH: Heinemann.

Clay, M. M. 1998. *By Different Paths to Common Outcomes*. York, ME: Stenhouse.

Clay, M. M. 2001. *Changes Over Time in Children's Literacy Development*. Portsmouth, NH: Heinemann.

Copenhaver, J. 2001. "Rushed Read-Alouds in a Primary Classroom: What Happens to Response When Time Runs Short?" *Language Arts* 79(2): 148-158.

Damasio, A. R. 1994. *Descartes' Error: Emotion, Reason and the Human Brain.* New York: Putnam's Sons.

Diaz, R. M., C. J. Neal, and M. Amaya-Williams. 1990. "The Social Origins of Self-regulation." In *Vygotsky and Education*, ed. L. C. Moll. New York: Cambridge University Press.

Diller, D. 1999. "Opening the Dialogue: Using Culture as a Tool in Teaching Young African American Children." *The Reading Teacher* 52: 820-828.

Dineson, I. 1992. *Out of Africa.* Modern Library.

Flippo, R. F. 1999. *What Do the Experts Say?* Portsmouth, NH: Heinemann.

Fountas, I., and G. S. Pinnell. 1996. *Guided Reading: Good First Teaching for All Children.* Portsmouth, NH: Heinemann.

Fountas, I., and G. S. Pinnell. 1999. *Matching Books to Readers: Using Leveled Books in Guided Reading, K-3.* Portsmouth, NH: Heinemann.

Fountas, I. C., and G. S. Pinnell. 2001. *Guiding Readers and Writers, Grades 3-6: Teaching Comprehension, Genre, and Content Literacy.* Portsmouth, NH: Heinemann.

Freedman, R. 1992. "Fact or Fiction?" In *Using Nonfiction Trade Books in the Elementary Classroom: From Ants to Zeppelins*, Freeman, E. B., and D. G. Person, 2-10. Urbana, IL: National Council of Teachers of English.

Gopnik, A., A. Meltzoff, and P. K. Kuhl. 1999. *The Scientist in the Crib.* New York: Morrow.

Greenspan, S. 1997. *The Growth of the Mind.* Reading, MA: Addison Wesley.

Hickman, J. 1992. "What Comes Naturally: Growth and Change in Children's Free Response to Literature." In *Stories and Readers: New Perspectives on Literature in the Elementary Classroom*, eds. C. Temple and P. Collins, 185-193. Norwood, MA: Christopher-Gordon.

Hiebert, E. H., P. D. Pearson, B. Taylor, V. Richardson, and G. S. Paris. 1998. *Every Child a Reader: Strategic Comprehension.* Ann Arbor, MI: Center for the Improvement of Early Reading Achievement.

Holdaway, D. 1979. *Foundations of Literacy.* Sydney: Scholastic.

hooks, b. 1995. *Killing Rage: Ending Racism.* New York: Henry Holt.

Huck, C. S., S. Hepler, and J. Hickman. 1993. *Children's Literature in the Elementary School* (5th ed.). Madison, WI: Brown & Benchmark.

Huck, C., S. Hepler, J. Hickman, and B. Kiefer. 2001. *Children's Literature in the Elementary School* (7th ed.). Madison, WI: Brown & Benchmark.

Huxley, E. 1981. *The Flame Trees of Thika: Memories of an African Childhood.* New York: Viking.

Keene, E. O., and S. Zimmerman. 1997. *Mosaic of Thought.* Portsmouth, NH: Heinemann.

Kingsolver, B. 1998. *The Poisonwood Bible.* New York: Harper/Perennial.

LeDoux, J. 1996. *The Emotional Brain.* New York: Simon & Schuster.

Lindfors, J. W. 1999. *Child's Inquiry: Using Language to Make Sense of the World.* New York: Teachers College Press.

Lyons, C. A., and G. S. Pinnell. 2001. *Systems for Change: A Guide for Professional Development.* Portsmouth, NH: Heinemann.

McCarrier, A. M. 1992. *Supporting Literacy Learning in At-risk Children: A Case Study of an Urban Kindergarten.* Unpublished doctoral dissertation. The Ohio State University. Columbus, OH.

McCarrier, A., G. S. Pinnell, and I. C. Fountas. 2000. *Interactive Writing: How Language & Literacy Come Together, K-2.* Portsmouth, NH: Heinemann.

McGee, L. M. 1995. "Talking about Books with Young Children." In *Book Talk and Beyond: Children and Teachers Respond to Literature,* eds. N. L. Roser and M. G. Martinez, 105-115. Newark: IRA.

Ninio, A., and J. Bruner. 1978. "The Achievement and Antecedents of Labeling." *Journal of Child Literature* 5: 1-15.

Pearson, P. David. 1985. "Changing the Face of Reading Comprehension." *The Reading Teacher* 38: 724-737.

Peterson, R., and M. Eeds. 1990. *Grand Conversations: Literature Groups in Action.* New York: Scholastic.

Pinnell, G. S., J. J. Pikulski, K. K. Wixson, J. R. Campbell, R. B. Gough, and A. S. Beatty. 1995. *Listening to Children Read Aloud: Data from NAEP's Integrated Reading Performance Record* (IRPR) at Grade 4. Report No. 23-FR-04. Prepared by Educational Testing Service under contract with the National Center for Educational Statistics, Office of Educational Research and Improvement, U.S. Department of Education.

Rasinski, T. 2000. "Speed Does Matter in Reading." *The Reading Teacher* 54 (2): 146-151.

Rosenblatt, L. M. 1969. "Towards a Transactional Theory of Reading." *Journal of Reading Behavior* 1 (1): 31-49.

Snow, C., and A. Ninio. 1986. "The Contract of Literacy: What Children Learn from Learning to Read Books." In *Emergent Literacy: Writing and Reading*, eds. W.H. Teale and E. Sulzby, 116-138. Norwood, NJ: Ablex.

Sparks, N. 1999. *The Notebook*. New York: Warner.

Stephen, J., and K. Watson. 1994. *From Picture Book to Literary Theory*. Sydney, NSW: St. Clair Press. Cited in *What's in the Picture?*, ed. J. Evans. London: Paul Chapman.

Tatum, B. D. 1997. *"Why Are All the Black Kids Sitting Together in the Cafeteria?" and Other Conversations about Race*. New York: Basic Books.

Taylor, D., and D. Strickland. 1986. *Family Storybook Reading*. Portsmouth, NH: Heinemann.

Teale, W. H. 1984. "Reading to Young Children: Its Significance for Literacy Development." In *Awakening to Literacy*, eds. H. Goelman, A. Oberg, and F. Smith, 110-121. Portsmouth, NH: Heinemann.

Teale, W. H. 1986. *Home Background and Literacy Development*. Norwood, NJ: Ablex Publishing Company.

Tharp, R. G., and R. Gallimore. 1988. *Rousing Minds to Life: Teaching, Learning and Schooling in Social Context*. Cambridge, UK: Cambridge University Press.

Thompson, J. 1987. *Understanding Teenagers' Reading*. London: Croom Helm/Methuen. Cited in What's in the Picture?, ed. J. Evans. London: Paul Chapman.

Vygotsky, L. S. 1978. *Mind in Society*. Cambridge, MA: Harvard University Press.

Wan, G. 2000. "A Chinese Girl's Storybook Experience at Home." *Language Arts* 77: 398-405.

Wells, G. 1986. *The Meaning Makers: Children Learning Language and Using Language to Learn*. Portsmouth, NH: Heinemann.

Wells, D. 1995. "Leading Grand Conversations." In *Book Talk and Beyond: Children and Teachers Respond to Literature*, eds. N. L. Roser and M. G. Martinez, 132-139. Newark: IRA.

Wertsch, J. V. 1985. *Vygotsky and the Social Formation of Mind*. Cambridge, MA: Harvard University Press.

Williams, J., P. L. Scharer, and G. S. Pinnell. 2000. *Literacy Collaborative 2000 Research Report*. The Ohio State University. Columbus, OH.

Wood, D. 1988. *How Children Think and Learn: The Social Contexts of Cognitive Development*. Cambridge, MA: Basil Blackwell, Inc.

Wood, D., G. S. Bruner, and G. Ross. 1976. "The Role of Tutoring in Problem-solving." *Journal of Child Psychology and Psychiatry* 17: 89-100.

Bibliography of Children's Literature

Adler, D. A. 1993. *Cam Jansen and the Chocolate Fudge Mystery*. New York: Viking Press.

Ahlberg, J., and A. Ahlberg. 1979. *Each Peach Pear Plum*. New York: Viking.

Bacon, R. 1989. *Why Elephants Have Long Noses.* Crystal Lake, IL: Rigby.

Baker, K. 1999. *Quack and Count*. San Diego, CA: Harcourt Brace.

Balinger, M. 1997. *Making a Memory*. New York: Scholastic.

Bloom, B. 1999. *Wolf!* New York: Orchard.

Bunting, E. 1994. *Sunshine Home*. New York: Clarion.

Cachemaille, C. 1996. *Sam's Mask*. Photographs by Terence Taylor. Wellington, New Zealand: Learning Media Limited.

Cameron, A. 1981. *The Stories Julian Tells*. New York: Alfred A. Knopf.

Cameron, A. 1995. *The Stories Huey Tells*. New York: Alfred A. Knopf.

Canizares, S., and D. Moreton. 1998. *Who Lives in a Tree?* New York: Scholastic.

Carle, E. 1969. *The Very Hungry Caterpillar*. New York: Philomel.

Chardiet, B. 1990. *Martin and the Tooth Fairy*. New York: Scholastic.

Climo, S. 1993. *The Korean Cinderella*. New York: HarperCollins.

Clyne, M., and R. Griffiths. 1999. *Trash or Treasure*. Littleton, MA: Sundance.

Costain, M. 1997. *Mom's Secret*. New York: Scholastic.

Cowley, J. 1983. *Greedy Cat*. New York: Richard C. Owen.

Cowley, J. 1986. *The Little Red Hen*. Auckland, New Zealand: Heinemann Education.

Cowley, J. 1986. *Splish Splash!* Auckland, New Zealand: Heinemann Education.

Cowley, J. 1987. *Goodbye Lucy*. Bothell, WA: The Wright Group.

Cowley, J. 1988. *Greedy Cat Is Hungry*. Wellington, New Zealand: Learning Media Limited.

Cowley, J. 1998. *Mrs. Wishy-Washy*. Bothell, WA: The Wright Group.

Cowley, J. 1999. *Red-Eyed Tree Frog*. New York: Scholastic.

Crimi, C. 2002. *Tessa's Tip-Tapping Toes*. New York: Scholastic.

Dalgliesh, A. 1952. *The Bears on Hemlock Mountain*. New York: Aladdin.

Davidson, A. 1998. *My Scrapbook*. Denver, CO: Shortland Publications.

Doyle, M. 2002. *Cow*. New York: Simon & Schuster.

Elya, S. M. 2002. *Eight Animals Bake a Cake*. New York: J.P. Putnam's Sons.

Eschbacher, R. 2002. *Nonsense! He Yelled*. New York: Dial.

Fleming, C. 2002. *Muncha! Muncha! Muncha!* York: Simon & Schuster.

Florian, D. 1999. *Laugh-eteria*. San Diego, CA: Harcourt Brace.

Fox, M. 1990. *Shoes from Grandpa*. New York: Orchard Books.

Fox, M. 2000. *Harriet, You'll Drive Me Wild*. San Diego, CA: Harcourt.

Fritz, J. 1992. *George Washington's Mother.* New York: Grosset & Dunlap.

Galdone, P. 1970. *The Three Little Pigs*. New York: Houghton Mifflin.

Galdone, P. 1973. *The Little Red Hen*. New York: Clarion Books.

Gardner, M. 1996. *My Cat Muffin*. New York: Scholastic.

Giles, J. 1996. *Out in the Weather*. Crystal Lake, IL: Rigby.

Gorbachev, V. 2002. *One Rainy Day*. New York: Penguin Putnam.

Hall, D. 1979. *Ox-Cart Man*. New York: Viking.

Henkes, K. 1987. *Sheila Rae, the Brave*. New York: Viking Penguin.

Hill, E. 1980. *Where's Spot?* New York: Putnam's Sons.

Hoffman, M. 1991. *Amazing Grace.* New York: Dial.

Hort, L. 2000. *The Seals on the Bus*. New York: Henry Holt.

Hutchins, P. 1974. *The Wind Blew*. New York: Macmillan.

Hutchins, P. 1983. *You'll Soon Grow Into Them, Titch*. New York: Greenwillow.

Hyman, T. 1983. *Little Red Riding Hood*. New York: Holiday House.

Jennings, P. 1995. "Licked." In *Unbearable! More Bizarre Stories*. New York: Viking.

Johnson, A. 1990. *Do Like Kyla*. New York: Orchard.

Jonas, A. 1985. *The Trek*. New York: Greenwillow.

Jordan, S. 1989. *The Wobbly Tooth*. Crystal Lake, IL: Rigby.

Keller, L. 2000. *Open Wide: Tooth School Inside*. New York: Henry Holt.

Kimmell, E. 1988. *Anansi and the Moss-Covered Rock*. New York: Holiday House.

Klein, A. 2000. *I Can See*. New York: Scholastic.

Lobel, A. 1970. *Frog and Toad Are Friends*. New York: HarperCollins.

MacLulich, C. 1996. *Bats*. New York: Scholastic.

Martin Jr., B. 1999. *A Beasty Story*. San Diego, CA: Harcourt Brace.

Martin, C. 1993. *My Bike*. Wellington, New Zealand: Learning Media Limited.

McMullan, K., and J. McMullan. 2002. *I Stink!* New York: HarperCollins.

Micucci, C. 1995. *The Life and Times of the Honeybee*. New York: Ticknor & Fields.

Mitchell, M. 1993. *Uncle Jed's Barbershop*. New York: Simon & Schuster.

Naden, N. 1989. *Dad Didn't Mind at All*. Crystal Lake, IL: Rigby.

Numeroff, L. J. 1985. *If You Give a Mouse a Cookie*. New York: HarperCollins.

O'Connell, N. 1989. *Too Many Bones and A Toothbrush Tale*. Austin, TX: Steck-Vaughn.

Opie, I. 1999. *Here Comes Mother Goose*. Cambridge, MA: Candlewick Press.

Osborne, M. 2000. *Kate and the Beanstalk*. New York: Simon & Schuster.

Parker, J. 1989. *Emma's Problem*. Crystal Lake, IL: Rigby.

Parkes, B., and J. Smith. 1986. *The Enormous Watermelon*. Crystal Lake, IL: Rigby.

Parrish, P. 1992. *Amelia Bedelia*. New York: HarperCollins.

Pinnell, G. S. 2000. *Lunch*. New York: Scholastic.

Plourde, L. 1997. *Pigs in the Mud in the Middle of the Rud*. New York: Scholastic.

Randell, B. 1994. *The Lion and the Rabbit*. Crystal Lake, IL: Rigby.

Randell, B. 1996. *Tabby in the Tree*. Crystal Lake, IL: Rigby.

Randell, B. 1997. *The Babysitter*. Crystal Lake, IL: Rigby.

Reid, M. 1993. *How Have I Grown?* New York: Scholastic.

Rockwell, A. 1989. *Apples and Pumpkins*. New York: Simon & Schuster.

Rylant, C. 1987. *Henry and Mudge: The First Book*. New York: Aladdin.

Rylant, C. 1989. *Henry and Mudge Get the Cold Shivers*. New York: Simon & Schuster.

Rylant, C. 1994. *Mr. Putter and Tabby Pour the Tea*. San Diego, CA: Harcourt Brace.

Salley, C. 2002. *Epossumondas*. San Diego, CA: Harcourt Brace.

Schwarz, V. 2002. *The Adventures of a Nose*. Cambridge, MA: Candlewick.

Sendak, M. 1963. *Where the Wild Things Are.* New York: Harper & Row.

Sharmat, M. W. 1981. *Nate the Great and the Lost List.* New York: Bantam Doubleday.

Sharmat, M. W. 1981. *Nate the Great and the Missing Key.* New York: Dell.

Shaw, C. 1947. *It Looked Like Spilt Milk.* New York: Harper & Row.

Skelly, A. 1989. *Roll Over.* Crystal Lake, IL: Rigby.

Stevens, J. 1995. *Tops and Bottoms.* San Diego, CA: Harcourt Brace.

Stevens, J. 1987. *The Three Billy Goats Gruff.* San Diego, CA: Harcourt Brace Jovanovich.

Sturges, P. 1999. *The Little Red Hen (Makes a Pizza).* New York: Dutton.

Wallner, J. 1970. *City Mouse-Country Mouse and Two More Mouse Tales from Aesop.* New York: Scholastic.

Walton, R. 1998. *So Many Bunnies: A Bedtime ABC and Counting Book.* New York: Lothrop, Lee & Shepard.

Walton, R. 2002. *Bertie Was a Watchdog.* Cambridge, MA: Candlewick.

Ward, C. 1988. *Cookie's Week.* New York: Putnam.

Ward, L. 1952. *The Biggest Bear.* Boston: Houghton Mifflin.

Wattenberg, J. 2000. *Henny-Penny.* New York: Scholastic.

Wildsmith, B. 1982. *Cat on the Mat.* New York: Oxford University Press.

Williams, V. B. 1981. *Three Days on a River in a Red Canoe.* New York: Scholastic.

Yolen, J. 1987. *Owl Moon.* New York: Philomel Books.

Zimmerman, H. W. 1989. *Henny Penny.* New York: Scholastic.

KEEP BOOKS®

Francis, J. (illustrator). 1995. *A Retold Tale: The Three Little Pigs.* Columbus, OH: The Ohio State University.

Fried, M. D. 1999. *Zoo Animals.* Columbus, OH: The Ohio State University.

Mann, C. 1996. *The Smoke Detector.* Columbus, OH: The Ohio State University.

McCarrier, A. 1995. *Growing a Pumpkin.* Columbus, OH: The Ohio State University.

McCarrier, A. 1996. *Clickety-Clack.* Columbus, OH: The Ohio State University.

Pinnell, G. S. 1996. *Mugs.* Columbus, OH: The Ohio State University.

Index

H

I

J, K

L

T

U, V

W, X, Y, Z